Rita Mulcahy's

Risk Management
Tricks of the Trade® for Project Managers

and PMI-RMP® Exam Prep Guide

A COURSE IN A BOOK®

Second Edition

RITA MULCAHY, PMP

Printed in the United States of America

First Printing

ISBN: 978-1-932735-32-1

Library of Congress Control Number: 2009913343

RMC Publications, Inc.

Phone: 952.846.4484
Fax: 952.846.4844
E-mail: info@rmcproject.com
Web: www.rmcproject.com

Cover design by Amy Svir

To Kerry, who sat next to me, at age one, through the creation of most of this book and smiled without complaint.

To the thousands of project managers around the world who realize that striving to be better has its rewards and who have made this book the most real-world and easy-to-use guide to project risk management in the world.

Reviewers

Rita Mulcahy thanks each of the following people for their contributions to this book:

Marwa Muhammad Aboulfadl, PMP
Sonja Almlie, PMP
Iris Arth
Heather R. Austin, PMP
Amy Jo Bloom, PMP
Lon Blumenthal
Rick D. Boshart, PMP
Barbara Brooker
Rose Colacicco
Constance DeVere, PMP
Laurie Diethelm, CAPM
Art Drake
Deborah Gay
Robert Halterman
David Jacobs, Lt. Col., USAF
Courtney Johnson
Mary Lofsness
Anne McDonley
Jean McKay, RMP, PMP
Jeff Nielsen, RMP, PMP, PGMP
Greg Olk
Cynthia Osborne
Marc Pravatiner, PMP
Karen Rainford, PMP
Kara Schmitz
Trish Sutter, PMP
Whitney Thulin
Witold Urbanowicz, PMP
Max Wideman

© 2010 RMC Publications, Inc. • (952) 846-4484 • info@rmcproject.com • www.rmcproject.com

● ● ● ● Table of Contents

● ● ● ● About the Author

Rita Mulcahy, PMP, is an internationally recognized expert in project management and a highly sought-after project management author, trainer, and speaker. She has over 30 best-selling project management resources to her credit. Rita has taught and spoken to tens of thousands of managers and executives, and her products, classes, and e-Learning courses have helped over 250,000 people become more effective at managing projects. The first edition of this book, *Risk Management, Tricks of the Trade® for Project Managers*, won the Professional Development Product of the Year Award from the Project Management Institute (PMI).

Rita is also the founder of RMC Project Management, an international project management speaking, training, and consulting firm, a Global Registered Education Provider with PMI, and one of the fastest-growing training companies in the country. RMC specializes in real-world project management training—interpreting the *PMBOK® Guide* for real-world use and helping companies use the latest project management tools and techniques to complete projects faster, with less expense, better results, and fewer resources. RMC provides training in basic and advanced project management for team members, project managers, project management offices, and senior management. RMC offers classroom and online training on topics including:
- Project Management Fundamentals
- Project Risk Management
- Determining and Managing Requirements
- Common Project Problems
- Troubled Project Recovery
- Negotiation
- Contracts and Procurement
- Best Practices

Please visit RMC's Web site, www.rmcproject.com, for more information about these and additional course topics.

● ● ● ● Introduction

Imagine you are the project manager assigned to build a supermarket in South America. The project is scheduled to begin during the dry season and will be built near a rain forest. Now imagine the risks you might encounter. Even if you are not a construction expert, you might have thought that rain could be a problem. In the construction industry, there is something called liquidated damages, money the seller pays the buyer for delay in meeting the completion date. Therefore, the seller would be worried about anything that might delay the project.

During the project, it starts to rain and rain. Your boss, very upset, comes down to the construction site saying, "It's raining. It's raining!" The buyer's project manager, also upset, comes down to the construction site saying, "It's raining! It's raining!" You say, "Don't worry; the helicopter will be here in a moment." Just as you finish speaking, a helicopter arrives and proceeds to use the speed of its rotors to blow the water off the construction site. No more problems! How can the boss not give you and your team some credit for such activity? How can he not assign you to the next project everyone else wants to be assigned to? The boss and buyer will probably tell everyone they know about this one for years! To them, it looked like magic. To you and your team, it was just project management.

....

While developing a new handheld computer, the customer learned that the keypad they requested would not work under the conditions necessary. Worried that the required end date could no longer be met and huge expense would be incurred, the customer held a meeting with the project manager to discuss the problem. The customer was shocked when the project manager said, "We expected this could happen and have an alternative keypad almost ready. The delay for this issue has been already planned into the project reserve and we will still be able to complete the project on time."

....

These stories are examples of successful risk management. However, in the real world, many project managers are unaware of the process of risk management, or they think risk management is too hard or is only for large projects. As a result, they are unable to achieve the level of success reflected in the previous stories.

RMC Project Management, founded by Rita Mulcahy, PMP, has conducted several international studies of the methods used in project risk management. Our conclusion is that the situation is dire! We found managers of US $700,000,000 projects in South Africa who were using checklists and believing that was risk management. A team on a US $300,000 project in France used only an interview technique to manage risk for a project that could have resulted in the death of many of its workers. Project managers in more than one country never looked at the causes of their risks to realize that a single cause could result in the occurrence of many low-ranking risks, thereby leading to project failure. Consultants speaking at "risk management" conferences were telling people that risk management is only the use of a stoplight evaluation of red, yellow, or green for a project, rather than detailed identification of individual risks. Project managers in the United States were using only Monte Carlo simulation, believing they were doing adequate risk management. Professional risk management associations were only accepting papers on quantitative risk analysis, excluding as unimportant all the other topics in risk management.

We have since found that industries are now taking risk management more seriously, and embracing and reaping the rewards of following more comprehensive risk management processes.

In 1999, the Committee on Banking Supervision of the Bank of International Settlements (Basel Committee) established minimum requirements to improve the measurement of risks in that industry. Banks are incentivized to invest in, develop, and implement project risk management. Ultimately, the institutions with more sophisticated risk management disciplines will be able to set their own capital requirements based on their own risk profiles. What does this mean? The better a bank's risk management, the more funds they are allowed to lend, thus, the more revenue they can earn.

In the construction industry, studies show that ignoring risk and simply trying to shift all risks to the seller results in 8 percent to 20 percent additional costs to the buyer.

In the software industry, the Capability Maturity Model (CMM) levels espoused by many different organizations require a documented and assessed risk management process.

In country after country, standard project management practices now focus on risk management. Yet, in reality, too many project managers and those who work on projects still ignore risks, doing nothing about them.

Can you imagine preventing 90 percent of your project problems? How helpful would it be to eliminate 35 percent of those problems on the first try? Can you imagine how much the quality, cost, and schedule of your projects could be improved?

After years of working with thousands of project managers from around the world, this book has been written to fill a substantial gap in international risk management knowledge. It also attempts to correct common errors flagrantly noted and taken as fact in poorly documented articles and project management literature.

Since this book covers the basics of risk management—plus advanced topics and Tricks of the Trade® from around the world—it is a must for project managers, management, team members, and those preparing for project management or risk management certification, whether through self study or in university or corporate risk management courses.

Using This Book to Prepare for Certification Exams

This book is designed to teach real-world risk management and to provide real examples of managing risk. Since most certification exams that test on risk management test your ability to apply risk management to real-world situations, rather than just testing your knowledge, this book is also the primary text for becoming risk management certified. It was designed as the primary resource for preparing for the Project Management Institute's Risk Management Professional (PMI-RMP®) exam. This book is also a key text to use in preparing for the risk management questions on the Project Management Institute's PMP® and CAPM® exams and the risk management questions on the PRINCE2 certification.

> Note: If you are using this book to prepare for PMI's Risk Management Professional (PMI-RMP®) exam, please start by reading Chapter 10 of this book. If you are using this book as part of your preparation for the PMP® or CAPM® exam, please start by reading Chapter 11 of this book.

This book may also be used to obtain up to 15 PDUs in the self study category for Project Management Professional (PMP) recertification or 7.5 PDUs in the self study category for PMI-RMP® recertification with the Project Management Institute.

This book has the following features:
- Tricks of the Trade® from 141 worldwide contributors and international risk management research
- Subjects and innovative tricks that no one else has written about
- Exercises to make all the concepts real
- Questions for discussion and other features needed for university courses that use this book
- Templates you can adapt to your real-world projects
- Exams, games, and exercises utilizing adult and accelerated learning to increase your knowledge in fast and fun ways
- Over a thousand sample risks and risk categories that will help you identify risks you have not previously thought about
- Access to free templates and additional risk information

This book:
- Shows how risk management fits into the project management process, especially in the areas of cost, schedule, quality, team building, and procurement.
- Emphasizes the areas that should get the most attention in the real world.
- Provides a methodology that prevents many of the problems faced on projects and shows how to do it, not just what to do.

How to Use This Book

Throughout this book, you will see many exercises. These have been developed based on accelerated learning theory and an understanding of difficult topics in risk management. It is important to make sure you do these exercises, rather than jumping right to the answers. Do not skip them, even if their value is not evident to you. The exercises and activities are key benefits of this book, whether your goal is to pass an exam or simply to improve your project management abilities.

Each chapter is concluded by a chapter review. This review includes key concepts, key terms, a matching game, and questions for discussion. Make sure you can honestly say that you understand each of the key concepts and know each of the key terms. If not, go back and reread the chapter. Then play the matching game to make sure you are comfortable with these concepts. Lastly try to complete the questions for discussion. These questions will help you think about what you read in the chapter in new ways and thus make sure you really understand the concepts.

Each chapter review also includes an opportunity for you to adapt what you have learned to your real-world projects. Again, this will help you because you have to apply what you have learned to a real-world situation—in this case, YOUR real world situation. In doing so, you can uncover gaps in your knowledge. Many of the templates included in the book are also available online for you to print and to adapt as the circumstances of your project dictate.

 Also included throughout the book are Tricks of the Trade®, a registered trademark of RMC. They are designated by this image and will give you some extra insight on what you need to know about project risk management. Many of the Tricks of the Trade® first described or promoted in previous editions of this and other RMC publications have since become industry standards!

Concepts such as risk tolerance and risk owners are similar across the different risk management approaches. In the PRINCE2 project management standard, qualitative and quantitative risk analysis are called risk evaluation. Risk response planning is referred to as identifying suitable responses to risk and selecting and planning resources. The risk register is called a risk log. Otherwise the concepts are similar.

No matter how much experience a person may have in managing projects, everyone has a few tricks for managing risk. Before you continue reading, take some time to list yours now, and then see how many more you have after reading this book. Have fun adding to your list!

PRETEST

Test your current knowledge of risk management. Using this score sheet, take the Pretest, and put a checkmark next to the ones you answered correctly. Then read this book and complete the exercises. A final exam is provided after Chapter 11 to test your knowledge in more detail.

Pretest Score Sheet					
Question	Answer	Check (✓) if Correct	Question	Answer	Check (✓) if Correct
1			14		
2			15		
3			16		
4			17		
5			18		
6			19		
7			20		
8			21		
9			22		
10			23		
11			24		
12			25		
13			Total Correct		

1. Which of the following best describes why a work breakdown structure is needed before you can complete the risk management process?
   A. It describes resources to be used on the project.
   B. It shows the interdependencies on the project.
   C. It shows the work to be done on the project.
   D. It shows the lack of organization on the project.

2. Of the risk management processes, which one might it be appropriate to omit on certain projects?
   A. Plan Risk Management
   B. Perform Qualitative Risk Analysis
   C. Perform Quantitative Risk Analysis
   D. Plan Risk Responses

3. What is the purpose of risk management?
   A. To plan how to deal with problems
   B. To uncover scope of work that needs to be accomplished
   C. To assign risks to risk owners
   D. To systematically manage things that can go right and wrong on a project

4. Which of the following processes uses a subjective evaluation of risks?
   A. Identify Risks
   B. Perform Qualitative Risk Analysis
   C. Perform Quantitative Risk Analysis
   D. Plan Risk Responses

5. A short list of risks is created during which risk management process?
   A. Identify Risks
   B. Perform Qualitative Risk Analysis
   C. Perform Quantitative Risk Analysis
   D. Plan Risk Responses

6. Which of the following is most likely to occur if risk management is not done on a project?
   A. Testing activities will fail.
   B. The project will cost more and take longer.
   C. The customer will appreciate how much less time it will take to complete the project.
   D. Team members will be unhappy.

7. Who is involved in identifying risks?
   A. The team
   B. The sponsor
   C. The project manager
   D. Everyone

8. What is the definition of a risk?
   A. An opportunity or threat that might affect the project
   B. A project constraint
   C. A problem that has occurred
   D. An issue that needs the sponsor's attention to resolve

9. Which of the following are needed before you can effectively perform the Plan Risk Management process?
   A. A work breakdown structure and a project charter
   B. Measurements
   C. The sponsor and some work completed
   D. An understanding of the calculations to be made to measure progress

10. Opinions or beliefs about the project that may or may not be accurate are called:
    A. Constraints.
    B. Assumptions.
    C. Dependencies.
    D. Risks.

11. Historical records are important to review in planning a project because:
    A. You can duplicate all the templates from another project, rather than creating your own.
    B. They document company policies and procedures for project management.
    C. You can save the time of identifying risks by using the risk register from a previous project.
    D. They include lessons learned from past, similar projects, which may help you plan your own project and benefit from previous successes and failures.

12. The role of the project management office (PMO) may include all of the following EXCEPT:
    A. Advising the project manager on processes and procedures.
    B. Authorizing the project charter.
    C. Providing standard reporting forms for use on the project.
    D. Measuring the effectiveness of corrective action on the project.

13. Someone who is risk averse:
    A. Is a risk taker.
    B. Is a risk management expert.
    C. Prefers to avoid risks.
    D. Will accept a particular category of risks on a project.

14. Affinity diagrams, nominal group technique, and brainstorming are all tools for:
    A. Developing the project charter.
    B. Quantifying risks.
    C. Responding to risks.
    D. Identifying risks.

15. Which of the following is NOT an example of a project risk?
    A. The temperature could drop below freezing earlier in the season than usual.
    B. An important delivery could be delayed.
    C. We do not have enough qualified technicians to complete the installation as required.
    D. Our competition could beat us to market with a similar product.

16. Which of the following risk identification techniques continues until a consensus of expert opinion is reached?
    A. Delphi technique
    B. Brainstorming
    C. Affinity diagramming
    D. Nominal group technique

17. The process of determining how well a risk is understood is called:
    A. Qualitative risk analysis.
    B. Data quality analysis.
    C. Earned value analysis.
    D. Assumptions testing.

18. Monte Carlo simulation is:
    A. A method of identifying risks.
    B. A response to risks not identified in the planning process.
    C. A way to calculate expected monetary value of risks.
    D. A method of analyzing the probability of completing the project within a range of time or cost.

19. Probability and impact of risks can be determined by all of the following EXCEPT:
    A. Referring to historical records of past, similar projects.
    B. Utilizing the Delphi technique.
    C. Network diagram analysis.
    D. Interviewing experts.

20. Which of the following is a risk response strategy for both threats and opportunities?
    A. Transfer
    B. Accept
    C. Mitigate
    D. Exploit

21. A secondary risk is a risk that:
    A. Has occurred twice during the project.
    B. Is generated by a response to another risk.
    C. Is not identified before it occurs.
    D. Is addressed by a fallback plan.

22. Contingency reserves can be used:
    A. To deal with unplanned risks that occur.
    B. Only with management's approval.
    C. To deal with specific risks as planned.
    D. By the project team as needed.

23. A risk trigger is:
    A. An individual assigned to manage a specific risk.
    B. An indication that a specific risk has occurred or is about to occur.
    C. An impact of a risk that is greater than expected.
    D. A risk that is planned for, but does not occur, during the project.

24. A risk review:
    A. Looks forward in time to ensure existing risk response plans are adequate.
    B. Evaluates the effectiveness of the team's risk management efforts.
    C. Indicates that an identified risk is about to occur.
    D. Is an evaluation by the project manager of the work done by risk owners.

25. Inputs to the Perform Qualitative Risk Analysis process include all of the following EXCEPT:
    A. Project scope statement.
    B. Watchlist.
    C. Risk management plan.
    D. List of potential risks.

© 2010 RMC Publications, Inc. • (952) 846-4484 • info@rmcproject.com • www.rmcproject.com

1. **Answer:** C

   Explanation: A work breakdown structure is used to help identify the work to be done and therefore allows risks to be identified by work package, a more detailed level than only identifying risks by project.

2. **Answer:** C

   Explanation: The Perform Quantitative Risk Analysis process is a more detailed, numerical method of analyzing risks. Depending on the size and priority of the project, the time and effort required to complete this process may not be worthwhile or necessary.

3. **Answer:** D

   Explanation: Notice that choice D includes addressing threats AND opportunities. It is more inclusive than choice A, and therefore more accurate.

4. **Answer:** B

   Explanation: Subjective evaluations of risk are done during the Perform Qualitative Risk Analysis process.

5. **Answer:** B

   Explanation: The purpose of the Perform Qualitative Risk Analysis process is to take the long list of risks created in the Identify Risks process and determine which ones warrant further analysis. These risks comprise the short list.

6. **Answer:** B

   Explanation: The process of risk management removes many of the things that can go wrong on a project and finds ways to save time and cost. Therefore, the project can generally be completed faster and cheaper.

7. **Answer:** D

   Explanation: All stakeholders should be involved in the risk management process, including the identification of risks. It is important to have input on risk identification from a variety of sources, to ensure that all possible risks are identified.

8. **Answer:** A

Explanation: Constraints (choice B) are facts, not risks. Risks are opportunities or threats that might affect the project for better or worse (choice A) and not problems that have already occurred (choice C). Risk resolution generally does not require the involvement of the sponsor (choice D).

9. **Answer:** A

Explanation: Choice A is the only choice that describes items needed before you can do risk management. Measurements (choice B) and completed scope (choice C) come after the Plan Risk Management process. Calculations (choice D) are not required.

10. **Answer:** B

Explanation: This is the definition of assumptions (choice B). Assumptions must be investigated and their validity determined, as incorrect assumptions can negatively impact the entire risk management process.

11. **Answer:** D

Explanation: Choices A, B, and C are incorrect statements regarding historical records. Although you may find some templates and/or the risk register from previous projects to be useful (choices A and C), your plan should be specific the needs of your particular project. Historical records are best used as a starting point, and adapted by the project manager. Policies and procedures (choice B) are parts of organizational process assets, and not specifically historical records. Choice D is the correct answer and describes the value of reviewing historical records from past projects.

12. **Answer:** B

Explanation: All of the choices except choice B are possible ways the PMO may be involved in a project. The project charter is authorized by the project sponsor.

13. **Answer:** C

Explanation: The definition of risk averse is "unwilling to accept risk."

14. **Answer:** D

   Explanation: These are all tools the project manager can use with the team and stakeholders in the Identify Risks process.

15. **Answer:** C

   Explanation: A "risk" that is at least 80 percent likely is not a risk, but a fact. Facts are addressed in other parts of project planning.

16. **Answer:** A

   Explanation: The Delphi technique involves getting opinions from multiple experts, compiling the results and then sending the feedback back to the experts until consensus is reached.

17. **Answer:** B

   Explanation: Data quality assessment analyzes the current understanding of the risk and the reliability of the data. This technique identifies risks that require further investigation.

18. **Answer:** D

   Explanation: Monte Carlo simulation is a tool used in the Perform Quantitative Risk Analysis process. It creates a probability distribution of completing the project within a range of possible dates or costs.

19. **Answer:** C

   Explanation: Although the network diagram (choice C) is used to identify risks on the project, it is not of value in analyzing the probabilities or impacts. All of the other choices may be used for that purpose.

20. **Answer:** B

   Explanation: Transfer (choice A) and mitigate (choice C) are response strategies for threats. Exploit (choice D) is a response strategy for opportunities.

21. **Answer:** B

    Explanation: Secondary risks must be identified in the Plan Risk Responses process, and response strategies must be created for them, as well as for the other risks.

22. **Answer:** C

    Explanation: Additional funds allocated for unplanned risks (choice A) are management reserves. Contingency reserves are included in the budget to be used for specific potential risks.

23. **Answer:** B

    Explanation: A risk trigger is an indication that a risk has occurred or is about to occur. The individual assigned to each risk is the risk owner. This person is responsible for watching for triggers and carrying out the risk response if the risk occurs.

24. **Answer:** A

    Explanation: Choice A is the correct definition of a risk review. A risk audit evaluates the effectiveness of the team's risk management efforts (choice B). Choice C is the definition of a risk trigger.

25. **Answer:** B

    Explanation: A watchlist includes non-top risks documented for later review during the Monitor and Control Risks process. It is an output of the Perform Qualitative Risk Analysis process, not an input.

CHAPTER 1

Risk Management Overview

The risk management process is a systematic and proactive approach to taking control of projects by understanding or decreasing uncertainties (unknowns). Tailored risk management can apply to projects with a range of durations from weeks to years and budgets ranging from a few thousand to millions of dollars.

Risk management involves minimizing the consequences of adverse events *as well as* maximizing the results of positive events. Therefore, risks can be good or bad events, referred to in this book as opportunities or threats.

It is essential that potential good events (opportunities) are included in risk management. Such identification allows the team to take advantage of opportunities presented by the project. The things that go right (cheaper parts, an activity completed faster than scheduled) are what give you an edge over the things that go wrong.

Look for the good AND bad things that can happen!

Risk management is a part of the project management process, and consistently following that process is important for getting results. It allows you to take control of the project, rather than letting the project control you. If the early steps of the project management process are not followed, the benefits of the later steps will not be realized.

The six individual risk management processes are outlined next. They will be described in detail in the following chapters.

Plan Risk Management

This process focuses on determining how risk management will be done on the project, who will be involved, and the procedures to be used.

Identify Risks

In this process, the stakeholders are involved in making a long, comprehensive list of specific risks (threats and opportunities). This does not mean five items, but hundreds of items. Risks to the entire project are identified, but risks are also identified at a lower level—by work package or by activity.

Perform Qualitative Risk Analysis

This process includes subjectively analyzing the risks obtained in the Identify Risks process and deciding which risks warrant a response—creating a "short list." Probability and impact are determined qualitatively, a choice is made about whether a quantitative evaluation is necessary, and the project risk score and the probability of meeting project objectives are determined.

Perform Quantitative Risk Analysis

If it is necessary for the project, this process is performed to numerically analyze the probability and impact of specific risks and the overall risk of the project.

Plan Risk Responses

This process involves determining what can be done to reduce the overall risk of the project by decreasing the probability and/or impact of the short-listed threats and increasing the probability and/or impact of opportunities.

Monitor and Control Risks

In this process, the risk response plans are implemented as risks occur throughout the course of the project. It includes looking for risk triggers, identifying new risks, and evaluating the effectiveness of risk responses.

Risk Management Is an Iterative Process

Risk management is not a one-time-only process. It is repeated throughout the life of the project. Therefore, risk identification starts in initiating. It is heavily addressed during project planning and continues during project executing and monitoring and controlling,

© 2010 RMC Publications, Inc. • (952) 846-4484 • info@rmcproject.com • www.rmcproject.com

as changes are made or issues are discovered. Each of the individual risk management processes should be done as completely as possible and then fine-tuned through iterations.

There are two types of risk:
- **Business risk:** A risk of a gain or loss (e.g., a product that can lose money or make money when sold)
- **Pure (insurable) risk:** Only a risk of loss (e.g., such as a risk of fire)

In any case, a risk is something that is less than 100 percent certain—if it is a fact, it is not a risk! Risk management involves determining the following risk factors:
- **Probability:** The likelihood that a risk (threat or opportunity) will occur
- **Impact (consequence):** The effect on the project if the risk (threat or opportunity) occurs
- **Expected timing:** When during the life of the project the risk (threat or opportunity) might occur
- **Frequency of the event:** How many times the risk (threat or opportunity) might occur during the life of the project

Risks are identified early in the project, but most do not impact the project until later (see the following diagram). Therefore, the risk management process helps prevent future problems from occurring.

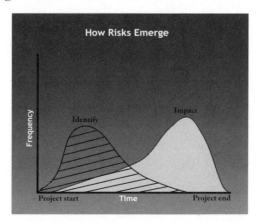

The following chart shows the entire risk management process that is described in this book. Use this chart to help make sure you understand how each part of the process fits together.

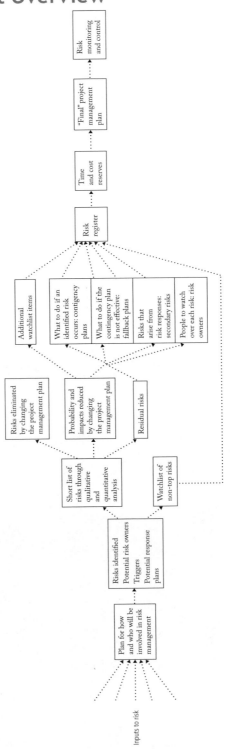

Chapter Summary

Key Concepts

- Risk management is a systematic approach with a process that must be followed in order to gain results.

- Risk management should be used on all projects.

- Risk management is an iterative process that recurs throughout the life of the project.

- A risk can be a threat or an opportunity.

- A fact is not a risk.

Key Terms

- Risk management process

- Uncertainties

- Risks

- Threats

- Opportunities

- Plan Risk Management process

- Identify Risks process

- Perform Qualitative Risk Analysis process

- Perform Quantitative Risk Analysis process

- Plan Risk Responses process

- Monitor and Control Risks process

- Iterative

- Business risk

- Pure (insurable) risk

- Risk factors

- Probability

- Impact

Matching Game: Overview

Instructions: Match the risk management key word to its definition.

Key Word

_____ **1.** Risk management process

_____ **2.** Uncertainties

_____ **3.** Risks

_____ **4.** Threats

_____ **5.** Opportunities

_____ **6.** Plan Risk Management process

_____ **7.** Identify Risks process

_____ **8.** Perform Qualitative Risk Analysis process

_____ **9.** Perform Quantitative Risk Analysis process

_____ **10.** Plan Risk Responses process

_____ **11.** Monitor and Control Risks process

_____ **12.** Iterative

_____ **13.** Business risk

_____ **14.** Pure (insurable) risk

_____ **15.** Risk factors

_____ **16.** Probability

_____ **17.** Impact

Definition

A. Repeated throughout the life of the project

B. A systematic and proactive approach to taking control of projects by understanding or decreasing the uncertainties

C. Determining specific risks by project and by activity

D. Unknowns

E. Numerically analyzing the risks obtained in the Identify Risks process and analyzing the extent of overall project risk

F. Determining how risk management will be done on the project, who will be involved, and procedures to be used

G. A risk of a gain or loss

Matching Game: Overview

H. Implementing the risk response plans as risks occur, looking for risk triggers, identifying new risks, and evaluating the effectiveness of risk responses

I. Possible events that may positively impact a project

J. Determining what can be done to reduce the overall risk of the project by decreasing the probability and impact of the threats and increasing the probability and impact of opportunities

K. Subjectively analyzing the risks obtained in the Identify Risks process and deciding which risks warrant a response; creating a "short list" of risks

L. Possible events that may positively or negatively impact a project

M. The likelihood that a risk (threat or opportunity) will occur

N. A risk of loss

O. Probability, impact, expected timing, frequency of the event

P. The effect on the activity or the project if the risk (threat or opportunity) occurs

Q. Possible events that may negatively impact a project

Answer Key

1.	B	10.	J
2.	D	11.	H
3.	L	12.	A
4.	Q	13.	G
5.	I	14.	N
6.	F	15.	O
7.	C	16.	M
8.	K	17.	P
9.	E		

Questions for Discussion

1. How do you currently manage risks on your real-world projects?

2. Why is following a process so important for achieving successful results?

3. Why should risk management include an analysis of things that could go right in addition to things that can go wrong?

4. Why should a company require that any risk that is 80 percent or more probable be considered a fact and included as a constraint in the project management plan?

What You Need Before You Can Effectively Begin Risk Management

An input is something that must be done or information that must already have been collected before you can adequately complete the next process. This is important! If risk management is going to be fast and effective, certain other items must be available before you begin.

Inputs are listed here because they are used throughout the risk management process. If you do not understand these after reviewing the following introduction and exercise, I suggest you spend a little more time understanding project management before you delve into risk management. Risk management should be addressed throughout an organization, and is a part of the project management process. Project management tools, documents, processes, and tricks will be referred to throughout this text.

● ● ● ● **Exercise** Test yourself! Explain why each of the following inputs to risk management are needed before you can adequately complete the risk management process.

Input	Why Is It Needed?
Project management process	
Project background information	

What You Need Before You Can Effectively Begin Risk Management

Input		Why Is It Needed?
Project charter		
Outputs from project planning for your project	Stakeholder register • Stakeholders from within your performing organization • Stakeholders from outside of the performing organization	
	Project scope statement	
	Project constraints	
	Assumptions	
	Work breakdown structure	
	Network diagram	

Input		Why Is It Needed?
Outputs from project planning for your project	Estimates for time and cost	
	Human resource plan	
	Communications management plan	
	Procurement management plan	
Organizational process assets	Risk management policies, procedures, templates	
	Historical records from previous projects	
	Lessons learned from previous projects	
	Risk tolerance areas	
	Risk thresholds	

● ● ● ● **Answer** The following is a detailed summary of these inputs. Spend more time on this if you have not had recent training in project management. Read carefully, and look for tricks to add to your list in the next few pages!

The Project Management Process

In order to complete projects faster, cheaper and with the highest quality, effective risk management must occur within a properly executed project management process.

The project management process begins with initiating, where the project charter is created and the stakeholders are identified. Project planning then involves creating a project management plan that is bought-into, approved, realistic, and formal. Executing involves completing the project to the plan and coordinating and facilitating the project team in completing the project work. Monitoring and controlling involves measuring progress against the project management plan. Executing and monitoring and controlling often overlap in time during the project management process. In closing, final acceptance is achieved and lessons learned and other historical records are created.

Risk management fits into the project management process as shown in the following chart.

What You Need Before You Can Effectively Begin Risk Management

INITIATING	PLANNING (This is the only process group with a set order)	EXECUTING	MONITORING & CONTROLLING	CLOSING
▶ Select project manager		▶ Execute the work according to the PM plan	▶ **Take action to control the project**	▶ Confirm work is done to requirements
▶ Determine company culture and existing systems	▶ **Determine how you will do planning—part of all management plans**	▶ Produce product scope	▶ Measure performance against the performance measurement baseline	▶ Complete procurement closure
▶ Collect processes, procedures, and historical information	▶ Finalize requirements	▶ Request changes		▶ Gain formal acceptance of the product
▶ Divide large projects into phases	▶ Create project scope statement	▶ Implement only approved changes	▶ **Measure performance against other metrics determined by the project manager**	▶ Complete final performance reporting
▶ Understand the business case	▶ Determine what to purchase	▶ Ensure common understanding		▶ Index and archive records
▶ **Uncover initial requirements and risks**	▶ Determine team	▶ Use the work authorization system	▶ **Determine variances and if they warrant a change request**	▶ Update lessons learned knowledge base
▶ Create measurable objectives	▶ Create WBS and WBS dictionary	▶ Continuously improve	▶ **Influence the factors that cause changes**	▶ Hand off completed product
▶ Develop project charter	▶ Create activity list	▶ Follow processes	▶ **Request changes**	▶ Release resources
▶ Identify stakeholders	▶ Create network diagram	▶ Perform quality assurance	▶ Perform integrated change control	
▶ Develop stakeholder management strategy	▶ Estimate resource requirements	▶ Perform quality audits	▶ Approve or reject changes	
	▶ Estimate time and cost	▶ Acquire final team	▶ Inform stakeholders of approved changes	
	▶ Determine critical path	▶ Manage people	▶ Manage configuration	
	▶ Develop schedule	▶ Evaluate team and project performance	▶ Create forecasts	
	▶ Develop budget	▶ Hold team-building activities	▶ Gain acceptance of interim deliverables from the customer	
	▶ Determine quality standards, processes, and metrics	▶ Give recognition and rewards	▶ Perform quality control	
	▶ Create process improvement plan	▶ Use issue logs	▶ Report on project performance	
	▶ **Determine all roles and responsibilities**	▶ Facilitate conflict resolution	▶ **Perform risk audits**	
	▶ Plan communications	▶ Send and receive information	▶ **Manage reserves**	
	▶ **Perform risk identification, qualitative and quantitative risk analysis, and risk response planning**	▶ Hold meetings	▶ Administer procurements	
	▶ **Go back—iterations**	▶ Select sellers		
	▶ Prepare procurement documents			
	▶ **Finalize the "how to execute and control" parts of all management plans**			
	▶ **Develop final PM plan and performance measurement baseline that are realistic**			
	▶ Gain formal approval of the plan			
	▶ Hold kickoff meeting			

What You Need Before You Can Effectively Begin Risk Management

Project Background Information

Information such as correspondence from before the project was approved, articles written about similar projects, and other such information will help identify more risks.

Though there are many steps in risk management, it does not need to be a lengthy process. To shorten the time, it is important to locate all relevant information before beginning the planning component; otherwise mistaken assumptions and miscalculations will affect your risk management efforts. Depending on the size of your project, you might consider collecting such information as:

- Corporate objectives
- Corporate risk management policies or procedures
- Priority of this project compared to all others
- Answers from management and the customer to as many of your questions about the project as possible so that you are clear about the project charter, constraints, and issues related to the project
- Supporting data for management's time or cost objectives (if available)
- Experts
  - Who are they?
  - How can they assist the project team with the customer, the project scope of work, and project management?
- Articles or publications on risk
- Cultural issues and suggested protocol, language barriers, and social customs
- Review of documentation relevant to the project:
  - All e-mails and meeting minutes from before the project was approved, including those from the customer
  - Technical and project management literature or articles
  - Copies of contracts, standards, or regulations related to the project
  - Technical drawings and specifications
  - Organizational charts
  - Résumés of potential team members
  - Marketing or sales reports

The following are questions about project background information to consider when identifying risks:

- What would e-mails tell you?
- Have you ever read the contracts related to your projects?

- How does your project relate to the strategic plan of your organization?
- What is the level of management support for your project?
- How do you know you have a clear understanding of the requirements and expectations of management and the customer?

Project Charter

A project charter is not a project management plan, but rather a high-level directive from management outlining the overall objectives of the project. It authorizes the existence of a project (the completion of work), gives the project manager the authority needed to complete the project, and provides some extremely important direction for the project. A project charter should be issued by management for every project. It should be no more than two sides of a page long, and contain the following information:

> **A charter should be in writing for every project.**

PROJECT CHARTER

Project Title and Description: This section should briefly describe the project.

Project Manager Assigned and Authority Level: This section should include the project manager's name and information about whether he or she can determine budget, schedule, staffing, etc.

Business Case: The business case addresses why the project is being done.

Resources Preassigned: This section describes how many or which resources will be provided.

Stakeholders: The stakeholders section addresses who will affect or be affected by the project (influence the project), as known to date.

Stakeholder Requirements as Known: This includes requirements related to project and product scope.

What You Need Before You Can Effectively Begin Risk Management

Product Description: The product description includes the specific product deliverables that are wanted and the end result of the project.

Measurable Project Objectives: This section describes how the project ties into the organization's strategic goals and what project objectives support those goals.

Project Approval Requirements: These requirements include what items need to be approved for the project, who will have sign-off, and what designates success.

High-Level Project Risks: This section describes potential threats and opportunities for the project.

Signature: The project sponsor signs the charter to indicate approval and authorization of the project.

The following are questions about the project charter to consider when identifying risks:
- What is included in the project charter?
- What is not included?
- How clear are the information and directions?
- Are the project objectives achievable?
- What is the degree of difficulty in completing the work described in the project charter?
- What is the level of the project manager's authority?

Outputs from Project Planning for Your Project
Stakeholder Register

Stakeholders are individuals and organizations who are actively involved in the project or may affect or be affected by the project.

The names, skills, abilities, and needs of the individual stakeholders are determined early in the project and documented in a stakeholder register. This document is updated throughout the project, as more information about the stakeholders and their preferences becomes known.

Stakeholders may include:
- People within the performing organization
  - Project sponsor
  - Management
  - Project manager
  - Project team
  - Project manager's boss
  - Team members' bosses
  - Procurement department
  - Marketing department
  - Salespeople
  - Quality assurance/quality control departments
  - Manufacturing
  - Legal counsel
  - Other departments
  - Project managers of previous, similar projects
  - Project managers who have worked with the customer before
- And people from outside the performing organization
  - Customer
  - Customer's competition
  - End users
  - Suppliers and vendors
  - Experts
  - Public
  - Funding sources

Since stakeholders will be affected by the project, they have an important role in risk management. Stakeholders outside of the team will be able to see risks that the team cannot. They can assist in each step of risk management and may even be assigned as the owners of some risks. Thus, they have specific roles and responsibilities. Documented information about stakeholders, their communication styles, and preferences will be an asset during the Identify Risks process and throughout the project.

It is important to understand the roles of all stakeholders, who is assigned to each risk, and what level of authority the project manager and others have on the project.

The following are questions about stakeholders to consider when identifying risks:
- Who are all the stakeholders for the project?
- What are their stated objectives?
- What are their expectations (intents that are not stated but are their motivators or non-motivators for working on the project)?
- What are their areas of influence/weakness?
- Do stakeholders understand their roles?
- What is the time commitment and availability required of them?

Project Scope Statement

Think of the term "project scope statement" as the approved project and product scope for the project. To perform risk management, it is important to have a finalized project scope statement that describes the complexity of the project.

The following are questions about the project scope statement to consider when identifying risks:
- What areas of the scope of work are incomplete?
- What did any of the stakeholders want that was ultimately not included in the project scope statement?
- What work has never been done before?
- What work are you, as the project manager, experienced with?
- What work are you inexperienced with?
- What parts of the project scope statement are unclear?

Project Constraints

The project scope statement includes information about project constraints, which are also important inputs to the risk management process. A project constraint is anything that limits the team's options.

Examples include:
- **Time:** Complete the project by June 15.
- **Cost:** Complete the project for less than US $125,000.
- **Scope/performance:** Complete all the work listed.
- **Quality:** There should be no more than three bugs per module.
- **Risk:** The risk score for the project should be no more than 60 on a 0 to 80 scale.

- **Resources:** Only three resources from the marketing department may be used.
- **Customer/Stakeholder satisfaction:** The customer satisfaction rating throughout the project should be at least 8.0 on a 1 to 10 scale.

The following are questions about project constraints to consider when identifying risks:
- After a high-level review, do any constraints on this project appear to be unrealistic?
- How does a constraint in one area affect other areas of the project?

Assumptions

The project scope statement also includes information about assumptions. Assumptions are things that are accepted as true, but that may not be true. Project assumptions may increase or decrease risks and help in determining risk impacts. Such beliefs or opinions about the project must be identified. The validity of the assumptions will be tested later in risk management, during the Perform Qualitative Risk Analysis process.

The following are questions about assumptions to consider when identifying risks:
- What assumptions might prove to be incorrect later in the project?
- How can you prevent problems by clarifying assumptions early?

Work Breakdown Structure

A work breakdown structure (WBS) is one of the key outputs of project management planning. It is an input to other processes and is essential for all projects. The work breakdown structure decomposes the project into smaller, more manageable pieces, called work packages. Those work packages then are managed by the project manager. A work breakdown structure can be created using many tools, but is often created using sticky notes with the project team.

A simple work breakdown structure may look like this:

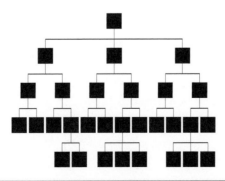

What You Need Before You Can Effectively Begin Risk Management

Many project teams mistakenly believe that risk management is only a high-level evaluation of the risks of the project. Instead, risk management concentrates on identifying the risks of the work packages and associated activities, as well as the overall risks of the project!

The following are questions about the work breakdown structure to consider when identifying risks:

- Are there any particularly risky work packages?
- How difficult was it to complete the WBS and to gain agreement or buy-in?
- Based on the WBS, are the time and cost requirements achievable?
- Is any part of the scope incomplete or not achievable?

Network Diagram

A network diagram is a dependency-sequenced organization of the project's activities. These activities are derived from the decomposition of work packages in the work breakdown structure. The network diagram shows the flow of activities to be completed from project beginning to end, based on the dependencies between the activities. This tool can be used to decrease project duration by organizing the activities into parallel activities (activities that can be done concurrently).

A simple network diagram may look like the following:

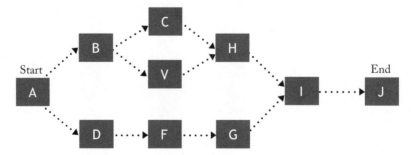

Once dates are assigned to each activity, it becomes a time-scaled schedule network diagram. The time-scaled schedule network diagram helps determine the critical path and the probability of completing the project within the required time objectives for the project; thus, it is a tool to help determine risks.

To evaluate risks, look at the network diagram for:

- **Estimates:** Estimates that contain padding or other hidden uncertainties add risk to the project.
- **Path convergence:** Places on the network diagram where many paths lead into one activity. Such convergence makes the activity riskier.
- **The allocation of resources and their skills:** An inexperienced person assigned to an activity on the critical path adds risk to the project. You may be able to move the resource to another activity that is not on the critical path to decrease that risk.
- **Parallel activities:** Parallel activities must be able to be completed at the same time in order to decrease risk.
- **The critical path:** The length of the critical path must be within the allocated time for the project.
- **The number of near-critical paths:** A near-critical path is close to the critical path in duration. Near-critical paths add risk to the project.
- **Dependencies:** Dependencies should be appropriate and logical to minimize risk.

Estimates for Time and Cost

In order to minimize risk to the project and to improve accuracy, estimates are created by the people doing the work, whenever feasible, and are based on the work packages identified in the work breakdown structure or the activities within those work packages.

Many project managers make the mistake of determining with the team one time estimate for each activity. Studies have shown that a schedule based on one time estimate per activity is only 5 to 15 percent likely to succeed! Time and cost estimates should be based on three estimates—optimistic, most likely, and pessimistic. The result is an indication of the risk involved in the estimate. If the range between the optimistic and pessimistic estimates is wide, the estimate includes more uncertainties. This tells you that there are more risks to be identified, and then eliminated or decreased.

To take this process a step further, let's say you need to shorten the activity or project time estimate. Why make the mistake of encouraging padding in future estimates and angering team members by telling them that they will have to complete the activity in a shorter period of time? Instead, identifying, eliminating, or decreasing the risks in the estimate will decrease the time estimate(s) and provide the project and the team members with a win–win situation.

What You Need Before You Can Effectively Begin Risk Management

The most professionally responsible way to shorten or decrease estimates is through identifying and eliminating risks by following the risk management process. The process of risk management can actually shorten the project schedule and decrease project cost!

The following are questions about time and cost estimates to consider when identifying risks:

- Who created the estimate?
- What is the estimator's knowledge of what they estimated?
- What is the estimator's confidence level regarding the estimate?
- Is the estimate based on detailed activities or work packages?
- Is the estimator generally overly-optimistic?
- What method was used for estimating?
- Does the estimate include padding?

Human Resource Plan

The human resource plan is a formal plan identifying when and how the team and other stakeholders will be involved in the project, and what roles they will perform.

The following are questions about the human resource plan to consider when identifying risks:

- Does such a plan exist?
- Are there any troublesome stakeholders involved?
- Are there any high-in-demand stakeholders involved? Remember that in a matrix environment team members may not be exclusively assigned to one project. The project manager will have to negotiate and communicate with functional managers to get, and keep, the people they need for the project.
- What is the knowledge level and skill set of the stakeholders? Will they need additional training?

Communications Management Plan

Communications planning is part of the project management planning process. Communication is a critical part of successful risk management. The communications management plan is created by the project manager and becomes part of the project management plan. It informs stakeholders how and in what form communications will be handled on the project. The creation of a communications management plan involves an analysis of the needs of each individual stakeholder. The plan may include the following information:

- What information needs to be collected and when
- Who will receive the information
- The method that will be used to gather and store information
- Limits, if any, on who may give direction to whom
- Reporting relationships
- Stakeholders' contact information
- The schedule for distribution of each type of communication
- Preferred methods of communication

The information in the communications management plan should include the communication of risks and risk management activities, and results of formal communication should be documented and reported throughout the risk management process.

Specific communication checkpoints include:

- When the charter is finalized
- When the work breakdown structure is created
- When risks are qualified and a risk score is determined
- When risk response plans are created
- Throughout completion of the project
- When creating the monthly report
- When creating team meeting agendas and meeting minutes

More formal checkpoints include go/no-go decisions made during the Perform Qualitative Risk Analysis and Plan Risk Responses processes.

The following are questions about the communications management plan to consider when identifying risks:

- Do you have people on your team who are poor communicators?
- What areas need specific and careful management of communications?
- Where are you most likely to have communications problems?
- How do you know your methods of communication are most effective for the stakeholder and the situation?

Procurement Management Plan

A procurement management plan is a formal or informal plan for a project that describes what part(s) of the project will be purchased under contract or purchase order. It also includes a plan for managing the sellers on a project. Procurements can be used to transfer risk, but they can add risk if the contracts were not created based on the needs of the project and with input from the project manager.

The following are questions about the procurement management plan to consider when identifying risks:
- Were you involved in creating the contract before it was signed?
- Was risk management done before the contract was signed?
- What is your level of expertise in managing contracts?
- Have you worked with the sellers before?
- What are the particular terms and conditions of the contract?
- What are the deliverables and performance periods?

Organizational Process Assets

Risk Management Policies, Procedures, and Templates

A company should already have in place company policies, procedures, and templates for risk management. These guidelines address such topics as procedures for risk management, forms to be used, processes to be followed, and a definition of standard roles and responsibilities. Such procedures and templates should be high-level in nature and should be adapted by the project manager to the needs and nature of each particular project. Common templates and procedures include:
- Reporting forms for risk
- Standard probability and impact scales
- Procedures for the involvement of stakeholders in risk management
- Policies identifying who needs to approve risk response plans
- Risk ranking standards for go/no-go decisions
- Procedures for risk audits

People are constantly looking for templates, as if the right template will make a great project manager. Doing risk management well takes cognitive skills. Though some templates are provided in this book and can be helpful tools, remember that templates can severely limit risk efforts if people don't adapt the templates to their projects and work only within the limits of the templates.

Historical Records from Previous Projects

Only a small percentage of project managers have historical records. It follows, then, that most projects start from scratch. What a waste of time! Can you imagine if you could have access to the brains and experience of everyone in your company? How helpful would it be to have a list of risks from all the recent projects your company or department has completed or is in the midst of? This is the value of historical records.

Historical records may include the following information from previous, similar projects:
- Historical context of past projects and project phases (e.g., economic conditions, organizational issues such as reorganizations, mergers, and company goals)
- Outputs from project planning
- Outputs from risk management
  - Lists of risks
  - Lists of risk categories
  - Probability and impact of risks
  - Risk response plans
  - Methods used to measure effectiveness of risk management efforts
- Metrics created
- Benchmarks found

Lessons Learned from Previous Projects

Historical records also include lessons learned, which document what went right, what went wrong, or what would have been done differently by past project teams if they could execute their projects again. Lessons learned can help identify and manage risks on your project.

Such information helps prevent rework on projects and helps ensure that the same mistakes are not made by other project teams. It can also provide a sanity check on the project's risk efforts and shorten the time it takes to perform risk management on the project. Like other historical records, lessons learned will also help make risk efforts on future projects easier, more complete, and more effective.

The following are questions about organizational process assets to consider when identifying risks:

- Has a project similar to yours been successfully completed in your organization?
- What risks did past, similar projects experience?
- What policies and procedures are to be used that no one follows, or that could be misunderstood?
- How can existing policies and procedures help prevent problems on your project?
- What opportunities might your project have to improve organizational policies and procedures?

Risk Tolerance Areas

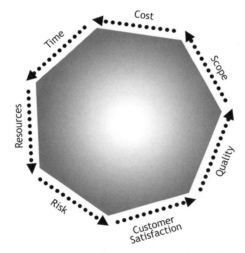

It is important to determine in what areas the company and key stakeholders are willing to accept risk. Risk tolerances are usually expressed in terms of the project constraints: scope, time, cost, quality, risk, resources, and customer satisfaction.

Other risk tolerances, such as the number of injuries, downtime, complaints, and more should also be determined in advance. Risk tolerances are reviewed after risks are identified to assist the team in prioritizing the risks to be addressed.

Individuals or organizations that are unwilling to accept risk are said to be risk averse.

Risk Thresholds

Risk thresholds are a companion to the concept of tolerance areas. The word "threshold" means "how much is too much" and can be used to refer to the whole project (e.g., risk threshold for the project) or to a risk tolerance (e.g., more than a two-day delay in the installation of X is unacceptable).

TRICKS OF THE TRADE®

Collect Risk Tolerance and Threshold Information During the Identify Risks Process

Stakeholders, project constraints, and project requirements are identified earlier in the project management process. This information will be used to help determine the impact of risks and the risk responses. The project manager may save time by collecting details on risk tolerance areas and thresholds at the same time that stakeholders and their project requirements are identified. See the following chart. The risk tolerance and thresholds are prioritized on each project, and the project is managed accordingly.

Stakeholder	Requirements	Risk Tolerances and Thresholds					
		Time	Cost	Quality	Down-time	Customer Satisfaction	Other
Manager of IT Department— Richard Kolb		More than a two day delay in the installation of X	None	None	None	None	None
		More than a five day delay in the completion of activity B					

Key Concepts

- Inputs are things that must be done or information that must already have been collected before you can adequately complete risk management.

- Without the necessary inputs, some risks will remain unidentified.

- Effective risk management must occur within a properly executed project management process.

Key Terms

- Inputs to risk management

- Project management process

- Project background information

- Project charter

- Outputs from project planning for your project

  - Stakeholder register

  - Project scope statement

  - Project constraints

  - Assumptions

  - Work breakdown structure

  - Network diagram

  - Estimates for time and cost

  - Human resource plan

  - Communications management plan

- Procurement management plan

- Organizational process assets

  - Risk management policies, procedures, templates

  - Historical records from previous projects

  - Lessons learned from previous projects

  - Risk tolerance areas

  - Risk thresholds

- Sponsor

- Project team

- Customer

- Stakeholders

- Expectations

- Risk averse

What You Need Before You Can Effectively Begin Risk Management

Matching Game: What You Need Before You Can Effectively Begin Risk Management

Instructions: Match the risk management key word to its definition.

Key Word

———— **1.** Inputs to risk management

———— **2.** Project management process

———— **3.** Project background information

———— **4.** Historical records

———— **5.** Lessons learned

———— **6.** Project charter

———— **7.** Project scope statement

———— **8.** Work breakdown structure

———— **9.** Network diagram

———— **10.** Estimates for time and cost

———— **11.** Human resource plan

———— **12.** Communications management plan

———— **13.** Procurement management plan

———— **14.** Stakeholder register

———— **15.** Sponsor

———— **16.** Project team

———— **17.** Customer

———— **18.** Expectations

———— **19.** Organizational process assets

———— **20.** Project constraints

———— **21.** Assumptions

———— **22.** Risk tolerance areas

———— **23.** Risk averse

———— **24.** Risk thresholds

Definition

A. A document that describes the approved product and project requirements

B. Those who will be executing the project management plan

C. A diagram that shows the decomposition of the project into smaller, more manageable pieces

Matching Game: What You Need Before You Can Effectively Begin Risk Management

D. A formal plan for when and how resources will be involved in the project, and what roles they will perform

E. A dependency-sequenced organization of the project's activities

F. Anything that limits the team's options, e.g., scope, time, cost, quality, risk, resources, and customer satisfaction

G. Things that must be done or information that must be collected before you can adequately complete risk management

H. A formal or informal plan that describes what part(s) of the project will be purchased under contract or purchase order; it includes a plan for managing the sellers

I. The individual or organization who will use the product of the project

J. Information from before the project was approved, articles written about similar projects, and other such information

K. Initiating, planning, executing, monitoring and controlling, closing

L. What went right, wrong, or would have been done differently by past project teams if they could execute their projects again

M. Unwilling to accept risk

N. Anticipated time or cost of project activities

O. Company policies, procedures, templates, and historical information

P. Things that are accepted as true, but may not be true

Q. Information from past, similar projects

R. High-level directive from the sponsor outlining the overall objectives of the project; it authorizes the existence of a project

S. Information about individuals and organizations who are actively involved in the project or who may affect or be affected by the project

T. The individual or group who authorizes the project and provides the financial resources

U. Amounts of risk the company and key stakeholders are willing to accept

V. Stakeholders' needs or intents that may be unstated, but are motivators or non-motivators for working on the project

W. Areas in which the company and key stakeholders are willing to accept risk

X. A formal plan documenting how and in what form communications will be handled on the project

Matching Game: What You Need Before You Can Effectively Begin Risk Management

Answer Key

1.	G	13.	H
2.	K	14.	S
3.	J	15.	T
4.	Q	16.	B
5.	L	17.	I
6.	R	18.	V
7.	A	19.	O
8.	C	20.	F
9.	E	21.	P
10.	N	22.	W
11.	D	23.	M
12.	X	24.	U

What You Need Before You Can Effectively Begin Risk Management

Questions for Discussion

1. Which of the inputs to risk management do you not have for your real-world projects? How will you go about getting or creating them?

2. What inputs do you not understand? How will you refresh your project management knowledge before reading more about risk management?

3. Why do you need iterations in project planning?

4. Why do you need a project scope statement, communications management plan, and procurement management plan before you can identify risks?

5. How does knowing the critical path help with determining risks?

Plan Risk Management

Objectives of the Plan Risk Management Process

The Plan Risk Management process sets the tone for the rest of the risk management efforts. It involves deciding how to proceed, who should be involved, when risk management activities should be done during the project life cycle, and how frequently they should be done.

The objectives of the Plan Risk Management process are to:
- Create a plan for handling risk management for the project
- Adapt any policies and procedures for risk to the needs of the project
- Tailor risk management activities to the needs of the project to make sure the level, type, and visibility of the activities are commensurate with:
  - The type and size of the project
  - The experience of the project team
  - The perceived level of project risk
  - The importance of the project to the organization

The risk management planning process could also include determining how you will measure the success of your risk efforts. You can create metrics such as:
- The number of unidentified risks that occurred in a reporting period
- The number of times risk owners were not prepared to handle an identified risk
- The amount of extra reserve requested
- The impact to the project of unidentified risks
- The number of fallback plans that needed to be implemented

Inputs to the Plan Risk Management process include the project scope statement; the schedule, cost, and communications management plans; and company historical records, policies, and templates for risk management.

The Importance of This Process

In my research, I have found that many project managers have difficulty convincing management and the team of the value of this planning process. People involved in the project may be more interested in beginning what they consider to be the "real" work of the project. However, in order for the risk management process to flow smoothly and produce a clear picture of the project risks, it is important to think about how the process will be completed BEFORE getting started. Therefore, the Plan Risk Management process allows the work, when it is done, to be completed faster, easier, and more effectively. With proper planning, you are less likely to miss something important!

So do not skip risk management planning. If you do, the project—and particularly quality—will be negatively affected. The quality process is often defined as plan, do, check, and act. Without planning, anything you do may be of lower quality.

Who Is Involved

To effectively perform risk management, the project team as well as the stakeholders should be involved.

The project manager directs the risk management planning process and may seek input from the sponsor, management, the project team, other stakeholders, and the project management office or a governance body, if one exists in the organization.

Project Management Office

The project management office, also referred to as the PMO, is a department that supports project management within an organization. For risk management, the project management office may provide the following:
- Activity estimating forms
- Procedures regarding who needs to approve risk response plans
- Procedures regarding the involvement of stakeholders in risk management
- Standard probability and impact scales

- Data quality standards
- Acceptable ranges of risk scores for activities and projects
- Standard decision points for go/no-go decisions
- Standard methods of determining and using reserves
- Standards for the probability or confidence level to use for estimating (e.g., 80 percent, 90 percent, etc.)
- Rules for contracting and including risk management in the procurement process
- Direction on when risk audits should be done and who should be involved
- Structure for the collection and dissemination of lessons learned
- Processes to incorporate the results of risk audits and lessons learned into the company
- Oversight assistance for measuring the effectiveness of corrective action
- Metrics to measure the effectiveness of the risk process

Risk Management Department

In some organizations, there is a separate risk management department (to address project risk, not other kinds of risk management). It may supply policies and provide assistance with project risk management efforts. This department generally performs functions similar to those of the project management office in the management of large projects. It mentors and coaches project managers on the use of risk management and ensures that risk management is done properly and given the appropriate level of attention throughout all projects in the organization.

Governance Body

Organizations that are more evolved in terms of risk management may even have some form of governance body that would be responsible for any or all of the items attributed to the PMO and risk management department in the previous sections.

Risk Team

On a large project, the project manager may require the help of others in managing risk. This group is called the risk team. It may include project team members, but not exclusively. For example, some stakeholders, the sponsor, and others could be on the risk team, depending on the needs of the project. The risk team solicits and considers everyone's ideas.

Plan Risk Management

Carefully Forming a Risk Team Is Time Well Spent

You may want to draw from your project team and any other stakeholders to form a team that will manage the potential range of risks on your project. A well-chosen risk team is one of the keys to identifying and addressing risks throughout the project. Don't forget to consider the sponsor and the customer.

Create a Chart of Responsibilities

Create a chart of responsibilities for individuals and groups working with the project manager on project risk activities. Such a chart with common responsibilities might look like the following:

	Sponsor	Project Manager	Risk Team	Team	Risk Owner	Other Stakeholders
Plan Risk Management		X	X			
Identify Risks	X	X	X	X	X	X
Perform Qualitative Risk Analysis	X	X	X	As needed		X
Perform Quantitative Risk Analysis		X	X	As needed		X
Plan Risk Responses	X	X	X	As needed	X	X
Monitor and Control Risks		X	X	X	X	

A Risk Management Plan

Here is a creative way to understand risk management plans. Imagine your project at its end. List the risk management activities that will help get you there. Next to each one, describe how you will do the activity. Now you have the beginning of a risk management plan.

The risk management plan may include:

- **Methodology:** This section defines how you will perform risk management for the particular project. Remember to adapt to the needs of each project. Low-priority projects will likely warrant less risk management effort than high-priority projects.
- **Roles and responsibilities:** Who will do what? Did you realize that non-team members may have roles and responsibilities regarding risk management?
- **Budget:** This section includes the cost for the risk management process. Yes, you must realize the cost of doing risk management, but know that risk management saves the project time and money overall by avoiding or reducing threats and taking advantage of opportunities.
- **Timing:** This section talks about when to do risk management for the project. Risk management should start as soon as you have the appropriate inputs and should be repeated throughout the life of the project, since new risks can be identified as the project progresses and the degree of risk may change.
- **Risk categories:** Look at historical records and other resources to find lists of areas or sources of risks experienced on similar projects. The value of risk categories will be further discussed in the Identify Risks chapter.
- **Definitions of probability and impact:** Would everyone who rates the probability a "seven" in the Perform Qualitative Risk Analysis process mean the same thing? A person who is risk averse might think of 7 as very high, while someone who is risk prone might think of 7 as a low figure. The definitions and the probability and impact matrix help standardize these interpretations and also help compare risks between projects.
- **Stakeholder tolerances:** What if the stakeholders have a low risk tolerance for cost overruns? That information would be taken into account to rank cost impacts higher than they would if the low tolerance was in another area. Tolerances should not be implied, but uncovered in project initiating and clarified or refined continually.
- **Reporting formats:** This describes any reports related to risk management that will be used and what they will include.
- **Tracking:** Take this to mean how the risk process will be audited, and the documentation of what happens with risk management activities.

Plan Risk Management

A risk management plan contains budgets and schedules for risk management, but it is created after the initial budget and schedule for the project and before the final schedule and budget are created in schedule development and cost budgeting. See the sample risk management plan at the end of this chapter.

Adapt and Tailor Risk Management Activities to the Needs of the Project

One of the top 10 reasons projects fail is that project managers do not adjust their project management process to the needs of each project. They use the same forms, processes, frequency of meetings, and management style on all projects.

> **Project failure can often be attributed to a lack of adaptation of organizational policies.**

All projects are different and need to be managed differently. If the project is a top priority for the company, then the risk management effort will be more extensive than if the project is lower priority. If the project has never been done before, more time will need to be spent on risk management than if the project had been done many times by the company.

Specific items to tailor include:
- When risk activities are done
- How much time is spent on the activities
- Who is involved
- What standard rating schemes are used
- What forms and processes are used

Adaptation also relates to company risk management policies. Do not laugh! Yes, it is true that companies should have these to help provide risk management direction, save time, and decrease the need for meetings. The project should make use of these procedures when planning risk management activities.

Risk Management Software

Risk management is a people-related process, not a software calculation. The best assets for risk management are the ideas and information possessed by people. Do not allow project and risk management software to be your main guide to managing projects. "Project management" software is most useful for scheduling and reporting. Understand what needs to be done for project management and risk management and use software accordingly!

Use Outside Risk Experts

If the company is inexperienced with risk, or is working on a type of project that they have never before completed, resources from outside the company might help ensure that risks are not missed. These people could be technical experts, project management experts, or risk experts. There are even consultants who specialize in risk identification.

Confusing Terms

Risk rating: A risk rating is a number between 1 and 10 chosen to evaluate the probability or impact of a risk.

Risk score for each risk: To calculate the risk score, you multiply probability times impact. This gives you a numerical value for each risk. That value is then compared to other risks in the project to determine the risk ranking for each risk within the project.

Risk score for the project: To obtain the project risk score, you add up the risk scores for each risk in the project.

Risk ranking within the project: To rank risks, you compare the risk scores for all the risks. The risk with the highest risk score becomes the highest ranking risk, the next highest becomes second, etc.

Risk ranking compared to other projects: The total risk score for each project can be compared to the risk score of other projects to rank projects by risk. Sometimes the total risk score is used, and sometimes the total risk score is divided by the number of risks and that number is compared to other projects.

So, to put it all together, the risk ratings are used to calculate the risk score, which is then used to determine the risk ranking of the risks and the project.

Plan Risk Management

Steps of the Plan Risk Management Process

The following are the recommended steps to follow in completing risk management planning.

1. Review available risk management procedures, historical records, and lessons learned.
2. Define what methodology you will use for the current project to identify risks.
3. Determine who will be involved in risk management (roles and responsibilities).
4. Determine how much the risk efforts will cost, and include those costs in the budget.
5. Determine the timing of the risk efforts throughout the project.
6. Establish the definitions of probability and impact you will use to qualify and quantify risks.
7. Determine the stakeholder tolerances and thresholds to consider in determining which risks to act on.
8. Define which risk categories will be used to identify risks.
9. Define how risks will be documented, analyzed, and communicated to the project team, other stakeholders, the sponsor, etc.
10. Determine how you will track and keep records of risks for use on future projects.

Output of the Plan Risk Management Process

The output of the Plan Risk Management process is a risk management plan. The following provides a description of a sample project and an example of what a risk management plan might look like for that project.

Project Description

- **Risk background:** The company has no risk management standards.
- **Project size:** It is a small project with a budget of $200,000 and is expected to be completed in three months. The project has 5 team members and 15 other identified stakeholders.
- **Complexity:** This project is thought to have low complexity.
- **Experience:** The project is similar to ones done before, so there is a lot of experience to tap into.
- **Skill level:** The team is not highly competent with risk management or project management.

- **The perceived level of project risk at this stage of the project:** After completing project planning up to this point, the project has a moderate amount of perceived risk.
- **The importance of the project to the organization:** The project is of moderate importance to the organization.

Based on this information, the project manager and team have decided to spend a moderate amount of time on risk management. They have created the following risk management plan:

Identify Risks			
Method	Details	Responsibility	Time Budget
Collect risks via e-mail	Three stakeholders; Eric (marketing), Jan (accounting), and Steve (IT), will be asked to e-mail the project manager with the risks they see on the project.	• Danny (team member), will compose the e-mail requesting the risks and make sure adequate responses are received.	0.5 hours
Risk identification meeting using individual thought/ brainstorming/ affinity diagram methods	The rest of the stakeholders (from different areas of the company) will be broken into three groups of four people. They will be brought into a meeting where they will first be shown relevant information about the project. They will be asked to write down the opportunities they see, and then the threats. Each person will be required to submit at least five threats or opportunities. Once completed, each group will immediately take part in a brainstorming session followed by the creation of an affinity diagram to look for additional risks.	• Mary (project manager) will coordinate this effort.	3 hours

Identify Risks			
Method	Details	Responsibility	Time Budget
Expert interview	It has been determined that there are questions and uncertainties about this project that only management can address. Therefore, there will be an expert interview with management.	• The team will provide the questions. • The project manager will conduct the expert interview. • Nicole (team member), will take notes during the interview.	0.5 hours
Risk identification meeting using individual thought/ brainstorming/ affinity diagram	Once threats and opportunities have been identified by others, the team will be asked to list, in writing, the opportunities they see and then the threats, followed by a brainstorming session. When no further ideas are forthcoming, the list of threats and opportunities from all other sources will be provided to the team for additional brainstorming. Lastly an affinity diagram will be used to look for any more risks.	• The project manager will conduct this team meeting.	2 hours

Perform Qualitative Risk Analysis			
What	Method	Responsibility	Time Budget
Data quality assessment	Each threat and opportunity will be analyzed and clarified if necessary so that the risks can be effectively assessed.	• The team will perform the data quality assessment.	2 hours
Definition of probability and impact	A 1 to 10 scale will be used for probability and for impact. Interpretation of the scale for probability: • 1 to 2 means very low • 3 to 4 means low • 5 to 6 means medium • 7 to 8 means high • 9 to 10 means it's a fact For impact: • 1 to 2 means little impact • 3 to 4 means possible delay that does not delay the overall project • 5 to 6 means possible delay of three days or less • 7 to 8 means possible delay of four to eight days • 9 to 10 means possible delay of more than nine days	• The team will use the agreed upon definitions of probability and impact.	0.5 hours

Perform Qualitative Risk Analysis			
What	Method	Responsibility	Time Budget
Application of the risk threshold	Any risk receiving a probability rating of 9 or higher will be considered a fact and will be addressed in the project management plan, not risk management. Any threat or opportunity with an impact rating of seven or higher will move forward in the process. Any threat or opportunity with a rating of less than seven will be included on the list of non-top risks.	• The project manager will determine which risks will move forward, based on probability and impact ratings.	0.5 hours
Calculating the risk score	The risk score for the project will be calculated. Our company does not have historical records of the risk scores of other projects to compare it to. This project will be used to begin the creation of historical records. The project as a whole must have a risk score of no more than 50.0.	• The project manager will calculate and document the project's risk score.	0.2 hours
Go/no-go meeting with management	A call will be placed to management to inform them of the risk score of the project. A decision will be made as to whether project planning should continue.	• The project manager will call management to discuss whether to continue planning.	0.5 hours

Perform Quantitative Risk Analysis
It is determined that this project does not require the time and effort needed to quantify the risks.

Plan Risk Responses			
What	Method	Responsibility	Time Budget
Determining risk responses	Responses to top risks will be determined in order to decrease the total threats and increase opportunities on the project. Secondary risks will be investigated, and threats will be eliminated when appropriate and possible.	• The team, other stakeholders, and management (if needed) will be involved in this effort.	2 hours
Reporting	Risk response plans and reserves will be created. The risk response plans will be sent to management for approval, and then used in the Monitor and Control Risks process.	• The project manager will obtain management approval and follow the plan approved.	0.5 hours
Go/no-go meeting with management	A meeting with management will be held to review the total impact of risk that remains on the project. We will show management the value of the efforts so far in decreasing threats and increasing opportunities, and the impact on project cost and time. A go/no-go decision will be made.	• The project manager will conduct the meeting with management.	0.5 hours

Monitor and Control Risks			
What	Method	Responsibility	Time Budget
Risk reviews	A risk review will be held once a week to review the top risks and their responses, measure the effectiveness of our risk activities, and update our risk response plans. It is expected that some changes will be made to the project as a result of these risk reviews in order to meet the project objectives.	• The project manager, team, and other stakeholders (if needed) will be involved in reviews.	3 hours
Tracking	Risk efforts will be monitored, and risk audits performed. The risk response plans will be kept updated for the benefit of future projects.	• The project manager will be responsible for managing these efforts.	3 hours
Reporting	The activity reporting formats will include reports on threats and opportunities. The project manager will be notified by e-mail when a trigger has occurred and the previously agreed-upon response has begun. Risk will be included in the monthly project status report and will be sent to the stakeholders. Attached will be the most current list of top risks and responses.	• Team members and risk owners will report to the project manager. • The project manager will maintain project documentation and provide reports to the stakeholders.	3 hours

Chapter Summary

Key Concepts

- The objective of this step of the risk management process is to decide how to approach risk management on the project. The level, type, and visibility of what is done must be commensurate with the complexity and size of the project, experience of the project team, perceived amount of project risk, and importance of the project to the organization.

- Companies should have risk policies, standards, and procedures so information from all projects can be interpreted properly and the risk process can be completed more quickly and effectively.

Key Terms

- Plan Risk Management process
- Project management office (PMO)
- Risk management department
- Risk management plan
- Risk team
- Methodology

- Budget
- Timing
- Definitions of probability and impact
- Reporting formats
- Tracking
- Roles and responsibilities

Matching Game: Plan Risk Management

Instructions: Match the risk management key word to its definition.

Key Word

_____ **1.** Plan Risk Management process

_____ **2.** Project management office (PMO)

_____ **3.** Risk management department

_____ **4.** Risk management plan

_____ **5.** Risk team

_____ **6.** Methodology

_____ **7.** Roles and responsibilities

_____ **8.** Budget

_____ **9.** Timing

_____ **10.** Definitions of probability and impact

_____ **11.** Reporting formats

_____ **12.** Tracking

Definition

A. Those helping manage the risk management process

B. Amount of resources allocated to be spent on the project

C. How records of risks will be documented for the benefit of the current project and future projects

D. A standardized interpretation of the numbering system used to evaluate risks

E. Determining how risk management will be done on the project, who will be involved, and procedures to be followed

F. How risk will be handled on the project and what data and tools will be used

G. A department that supplies policies and assistance with project risk management efforts

H. Who will do what on the project

Matching Game: Plan Risk Management

I. A department that supports project management within an organization

J. How the results of risk management will be documented and communicated

K. When/how often risk management activities will be performed throughout the project

L. A plan for how risk management will be done on a project; who should be involved, when risk management activities should be done, and how frequently they should be done

Answer Key

1.	E	7.	H
2.	I	8.	B
3.	G	9.	K
4.	L	10.	D
5.	A	11.	J
6.	F	12.	C

Questions for Discussion

1. How are projects different with a risk management plan?

2. How will you complete risk management planning for your real-world projects?

3. How will you determine risk tolerances on your real-world projects?

4. Why is it not possible to perform the Plan Risk Management process until after other parts of project planning have been completed?

5. Why would risk management planning need to be performed a second or third time during a project?

CHAPTER 4

Identify Risks

Objectives of the Identify Risks Process

Now the fun begins! Risk identification is really playing detective. It takes interaction with people to identify risks.

The objectives of the Identify Risks process are to:
- Identify and record a long list of threats and opportunities for the project and by work package; for many projects, the word "long" means hundreds of risks
- Make sure all risks are in the cause-risk-effect format
- Understand the risks

> **Risks include what can go RIGHT (opportunities) as well as what can go WRONG (threats)!**

As risks are being identified, it is logical and efficient to capture more information than just the risk. Some of the other information that could be captured at this time and used later in the risk management process includes the potential risk owner for each risk, triggers (indications that a risk is about to occur), and potential risk response strategies.

The inputs to the Identify Risks process include:
- Project charter
- Risk management plan
- Outputs from project planning—such as the work breakdown structure, estimates, and management plans

- List of common risk categories
- Historical records and project documents
- Stakeholder register

Determine What Additional Information Is Needed

Inputs are one thing, but are you really ready to start identifying risks? Have you had all your questions about the project answered? Many questions about the project and the scope of work or requirements will arise as you and your team identify risks. These may include, *"Is training included in this project?"* or, *"Now that we have looked closely at the project, I am not sure we know enough about what is meant in the project description section of the project charter."*

Such questions can be a major stumbling block in risk management because it can become impossible to move forward until they are answered. A smart project manager will spend time *before* risk identification to accumulate as much information as possible about the project and to ask the signer(s) of the project charter enough questions to minimize the need to ask additional questions later. (See project background data discussed earlier in this book for additional items to collect.) Expect questions to arise, however, since it is not possible to have all information complete before starting the Identify Risks process.

Have a Complete Scope of Work and Complete Requirements Before You Begin the Identify Risks Process

Unclear requirements and scope of work are a risk to the project and have cost and schedule impacts. Completely defining requirements is a tough challenge and one that many people think they are too busy to do. Those people think it is the project manager's job, when in fact it is only the project manager's job to manage the requirements, not to determine the requirements.

Reasons Requirements Are Difficult to Determine for Many Projects

- Stakeholders grab onto the first or most obvious solution to a problem instead of working toward the best solution
- Changing environments
- Differences in language or culture

© 2010 RMC Publications, Inc. • (952) 846-4484 • info@rmcproject.com • www.rmcproject.com

- Lack of support from management
- Determining requirements seems to take too much time
- Inexperienced project manager
- Unclear methodology for determining requirements
- Lack of historical records
- Tendency to avoid arguments
- Bureaucratic problems require the team to start the work before there is a final determination about what the organization wants
- Stakeholders are trying to fast track the project
- Stakeholders do not realize the consequences of providing unclear requirements
- Stakeholders do not want to commit in case they change their minds later, keeping options open

How to get complete requirements is complex and cannot be fully described here. I can provide a trick, however.

Show Them the Consequences

In the case of risk, this means adding such line items as the following to the list of project risks:

> **Unclear requirements or scope of work are a risk to the project and almost always have a negative cost and schedule impact.**

- Because the customer is not sure of the functionality of the X system, changes are expected. For every change in this area, there will be a three- to six-day delay of the project with a US $10,000 to US $20,000 cost for each occurrence.
- Because there is a lack of final approval of the feasibility of the X system design, component changes are expected. For every change, there will be at least a two-week delay and a $12,000 to $21,000 impact.

It may not be possible to have finalized requirements, but a serious effort must be made to determine them; otherwise project schedule and costs will be increased. It is the project manager's role to make sure consequences are known to all stakeholders in order to encourage the finalization of requirements. (For more on determining requirements, visit www.rmcproject.com for courses and products about this topic.)

Determine Who Has Insight into Risks

This is where the stakeholder register created earlier in the project management process comes in handy during the risk management process. Determining who has insight into risks is also one of the common stumbling blocks for risk management efforts. Can you imagine how many more risks can be identified and how much closer to identifying all the major risks you will be if you involve the right stakeholders in the Identify Risks process?

In informal studies conducted during risk management classes, there was an approximately 50 percent increase in the number of risks identified on small projects when stakeholders were involved. The difference is even greater on large projects where the project manager may not have day-to-day contact with many of the stakeholders. All impacted groups should be represented on the risk team. This includes individuals from any of the stakeholder groups listed in the Inputs to Risk Management chapter.

TRICKS OF THE TRADE® ### Gain Support for Risk Identification Before You Begin

Introduce the risk management process to your team and stakeholders by "setting the stage." Tell stories of past projects and the problems that were incurred. Then ask your team and other stakeholders if they would like to avoid those problems on the current project. When they say "yes" (which of course they will), you will have gained their participation in the risk management process.

TRICKS OF THE TRADE® ### Look Throughout the Organization for Risks and Risk Responses

There are many stories in business magazines and books that describe instances where those implementing the work (manufacturing, laborers, maintenance workers, and others in the organization) had ideas for major business improvements—but no one thought to reach into the organization to ask them. Do not make the same mistake. Consider including them on the risk team. The larger the project, the better it is to include representation from all levels of the organization for risks and risk responses.

Use Published Articles

Today, many executives write magazine articles—and even books—about their projects. Why not look for something written about a project comparable to yours? This will offer you a succinct overview of some of the risks others have faced in similar situations.

Use Involvement with Associations

If you are a member of a professional association, you might take advantage of your membership by mining the members for information and providing information in return. When you go to association meetings, ask those you meet for ideas about potential risks. You might think others who work on projects that are not similar to yours couldn't help you. That would be a mistake. When I teach risk management workshops, the attendees often consist of people from four or five industries. I strongly encourage the attendees to talk with each other, and when they do, they are surprised at the benefit they get from it. Try it.

Utilize Your Competition

Sometimes the competition even becomes a part of the risk team. In one case, a company was going to introduce a new product. If successful, the product would create a new industry. In this case, the company's competitors had a vested interest in seeing the company succeed, because all could be involved in offering products in the new industry. So a few competitors became members of the project risk team. Consider whether this could be the case on your project.

Include Your Customers

What about having your customers on the risk team? On one project, a designer of windows for fast food restaurants' drive-through windows wanted to create a dramatically new window. To make it better, they invited customer representatives to participate in identifying the risks of using the new window. As a result of involving those stakeholders, 11 additional risks were identified that the project team would not have been able to determine on their own. Of course, there was a side benefit. All the customers placed orders for the windows, months in advance of them becoming available.

Who Else Should Be Involved?

Ask those stakeholders involved with risk management to identify anyone else who should be involved on the risk team.

Limit the Use of Software

Software has little use in the Identify Risks process; it is a people process, not a computer process. In informal tests I have conducted in risk management classes, those teams that relied on software for initial risk identification produced 25 percent fewer risks. This is a huge difference and one that you cannot afford on your projects!

Plan for Risk Identification Meetings

When meeting with the team, starting by asking others what risks there might be will not only help identify more risks, but will also show that you are interested in the thoughts of your team and other stakeholders. You may need to suggest some risks to get the meeting started, but try to contribute most of your suggested risks toward the end of the session.

Your major contribution of risks should be related to business and project integration risks; you should also contribute risks related to project management or the lack of its application on the project. These items are added for discussion to the list that the risk team sees only toward the end of the Identify Risks process.

Meet Face-to-Face if Possible

I have to say it—you will identify substantially more risks if risk identification is done face-to-face. You know this is true. You can get a much better understanding when you are able to read body language and see the expressions on people's faces. Meeting virtually or using e-mail for risk management decreases the quantity and quality of risks identified.

This does not mean that lots of meetings are required. Many teams hold one project planning session where the charter is reviewed, the work breakdown structure is created, activities are sequenced, and risks are identified.

Risk Identification With Virtual Teams

In cases where it is impossible to physically gather a team, here are some tips to make working with a virtual team a success:

- Provide as much information as possible, including the project charter, WBS, project scope statement, etc.
- Clearly define your objectives, process, and "rules" for risk management
- Strive to obtain individual thought from virtual team members
- Use brainstorming on an anonymous Web site (where everyone has the same user name and password), expert interviews, and the nominal group technique to gather risks
- Create and distribute the full list of risks for qualitative risk analysis
- Have another (virtual) meeting

Meet Offsite

Have the risk team meet offsite to reduce interruptions and improve focus.

Properly Name Risks

One of the most commonly made risk-identification-related mistakes is to consider things as risks when they are not. One approach is to treat anything with a probability of greater than 80 percent as a certainty. "Lack of resources" is not a risk, nor is "not enough time to complete the project." If it is known that the required length of time for the project is shorter than the time allocated to complete the project, this is not a risk, but a fact. Such facts should be addressed in the project management plan through crashing, fast tracking, reestimating, removing scope, using other forms of schedule compression, and addressing the situation with management, not as part of risk management.

An opportunity should also not be a fact. The following examples describe circumstances that are 100 percent probable if basic project management is done on a project.

- Due to effective project team management, high team morale might occur, which may lead to high team satisfaction and productivity.
- Due to effective scope and change management, the project will be delivered on time, on budget, and according to approved scope, which may lead to high client satisfaction.

Identify Risks

To differentiate risks from facts and to adequately define risks, use the "cause-risk-effect" format for naming risks: As a result of (definitive cause), (uncertain event) may occur, which would/could/may lead to (effect). Such definition of risks provides enough information for the team to follow the rest of the project management process. See the following examples of risks in the "cause-risk-effect" format:

As a result of lack of clear direction for the scope of work for the XYZ component, there could be rework and wasted efforts, which could delay the project completion from two to four weeks.

As a result of the amount of work the customer is trying to accomplish on many projects during this project's completion, a delay in the customer's response to our requests for approvals may occur, which could result in a two-week delay in project completion.

Effects could relate to project objectives, project constraints, and risk tolerances.

What Is a Well-Defined Risk?

People often ask me what makes a well-defined risk. To answer that question, let's look at specific examples. Here is one submitted in our risk study.

- Due to the team not being co-located, communications might take a long time, which may lead to milestones being missed.

This is not a risk. Not being co-located is not the root cause of this risk. With a little further investigation, the real cause and risk might be uncovered. The real risk might be:

- As a result of the project manager's inexperience with virtual teams, work may take more time than allocated in the schedule, which may lead to milestones being missed.

Take a look at the following risk. Do you notice that it does not have much detail?

Cause	Risk	Effect
The market research function stopped focusing on the product while doing marketing research	thus missing a new trend in requirements	resulting in scope changes

© 2010 RMC Publications, Inc. • (952) 846-4484 • info@rmcproject.com • www.rmcproject.com

A well-worded risk is specific to the project. See the following reworded version.

Cause	Risk	Effect
The number of inches apart the seats should be spaced will depend on market research, which, due to changing consumer needs, will not be done until late in the project. The market research department has many products it will be researching	which may mean that seat-spacing requirements could be ignored or come even later than planned	causing the need to eliminate one row of seats and redesign the locking mechanism if the research shows changes in needs

Causes could really be threats. Let's look at the following threat submitted in one of my risk studies.

Cause	Risk	Effect
The system backup/disaster recovery mechanism may not work	which could lead to a loss of programming code or data structures and test data developed to date	None provided

Is the "cause" a cause or a threat? Let's see what it looks like after further analysis. You should ask, "Why would the system backup not work?" Knowing the real cause will be critical to analyzing the threat in the Perform Qualitative Risk Analysis process.

Cause	Risk	Effect
There have been three instances in this company where the backup/disaster recovery mechanism has not worked. Though that system is being investigated, no changes will occur before this project is completed	which means the system backup/disaster recovery mechanism may not work	which could lead to a loss of programming code or data structures and test data developed to date

Identify Risks

Causes Are Needed

Look at the following threat. Notice how much more you understand the potential threat when the cause is detailed? Also notice how ideas for responses to the threat come immediately to mind with such a detailed cause? This is one of the benefits of using the cause-risk-effect format for risks.

Cause	Risk	Effect
Because this contract is a time and materials contract, unlike previous releases that were done under fixed price contracts, and because the supplier is seldom critical of a customer-requested change	scope could creep	which could cause the project to be late and more costly

Look for the Root Cause Risk

Would you like to know a secret? Many of the risks identified are not the real risks, but causes. Look for the root cause (underlying risk) to make sure you understand the risk. For example, a threat of "customer delay in review of a submittal" might really be a threat that "the project has a low priority for the customer." It will do little good to create multiple ways to prevent the customer from delaying their review if the real threat is something else.

You should be constantly thinking, "What is the root cause?" while risks are being identified. You might explain this concept to those identifying risks to gain their assistance. Remember to review all risks before proceeding, to ensure the root cause risks have truly been identified.

Effects Can Be More Than Just Time and Cost

In the threat below, it would be easy to just list "delayed project," but would that be accurate? You do not know that this situation may cause the whole project to be delayed; it may just delay an activity that is not on the critical path. Also, just listing time or cost delay does not provide enough information to really understand the concern. Here, the specific concern is with meetings and hand-holding efforts. That wording provides more detail and thus more information for risk analysis and response development.

Cause	Risk	Effect
We are not able to maintain a good relationship with customer	causing lack of trust with customer	which may require more meetings and extra hand-holding

A Threat Is Not an Excuse for Poor Project Management

I was shocked at some of the threats submitted to me in my risk studies. It seems that some people who submitted threats tried to blame their problems on everyone but themselves. Let's look at this one. Does it seem like a well-defined threat to you?

- Due to upper management not supporting the project, resources will not be available, resulting in not being able to complete the project on time.

We could put it in the cause-risk-effect format and get the following:

Cause	Risk	Effect
Due to upper management not supporting the project	resources will not be available	resulting in not being able to complete the project on time

This doesn't get to the root cause of the impact. Such as with proper project management, issues like lack of support or lack of resources MUST be dealt with before the project starts. The project management plan must be achievable and bought-into before starting work. There is no other ethical option for a project manager.

Therefore, the project manager should not have agreed to an unrealistic timeframe or should have proven that the set timeframe was unrealistic. This "threat" is really a lack of the project manager doing what he or she should be doing. The project manager should have cut scope, crashed, fast tracked, adjusted quality, or taken some other measure to deal with the resources issues, rather than waiting until the risk identification process, and then sitting back and saying that the project cannot be completed on time.

Make Separate Lists of Threats and Opportunities to Prevent Identifying Only Threats

Opportunities should be identified to balance out the negative occurrences (threats), as well as to take advantage of additional benefits of the project.

It is hard for people to think of opportunities that may occur, as most people are used to thinking of risks as only bad things. I have found that having the team create a separate list of opportunities before threats helps increase the number of opportunities identified and gives people practice looking for the opportunities. Revisit opportunities after identifying threats to try to uncover even more opportunities.

The following are examples of opportunities:

Cause	Risk	Effect
Because there is a lot of research and development in this area a competitor may release new technology	that could also be available for our project	which could help save time on the project
Because we will be advertising our new products as part of this project	consumers who have not heard of us before may be introduced to our company	which will increase interest in our products
Because this project involves our new products as part of the project	new skills could be acquired	which could be sold to others and thus increase company revenue
Because we will be extensively working with a wide variety of customer information systems on this project	we may acquire the expertise to improve our own systems	thus allowing our existing customer service staff to do more work in a shorter period of time

Work should be done during planning to make sure the opportunity is investigated and specific plans undertaken to make it more likely. You can take advantage of an opportunity in the project management plan.

© 2010 RMC Publications, Inc. • (952) 846-4484 • info@rmcproject.com • www.rmcproject.com

Cause	Risk	Effect
As a result of the amount of information available from the prior Latin American eBusiness project (including payloads for order create/order response/order cancel response transactions)	we may be able to leverage the work from that project	which could make the work on this project easier and result in decreased cost and schedule duration

Can you leverage the work? It is part of planning to investigate further and clarify this opportunity so that specific plans can be made to take advantage of the opportunity.

Risks Should Be Clarified

Imagine someone identifies the following threat:
* Customer doesn't convey the problem clearly, either from RFP or during program execution.

Doesn't this situation need investigation and clarification while still in planning? In this case, there could be a further meeting with the customer, the sales department could talk to the customer, or questions to clarify this risk could be sent via e-mail to the customer.

Let's look at a few more examples where more detail or clarification is needed before qualitative analysis of the threat:

Cause	Risk	Effect
Misinterpretations of EPC contract/other reasons	may cause a delay on account of dispute between us and the customer regarding payment	leading to a delay in project implementation

What part of the contract? When is this most likely to occur?

Cause	Risk	Effect
Inefficiency of the supplier	may cause payment disputes between the supplier and his employees/workers	leading to a delay in the project schedule

Is there something specific behind these general statements? If so, that would have to be identified and clarified and a new threat or threats uncovered.

Cause	Risk	Effect
Due to sole sourcing equipment	the supplier may not be concerned about delivering on time	which could impact the project schedule and cost

A good project manager would ask about the threat above, "Do you have any specific reasons for concern? Has this supplier delayed delivery before to us or anyone else? What leads you to think this is a possibility on this project?"

Cause	Risk	Effect
Due to wrong date mis-entry (US system vs. UK system)	the computer outputs may give wrong validity/expiration dates	causing system failure

If this is one of the top threats, the solution during planning would be to add an activity to make sure that the correct entry format is used. The risk would be mostly eliminated in planning.

Include Risks Relating to Integration

Integration is the project manager's role of putting all the pieces of the project together into a cohesive whole that meets the customer's needs. You should include risks relating to integration in the Identify Risks process.

Here are some examples of integration risks:
- *Activity A may not provide the information that Activity B needs.*
- *Activity A may not complete in time for Activity B to start.*
- *Activity B may become dependent on Activities A and C being completed.*
- *The person doing Activity B may determine that the input of Activity A is incomplete.*

Look at Assumptions

Assumptions are often unidentified and if they are major ("I assume that the software will be received without any bugs"), the project could be impacted. Therefore, in addition to looking at the project and the activities for risks,

© 2010 RMC Publications, Inc. • (952) 846-4484 • info@rmcproject.com • www.rmcproject.com

a great project manager will also look at the assumptions to see if they add to the list of risks.

Some people treat assumptions as a risk category. In any case, assumptions must be identified, and they need constant review during the life of the project.

Quantity Is Quality

During the Identify Risks process, you are striving to identify as many risks as you can. The more risks, the better the risk identification session. Groups that are prepared and are led with a plan for risk identification in mind create the longest list and have the best results. A group of six people should be able to identify 100 to 150 risks in one-and-a-half hours, assuming that they are technically literate about the project. Many risk identification techniques will be described later in this chapter.

Dealing with Team Member Discouragement

When a project is in trouble before it even begins, the Identify Risks process could make the team members feel discouraged. Such discouragement should be a warning sign.

If you are in this situation, I suggest spending time on opportunities first (as noted previously) and then quickly moving through the risk management process to the Plan Risk Responses process, as this step tends to create more optimism.

Methods of Documenting Risks

One of the ways to speed up the risk management process is to have efficient methods. Think about how you are going to collect risks. Poor project managers will have to do a lot of recopying of risks. Great project managers will think through what they are going to do with the risks and make a determination on how to collect them without much rework. There are two main choices for recording risks: sticky notes or forms.

Sticky notes can be more versatile and useful throughout the Identify Risks process, but there will be times when forms are more practical.

Identify Risks

Forms

Too many people think that risk management involves just sending out a form for people to fill in risks. This is a mistake, as it will not on its own produce a complete list of risks for the project.

In my risk management studies, many multi-million dollar projects were relying on forms as their only risk management tool. Let me share with you some secrets about forms so you can make an informed, intelligent decision.

Forms have the following benefits:
- They are fast.
- They are commonly used for other work activities, so many people feel comfortable with them.
- They help accumulate the input of many people in a relatively short time period.
- They are a convenient way to gain the contribution of those who do not want to spend much time on the project.

Forms have the following disadvantages:
- They do not allow for group thought or opinion.
- They do not encourage people to think "outside the box." People will just fill out the form.
- They do not allow for in-depth analysis of risk.
- They do not allow discussion. Some people are more verbal and require a verbal method to come up with the best list of risks.
- They do not allow for unlimited ideas. People will come up with a few risks and stop.
- They are not always taken seriously. People will not view risk identification as seriously as they would if other methods are used.
- They limit responses.

During my risk management classes, people get a chance to apply what they are learning to their real projects. In these classes, I have seen the following actions—people stop when they run out of blank rows to enter risks, or they leave only one blank space for risks. When people in the first group are asked if they can think of any more risks, they respond, "Sure, but there is no more room on the form." People in the second group say they somehow felt it was not appropriate to use the entire form. Yes, that is what they say. Watch out if you are relying on forms. You will not identify all risks using a form!

Filling out a form is often viewed as boring. People usually have little incentive to really think through their ideas about risks. They frequently just provide a few and then get back to their "real" work.

In other instances, students have told me that they are not comfortable or as productive when they are writing. In order to really think, they need a more verbal tool. Informal studies of this issue conducted during my risk management classes show that one-third of those surveyed agreed that a form would not get their best contribution of risks. That is an astounding number!

There is an endless variety of forms used to obtain risks. Consider these options, but bear in mind the limitations of using forms for risk identification. Adapt one to your real-world project situation.

A basic form might look like the following:

Threats and Opportunities Identification Chart		
Overall project risks		
Risks per activity		
	Activity A	
	Activity B	
	Activity C	
	Activity D	

Checklists

A checklist is a form with more data. It might look like the following:

Risk Checklist			
Category	Cause of Risk	Relevant to This Project?	Impact (High, Medium, Low)
1. Technical	Unique or special resources		
	Proven or unproven technology		
	System or functional complexity		
	Interface complexity		
	Design clarity/ stability		
	Requirements or scope changes		
	Physical and/or material properties		
2. External Influences	Material availability		
	Regulatory changes		
	Schedule constraints		
	Funding priorities		
	Personnel skills		
	Unique communication problems		
	Objectives change		
	Personnel availability		

Risk Checklist			
Category	Cause of Risk	Relevant to This Project?	Impact (High, Medium, Low)
3. Internal Factors	Training and training support		
	Project manager experience		
	Facility		
	Policy changes		
	Equipment		

Note that each of these general categories could result in either threats or opportunities on the project. But watch out—only using a checklist would be a big mistake! Yet many companies think such a checklist is the entire risk management process.

Checklists have the following advantages:
- They are great tools to get a quick sense of the level of risk in the project during initiating—before a charter is created and before formal risk management begins.
- They give a quick overview of the risk on a project.
- They help generate conversation about the risk on the project before doing detailed risk identification.
- They are useful memory joggers.

Checklists have the following disadvantages:
- They do not identify risks by activity or work package.
- They do not provide enough details of the risks, their causes, or effects.
- They do not provide a chance for someone to add a risk that is not on the form!
- They are not project-specific. Checklists are usually used for all projects in a company or department.
- They provide a false sense of security that all risks have been uncovered.
- They lead to thinking "in the box" (i.e., not thinking about what is not on the list). It is extremely hard to think beyond what is on the list after one has read through the entire list and filled out the form.
- They do not help to assess, qualify, or quantify risks specific to the project being examined.

Sticky Notes

Sticky notes can be used to record risks as they are identified.

Sticky notes have the following advantages:
- They are easy.
- They equalize participation because all attendees may be required to provide the same number of sticky notes.
- They help satisfy the need for anonymity.
- They gain participation from people who are not comfortable speaking in front of a group. Many people are not very verbal and will therefore not contribute ideas during a meeting if the only opportunity to do so is to talk.
- They gain individual thought.
- They can be used to record risks uncovered through a variety of risk identification methods, described in the following sections.
- They help you keep track of lots of data while the data is manually sorted.

Sticky notes have the following disadvantages:
- It is hard (but not impossible) to use them with virtual teams.
- They cannot be e-mailed.
- They may be too small to be seen from a distance.
- They cannot automatically total or calculate probability and impact results like a form and software can.
- The information must be transferred to an electronic format.

Why use sticky notes and not just paper? You could use plain paper, but as you will see, having sticky notes and the ability to sort and re-sort them may dramatically speed up the subsequent risk steps.

TRICKS OF THE TRADE® RMC Risk Notes

Using a sticky note specifically designed for risk management purposes will further enhance and speed up the Perform Qualitative and Quantitative Risk Analysis processes. We call these tools RMC Risk Notes. The RMC Risk Notes format allows you to keep track of necessary risk information as you sort risks during the risk management process.

The following is an example:

Activity		Name of source	
Design the installation system		*Daniel from the end-user department*	
Probability	Risk		Impact
	Because we will not see component X until delivery from our supplier, component X may not adequately connect to component Y, resulting in a three-month delay while the part is reworked.		
When it might occur	Trigger		Potential Risk Owner
During the development phase			*Whitney*

Recording the name of the person or source of the risk will allow you to go back to that source if more information is needed during later steps of the risk process. Knowing how often the risk may occur (the risk frequency) and when it may occur will enable you to evaluate the risk during the Perform Qualitative and Quantitative Risk Analysis processes. All in all, capturing risks on these sticky notes is a very fast way to work the risk process.

Remember that you are just identifying risks now. The RMC Risk Notes are used throughout the risk process, as will be described throughout this book. As you work through the risk processes, you will add more information to these notes.

Methods to Identify Risks

Let me offer you another secret. Risks that are identified are less likely to occur simply because they have changed from unknown unknowns to known unknowns. In other words, simply identifying risks will decrease the overall risk for the project.

Methods to identify risks include the following (which will be explained later in this chapter):
- Use a prompt list
- Review the list of risks provided in this book
- Review your own company's historical records and other documentation

- Brainstorming
- Conduct a "pre-mortem"
- Affinity diagrams
- Expert interviews
- Nominal group technique
- Delphi technique
- Cause and effect diagram
- Failure modes and effects analysis
- Strengths, weaknesses, opportunities, and threats (SWOT) analysis

Use a Prompt List

A prompt list is a generic list of risk categories. This can be used as a starting point to customize a list of risk categories most relevant to projects within your organization. Using such a list has long been a trick recommended by RMC. It is now included in risk management standards as a tool of the Identify Risks process.

A prompt list of risk categories can be extremely beneficial in risk identification, but only when used properly. Watch out—identifying risks by category should not be the primary method (*"Let's determine what technology-related risks we have on this project."*). With any method of risk identification, risks should be identified for the project as a whole and by activity (*"What are the main concerns about completing this activity?"*). When the group has gone as far as they can, offer lists of risk categories and a risk list to uncover any risks that may have been missed.

A common error is to forget whole categories of risks. Can you imagine the impact to the project if a whole category of risks (like cultural risks) was forgotten in risk identification? Just look at any of the projects that have made news lately. Was the root cause of them being newsworthy that they forgot whole categories of risk?

Recently, a state governing body in the United States demanded that the seating arrangement in their meeting room be returned to the original configuration. They became unhappy with the new seating configuration after the building was renovated. The issue made news when it was discovered that such a change would cost about US $150,000. Why did the project manager not identify a risk that the new facility would not meet the end users' needs? Why were the end users not involved in making such a decision? It appears that the category of stakeholder satisfaction (of which end users are a part) was overlooked. End users often identify risks that the core team does not.

Using a Prompt List of Risk Categories

A truly great project manager will carry a list of risk categories (a prompt list) with him or her during the Identify Risks process and make sure that no matter how risks are identified, risks in all categories are unearthed. A generic list of risk categories includes:

- Technical, quality, or performance
- Project management risks
- Organizational risks
- External risks

Some of the most commonly missed risk categories are:

- Project management (such as lack of support, inexperience with estimating, inadequate quality of the project management plan)
- Culture (even for projects that occur only within your own country)
- Quality
- Stakeholder satisfaction
- Company organization (or lack thereof, including lack of prioritization of projects, inadequate funding, lack of focus on managing multiple project interactions, lack of proper signoff of the project charter)
- Contracts
- Sellers (vendors and suppliers)
- Changes in the marketplace
- Changes to the competitors' customers

Using the Prompt List of Risk Categories with the Cause-Risk-Effect Format

When identifying risks by category, you could put them in the format where the category is listed in the cause column and expanded upon based on the specifics of the project. Then the other columns are filled in.

Cause	Risk	Effect
Customer's competition		

A new threat is identified:

Cause	Risk	Effect
The customer's competition on this project is more scientifically advanced than the customer	which could cause new use of existing technology that we have little experience with to be requested by the customer	which could result in depletion of resource time to create a change order and learn the skills

Then try to put the category into the risk column and see if that helps you identify more threats and opportunities.

Cause	Risk	Effect
	Customer's competition	

A new threat is identified:

Cause	Risk	Effect
We are being asked by our customer to come up with a unique product that will create a totally new market. Unfortunately, the customer has competitors that are cash rich	which means the customer's competition may retaliate with a new product of its own before we finish this one	causing the loss of about 50% of the work at the time this occurs and extensive redesign and additional cost

Then try to put the category into the effect column and see if that helps you identify more threats and opportunities.

Cause	Risk	Effect
		Customer's competition

A new threat is identified:

Cause	Risk	Effect
This project is so unique that we might be asked to write about it in trade magazines	which may cause everyone to learn about the project	leading to the customer's competition announcing a new product of its own, creating a risk that we need to add scope to the existing project

Remember that not all the categories apply to all projects or apply in more than one column above. The concept is to uncover more risks by forcing the risk team to look at risks from different perspectives.

Risk Breakdown Structure

If your project is large enough to have many categories and subcategories of risks, those categories might be illustrated graphically in what is called a risk breakdown structure to better help in the process of identifying specific risks for your project.

Review the List of Risks Identified in This Book

What if you had a list of all the risks and risk categories your company had previously faced on similar projects? How valuable would that be?

Most project managers and companies do not have such lists. Therefore, they miss whole categories of risks and major individual risks. Not you! Appendix 2 of this book contains over 80 pages of risk categories and lists of risks for many types of projects submitted by project managers from around the world.

Be careful how you use the list of categories and the risk list. Present a list of risk categories to the risk team only after a substantial number of risks and risk categories have been identified, to see if the list provides them with any new ideas. Though the risk list is extensive, it does not contain all risks. As in the other risk identification techniques, it is better to utilize individual thought before you use groupthink. If you use the risk list after individual thought, you will uncover risks that are not on the risk list. In my informal studies, the risk list has been able to increase the number of risks identified by over 30 percent!

Review Historical Records

As noted in the previous section, risks can come to light by looking at historical records from past projects, including:

- Lists of risk categories
- Lists of risks
- Probability and impact of risks
- Risk response plans
- Lessons learned

Looking at records from past projects will save time in risk management and help you avoid repeating the mistakes of others.

Review Other Documentation

Risks can also come to light by looking at documentation regarding the current project, including:

- Inputs to risk management
- Requirements documentation
- Drawings
- Specifications
- Contracts and purchase orders
- Requests for proposal
- E-mails and other correspondence

Of course, not having a project charter, work breakdown structure, and other project management deliverables is not only unethical (yes, unethical in terms of a project manager's professional responsibility, because it causes wasted time, effort, and rework on the project), but also adds substantial risk to the project.

Brainstorming

Did you look at the "Brainstorming" title and say, *"I know that one?"* Do you really? As you read on, highlight anything mentioned in this section that you were not aware of. You may find you have more highlighted areas than you expected.

Brainstorming is a meeting to come up with ideas or solve problems. It can be used in the Identify Risks process as well as for other project management issues.

 Follow the Steps for Brainstorming to Identify Risks

1. Determine who to involve in the sessions(s). You may choose to have multiple sessions with different groups of people, such as end users, risk team, and other stakeholders.
2. Find two scribes. A person cannot facilitate and accurately record ideas. Having two people to write down ideas ensures all are captured. A scribe could be another project manager or a colleague.
3. Have a comfortable room set up with comfortable chairs, and a flip chart or sticky notes to record ideas.
4. Instruct the scribes to record risks on sticky notes or into a computer application.
5. State the objectives. For example, *"The objective of this session is to collect the longest list of risks in the shortest possible time. Please DO NOT EVALUATE ideas as they come up."*
6. Ask *"What are the risks related to this project as a whole?"*
7. Ask *"What are the related risks for each activity?"*
8. Ask *"What are the risks by category?"*
9. Either in this session or later, group risks into like categories.
10. Ask for clarification of the risks, and discuss them.
11. State risks in the cause-risk-effect format if possible.
12. Optional: Rank the risks.
13. Further analyze the risks.

The advantages of brainstorming include:
- It is familiar.
- Most people already understand many of the rules for brainstorming sessions.
- It can generate a large number of risks quickly.
- One idea will bounce off another.

The disadvantages of brainstorming include:
- It can be boring because it is familiar.
- Many people avidly hate these sessions.
- Not everyone will contribute because some attendees are quieter, do not like to talk in front of others, or are overshadowed by other attendees.
- There will be unequal contribution because some people will talk too much.
- It is not possible for brainstorming to uncover all possible risks.
- Brainstorming does not allow for the collection of thoughts that arise after the session is over.

The outputs of brainstorming are the group's thoughts (groupthink), not individuals' thoughts. During such a session, a risk idea will arise as a result of hearing a risk someone else identifies.

A brainstorming session can be led by an outside facilitator to keep everyone focused and to add direction.

Brainstorming is not necessarily the best choice, nor should it be the only choice for identifying risks. It cannot help determine all the risks on the project.

 ## To Get the Most out of a Brainstorming Session

Follow these rules:
- Do not evaluate responses. Evaluation while identifying risks slows progress and discourages participation.
- Find a way to make sure everyone participates by using sticky notes, or by simply asking, *"Jane, what are your ideas?"*
- Make sure no one person takes up too much time.
- Facilitate the meeting with a set of rules. Stick to them!
- Make the list of risks as long as possible.

 ## Collect Risks from All Stakeholders

Compile and send the risks identified from all stakeholders to the core team in advance of the brainstorming session. This will help the core team come up with more risks they would not otherwise have thought of and produce higher quality risks.

Conduct a "Pre-Mortem"

Like a brainstorming session, a "pre-mortem" is a meeting to come up with ideas. However, in this case, the assembled group is asked to imagine that the project is completed or has been terminated. It has failed to meet one or more of its objectives. The group is then asked to describe why the project has failed. To find the opportunities, the group is asked to imagine the project is a success.

The advantages of conducting a pre-mortem include:
- It is fun.
- It is unusual.
- It is non-threatening.
- It involves looking at a project from a different perspective.
- It is useful in instances when the participants are too familiar with the details of the project to view it from another perspective.
- It encourages thinking "outside-the-box."

The disadvantages of conducting a pre-mortem include:
- It cannot be used by itself.
- It will not result in identifying all known risks.
- Some people have a hard time imagining failure.

Affinity Diagrams

Would it be helpful to discover a technique that can add 20 percent more risks even when you think you have identified as many as is possible? The trick is to look for missing categories using affinity diagrams.

In this technique, the ideas generated from any other risk gathering techniques are sorted into groups by similarities. Each group of risks is then given a title. This sorting makes it easier to see additional risks that have not been identified.

What is great about this method is that it is different from the others. It is fun, will make people laugh, and it is incredibly effective.

Follow the Steps for Using an Affinity Diagram

1. Tell the group/team that, without talking, they should put the created RMC Risk Notes in columns of "like" things. All must participate. Watch how they laugh as they argue with expression only and communicate without talking. This will liven up the group and help increase productivity if the meeting has been in progress for some time.

2. Instruct the group that they can now talk. As a group, they should create titles for each of the columns and then add new columns and risks that may be missing. While this is occurring, you can compare their results with the list of categories and suggest categories that are missing.

Affinity Diagram

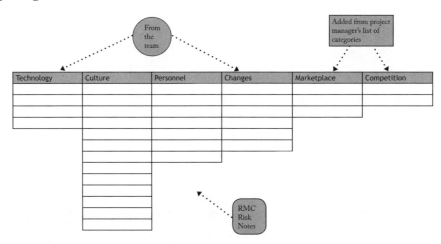

Affinity diagrams have the following advantages:

- They are fast.
- They make people laugh.
- They gain more participation from those who have never used this technique before. The method is inspiring because it is fast and efficient.
- They produce more risks even after all other risk identification tools have been used.
- They change the pace of the risk identification effort, thus keeping people interested.
- Twenty percent more risks can be uncovered.

Affinity diagrams have the following disadvantages:
- People need to be in the same room.
- Other risk identification methods such as brainstorming and document reviews need to be completed before using affinity diagrams.

Expert Interviews

Any time you ask people for their opinion or assistance, you are really holding an interview. Expert interviews can be used during all steps of the risk management process to gain expert opinion.

In risk management, it is often experts, the customer, and senior management that a project manager needs to interview to obtain risks. Therefore, good use of expert interviews is more important than you may have thought.

Expert interviews may take the form of meetings, e-mails, telephone calls, and letters. They are not informal discussions. They need to be planned, organized, and controlled during delivery in order to be most effective.

Carefully read the following. In my risk management classes, everyone seems to think an expert interview is easy when it is explained, but then they try it and fail miserably. Considering who you are interviewing in a project situation, you cannot afford to fail in an expert interview.

Follow the Steps for an Expert Interview

1. Be prepared with:
   - What you want to gain from the interview
   - Specific question

   This will help you look professional and give you the freedom to adjust the conversation without losing your direction.

2. Start by explaining why you are there and why you need to talk to them. Tell the truth, and compliment when appropriate.

   "I wanted to ask your advice because I heard you have a lot of experience with this issue!" This will get them more interested in helping you. Watch out, though—your compliment must be a real one and not just fluff such as, *"I heard you are great."*

3. I have found that only 60 percent of the verbal and nonverbal information communicated by the interviewee will be noticed if just one person from the risk team attends the interview! Roles of the attendees should be determined in advance in order to prevent distractions. Generally, one person asks the questions, another writes down the answers, and a third looks for nonverbal communications. Introduce those who came with you, and explain their roles. This will make the interviewee feel more comfortable with those taking notes.

"I have brought with me Nicole from the design team and Joe from the integration team. They will both be helping me by taking notes so that I can concentrate on the questions. Will that be all right with you?"

4. Ask an open-ended question to get their individual thoughts before you cloud their thinking by asking your prepared questions. Examples of open-ended questions include:

   - *What problems do you foresee if we use this method?*
   - *What problems have you had on similar projects in the past?*
   - *What are you most worried about on this project?*
   - *What might go wrong?*
   - *What might go right?*
   - *What additional opportunities do you see us being able to realize as a result of this project?*

5. Ask questions to clarify the interviewee's responses.

   "You said you were most worried about the software delivery being late. Why does this concern you? What impact do you see it having on the project? What would you estimate is the probability of it occurring?"

   Notice that there is more than one question about each of the risks identified and that the questions are digging or mining for information. This is an excellent procedure.

6. Ask the prepared questions. Such questions could include:

   "I have talked to others and analyzed the project requirements, and we are worried about a particular problem. Do you think this problem might occur? When? How many times?

What specifically might happen if this problem occurs? What do you estimate the impact to the project to be in hours if this problem occurs? In days? How likely do you think it is that this problem will arise, on a scale of 1 to 10?"

7. Ask follow-up questions for each question you ask.

"You mentioned that we should be concerned with the source of the equipment we purchase for the project. Why would this be a major concern? What sources should we avoid? How can we be sure to get a good source?""

People often make the mistake of asking one question after another without asking follow-up questions to dig into each area of inquiry.

8. Clarify responses.

Some people think it is a good idea to repeat all the responses received from the interviewee before continuing. However, interviewees may become annoyed at what they perceive as a waste of their time. Watch the reaction of the interviewee, and skip this step if it seems disruptive or does not add any value.

9. Ask for other ideas.

"Have any other ideas come to mind as we have been talking?"

Often the person asking the questions spends too much time asking and not listening or picking up body language indicating that the interviewee has more to say. Asking for any last ideas will give them an opening to offer additional thoughts.

10. Tell them you may need to meet with them again.

"You have given me a lot of new ideas. In the next few days, I will be investigating them and may need to ask you some follow-up questions. I may also get some ideas from others and want to get your opinion on those. Would it be all right if I were to contact you again?"

It is impossible to be able to think in advance of all the questions you will need to ask the expert. Later project activities will cause you to come up with additional risks. Going back to talk to the expert can be seen as wasting his or her time and may backfire by decreasing the expert's buy-in to the project. But, if you tell them that you may need to talk to them again, these negative impacts rarely occur. Instead you appear to be "on top of" the project.

11. Tell them how to get in touch with you.

   "It always happens that while you are going home at night or the next morning in the shower you will think of things you forgot to mention. Here is my e-mail address (or business card). I will be looking for other ideas from you in the next few days. Please feel free to contact me."

   This is the "shower effect" (a term I created). Most people do their best thinking while they are in the shower, exercising, or driving. You should realize that not all ideas have come out during the interview. The trick is to plant the idea in the interviewee's mind that they may think of things after the meeting and that you would like them to contact you with other ideas. You will not believe how many more risks you can determine simply by planting this idea!

12. Thank them for their time.

   "Your input will really help this project meet its objectives. Thank you so much for taking the time to talk to me!"

   ....

Expert interviews have the following advantages. They can help you to:
- Obtain an understanding of unfamiliar parts of the project.
- Uncover new risks that could not be uncovered from other sources.
- Gain information about probability, impact, contingency, and fallback plans for use in qualitative risk analysis, quantitative risk analysis, and risk response planning.
- Gain the expert's support for the project.
- Show your knowledge, skill, and competency.

Expert interviews have the following disadvantages:
- They take time.
- They require careful preparation.
- They can hurt reputations if done poorly.
- They are hard to correct if done poorly—you might only have one chance to do it right.
- Experts are hard to reach and gain cooperation.
- They require the assistance of others to do well.

Make Your Interview Even More Successful

- Show as much detail as possible.
- Use drawings or pictures whenever possible to enhance understanding.
- Know what you want to gain from the meeting and keep focused on that objective.

....

Pause After Asking Your Question and After Each Answer Before You Ask Your Next Question

Pausing gives you time to consider what your next question will be, and it gives the interviewee time to completely finish answering the question.

It is hard to be silent. To give yourself more experience with silence, try conducting a conversation, but hold your thoughts for five seconds before speaking. You will see how difficult it can be.

....

Look for More Than What Is Said

Research shows that about 55 percent of communication is nonverbal. Much of what is communicated in an interview is through the way things are said and the physical mannerisms used.

Did the person give you their full attention or did they interrupt or answer the telephone? If they did the latter, that may tell you they consider the project to be unimportant. Can you notice if someone is hiding something or if they are telling half-truths? An expert interview will help you discover these things in addition to acquiring a list of risks.

....

Watch What Is Reported Back to the Risk Team

When the interview is completed, the interviewers should tell the risk team what questions were asked, what answers were received, and their interpretation of them, rather than making the mistake of saying, "Here is what he said." Lastly, have the other attendees of the expert interview confirm or add to the comments, and have the rest of the risk team confirm the interpretation. An expert interview is too important to miss something that has been communicated.

....

Nominal Group Technique

The nominal group technique is used when you need a technique to gain a group's opinion (groupthink), rather than individual opinions. Sometimes the group could be a department or people who want to be or are only marginally stakeholders. The result of nominal group technique is the group's buy-in to the total group opinion on the specific risks of the project.

 Follow the Steps for Nominal Group Technique

1. Determine who should be invited to suggest risks.
2. Form groups of invitees.
3. Collect a list of risks from each group member. For efficiency's sake, input these ideas into a computer immediately or collect them before the meeting using a form.
4. Provide the group with a list of all their risks.
5. Ask each group member to rate each risk using a rating scale of 1 to 10, with 10 indicating "very important."
6. Tabulate all the ratings to obtain the group's opinion of the top risks.

....

Nominal group technique has the following advantages:
- It is a fast way to get groupthink.
- Its use of ranking gains buy-in to the results.
- It can be used to include people on the periphery of the project.
- It can be used to explore for high-level risks.

Nominal group technique has the following disadvantage:
- A major risk may be identified by a member but not accepted by the group in their final top list of risks. Therefore, selection of group members is very important.

Delphi Technique

This technique can be used to obtain a consensus of expert opinion on what work should be performed, what risks exist in the project, or the quantitative analysis of identified risks.

Follow the Steps for the Delphi Technique

1. Determine which experts can help you ascertain risks, but keep the list of names anonymous.
2. Send out a specific request with attached details of the project to each expert and request his or her opinion.
3. Collect all expert opinions and compile them into one list, keeping the experts' names anonymous.
4. Resend this list to every expert so they can review all the thoughts. Ask them for further comments based on the compiled list.
5. Try to reach consensus.

....

The advantages of using the Delphi technique include:

- It gets consensus of expert opinion.
- It can be done virtually.
- It can focus on details of the project or overview risks.

The disadvantages of using the Delphi technique include:

- You may need to wait long periods of time for experts to respond.
- It requires the ability to interpret expert opinions.

Cause and Effect Diagram

Cause and effect diagrams can be used to evaluate the causes of any events, such as quality problems or risks. Often in the risk identification process, a "risk" will be identified that is not really a risk. Risks should be specific, but often the risks that are identified are general and need more analysis to determine what the real problem is. This effort can be done in many ways, by simply discussing what the real cause is, by making lists of possible causes, or by using a cause and effect diagram.

For example, imagine you estimate that there is likely to be late delivery of software on your project. It might help your risk management process to determine the probable cause of this event and then try to deal with the cause as part of risk management. A cause and effect diagram is a visual tool to help a person or group see the potential causes and identify new ones. Let's say that a group is evaluating this problem and determines that some of the causes are:

- The software has never been created before.
- There are too many changes.
- There is a loss of team members.
- There is a lack of technical knowledge.

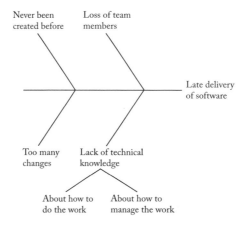

The person or group could continue adding potential causes as necessary until they agree on the most probable cause. If that cause is 100 percent likely to occur, then it is handled as a fact and managed as a formal part of the scope of the project. If it is uncertain (i.e., less than 80 percent certain), it is handled as a risk and included as part of the risk management process.

Failure Modes and Effects Analysis

Failure Modes and Effects Analysis (FMEA), also known as fault tree analysis, is a technique that can be used to assess the potential reliability of products. Aerospace programs in the 1940s were among the first to use this methodology. FMEA looks at possible "failure modes"—the ways a product or part of the product or process used might fail. It also looks at the potential impacts of failure and ways to reduce the probability or mitigate the impacts of such failure. The goal of FMEA is to design the failure out of the product.

Function	Failure Mode	Effects	Severity	Causes	Occurrence	Controls
Database query	Query returns inaccurate results	Wrong data is used for analysis	9	Query statement is wrong	7	Predefined queries saved but not required

Detection	Critical Characteristic	RPM	Recommended Action	Responsibility	Due Date	Action Taken
4	None	95	Always require predefined query or provide array in query fields to add partial level of sensible request statements	Mary	1 month from report	

Just like any other list of risks, a FMEA will rate the different risks associated with each failure mode. The failure modes with the highest ranking—their risk priority number (RPN), which is found by multiplying the severity times the occurrence rating times the detection rating—are handled in the risk management process as risks. There are no standards that describe which RPN numbers qualify to be added to the risk management process and which do not.

Strengths, Weaknesses, Opportunities, and Threats (SWOT) Analysis

This analysis looks at the project to identify its strengths and weaknesses and thereby identify risks (opportunities and threats).

Other Tools for Risk Identification

Risk identification should be easy. It does not require advanced tools. However, there are many people who write about all sorts of tools that can be used for risk management that were created in other disciplines, like quality management or engineering. None of these tools are any better than others, nor do they necessarily result in more risks being identified. They are usually just other methods to do the same thing that this book has already given you detailed help with—identify risks. These tools include:

- Force field analysis
- Influence diagrams including system dynamics

All these tools use visual diagrams that model a problem, cause, or part of the work, like the cause and effect diagram shown previously. Some tools, like decision trees and FMEA, include calculations to quantitatively analyze risks. Because they are visual, they help those working with them "see" the risks in ways that just talking about risks might not. If you are very familiar with any of these, then use them by all means. If you are not, then your lack of familiarity will just get in the way of your effectiveness in identifying risks. They will not add any value.

Tricks for Identifying More Risks

Equalize Participation

Imagine that not everyone has had a chance to contribute or that one person is monopolizing the conversation during a brainstorming session. Simply hand out some sticky notes or RMC Risk Notes and say: *"Before you leave, please take three (or four or five) RMC Risk Notes and write one risk on each note. You must hand them in before you leave."* Or, *"Before we leave, I would like you to write down four more risks pertaining to___ on four RMC Risk Notes!"*

Use Anonymity

It is not easy for someone in a meeting to admit out loud that they or their department might cause a risk. They may reveal it if provided an anonymous method like sticky notes or RMC Risk Notes. In situations where anonymity is obviously needed, simply add to your comments: *"Your contributions will be anonymous."*

Virtual Teams

Obviously, RMC Risk Notes can most easily be used when people are physically present. If you are working in a virtual environment, have virtual team members send you the filled-in RMC Risk Notes.

Use a Combination of Methods (e.g., Brainstorming and Sticky Notes)

This can be critical. As you have read, brainstorming cannot provide all risks, but using it in combination with other methods will provide opportunities for those who need anonymity, individual thought, group thought, verbal tools, etc., to contribute more risks. I have seen people who have not contributed anything in a brainstorming session be given another method to contribute—and then present a major risk.

My Favorite Choices

I send a form (by e-mail) to some of those on the periphery of the project with a letter telling them why I have selected them for their input. Then I ask them for risks. Other groups closer to the project are interviewed by my risk team members or are invited to brainstorming sessions. I then compile all the risks.

Next, I ask the risk team to complete a form and participate in a brainstorming session. When the session is reaching its conclusion, I provide the risk team with the compiled list and ask if it offers other ideas for risks. At the end of the session, I use RMC Risk Notes and then do an affinity diagram with all the risks identified on the project.

How Do You Know When You Are Finished?

Although risk management is iterative, that should not be an excuse for missing risks early and having to figure them out later. There should be a concerted effort to identify as many risks as possible (though others will come to light throughout the project).

Many companies believe that coming up with five risks is enough. The best answer to this is a phrase that may not make sense until you actually follow the processes in this book and try this suggestion. *Do it until it seems stupid.*

Many people will not divulge the real risks they are aware of until later in the Identify Risks process. It is a good idea to let the Identify Risks process get silly (*"An alien comes down from outer space and steals all the computer hard drives used on our project!"*), as this will make many people feel safe enough to state the truth. It is when the ideas become stupid (a level worse than silly) that you can usually determine that all risks have been identified. This may take a gut feeling rather than an analytical decision, but look for it in the Identify Risks process. You will see it occur, and then you can decide for yourself if this is a good way to judge.

Another way to determine if you are finished is to ask the team to rate how confident they are that all the major threats and opportunities have been identified. If the rating is too low, continue the Identify Risks process. It is up to you to determine what rating is too low. If the project is generally a low-risk project, then a 7 on a 1 to 10 scale (with 10 being the highest) will probably be sufficient. If the project is a high-risk and high-priority project, a confidence rating of 9 would be more appropriate.

Before moving on, make sure you have spent adequate time on the Identify Risks process and that there is no more to be done in this step. Ask yourself:
- Is risk identification worth more effort?
- Are there people who have not been consulted?
- Have we forgotten to research any literature, magazines, or other documents?
- Are there ways to identify risks that we did not use? Would they help?
- Are the risks identified adequately understood to move on to qualitative risk analysis?
- Have we really given the Identify Risks process the committed effort it requires?

Regardless of the method used to identify and document risks, all contributions are reviewed by the project manager and shared with the risk team for consideration. Input from sources outside of the risk team will stimulate ideas and give more information to the team, which will improve their understanding of the risks of the project.

Risk Register

The risk register is the place where most of the risk information is kept. Think of it as one document for the whole risk management process that will be constantly updated with information as the Identify Risks process and later risk management processes are completed. The risk register becomes part of the project documents and is also included in historical records that will be used for future projects. With a team experienced with risk management, the project manager could begin to collect additional information during the Identify Risks process along with the list of risks identified. Following is a sample risk register. Remember that information is added to this document throughout the project. This example includes information you could add at this point in the project.

Risk Register								
	Threats and Opportunities			Root Cause	Potential Risk Owner	Potential Responses	Triggers	Category
	Cause	Risk	Effect					
Overall Project Risks								
Risks per Activity								
A								
B								
C								
D								

Triggers

Triggers are early warning signs that a risk has occurred or is about to occur. List any triggers that come to light during risk identification so that they are not forgotten, but revisit them during the Plan Risk Responses process.

Will You Assign Risk Owners Now or Later?

A risk owner is the person whom the project manager assigns to watch for triggers, and manage the risk response if the risk occurs. A risk owner is a stakeholder who could also be a project team or risk team member who has particular knowledge about a risk, or expertise in handling the risk (or the activity to which the risk relates).

Some project management standards state that risks will be assigned to risk owners in the Plan Risk Responses process. Since most people become risk owners because of unique expertise with the issues relating to the risk, or because they have some responsibility and control over the risk, it may be a better idea to consider assigning risks to owners earlier in the process. Risk owners could have valuable insight into qualitative and quantitative risk analysis, as well as planning responses and managing risk. It is a good idea to make note of a proposed risk owner at this time. That assignment may be confirmed in the Plan Risk Responses process.

Steps of the Identify Risks Process

There is limited literature available about how to identify risks. Here is an efficient process that works for small to multi-million dollar projects.

1. Collect historical information.
2. Determine who may have insight into risks.
3. Determine which risk identification methods to use, and with what groups.
4. Identify risks with others (e.g., brainstorm with the team, provide the team with a list of risks from all sources—including the risk list from this book—and continue brainstorming, and then do an affinity diagram with the team to look for any remaining risks).
5. Make a list of all identified risks on a risk register.
6. Determine, with the risk team's assistance, how confident you are that the major risks have been identified.
7. If you are not confident that you have identified all the risks, redo the previous steps. If you are confident, determine whether questions remain and what information is still needed to understand and analyze the identified risks.
8. Ask the remaining questions, and collect the information.
9. Add new risks to the list and eliminate any items identified as not really risks in your data collection.
10. Discuss remaining risks as necessary to understand them.

11. If you used RMC Risk Notes, mark each note (if you have not already) with the activity, source, and other appropriate information to avoid losing the information as you move through risk management.
12. Move on to the Perform Qualitative Risk Analysis process.

Output of the Identify Risks Process

The output of the Identify Risks process is the risk register. At this point in the risk management process, the risk register may contain the following information.

Risk Register

- **List of risks**
- **Root causes of risks:** The root causes of risks are documented.
- **Potential risk owners**
- **List of potential responses:** Though risk response planning occurs later, one of the things experienced risk managers know is that it is not always logical or efficient to separate work on each part of risk management. There will be times when a response is identified at the same time as a risk. These responses should be added to the risk register as they are identified, and analyzed later as part of risk response planning.
- **Triggers:** Triggers or trigger conditions are noted to enable timely responses to identified risks when they occur.
- **Updated risk categories:** You will notice a lot of places where historical records and company records are updated throughout the project management process. Make sure you are aware that lessons learned and communicating information to other projects does not just happen at the end of the project. Here, the project is providing feedback to the rest of the company regarding new categories of risk to add to the organization's risk checklist.

Chapter Summary

Key Concepts

- The objective of the Identify Risks process is to devise the longest list of risks possible using a combination of methods.

- To prevent rework, be prepared with historical and project information before you begin to identify risks.

- Everyone, including all stakeholders, should be involved in the Identify Risks process.

- Risks should be identified in all relevant risk categories.

- Each risk identification method has rules to follow in order to get the most out of the method.

- Remember to identify opportunities as well as threats.

Key Terms

- Identify Risks process

- Risk categories

- Cause-risk-effect format

- Root cause

- Forms

- Checklists

- Sticky notes

- Brainstorming

- Pre-mortem

- Affinity diagram

- Expert interview

- Nominal group technique

- Delphi technique

- Prompt list

- Risk register

- Cause and effect diagram

- Failure Modes and Effects Analysis (FMEA)

- Strengths, weaknesses, opportunities, and threats (SWOT) analysis

Matching Game: Identify Risks

Instructions: Match the risk management key word to its definition.

Key Word

_____ **1.** Identify Risks process

_____ **2.** Prompt list

_____ **3.** Cause-risk-effect format

_____ **4.** Root cause

_____ **5.** Cause and effect diagram

_____ **6.** Brainstorming

_____ **7.** Pre-mortem

_____ **8.** Affinity diagram

_____ **9.** Expert interview

_____ **10.** Nominal group technique

_____ **11.** Delphi technique

_____ **12.** Risk categories

_____ **13.** Risk register

_____ **14.** FMEA

Definition

A. A tool to identify potential failure modes, determine their effects, and identify actions to mitigate the failures

B. A process of seeking consensus of expert opinion

C. Common areas or sources of risk on similar projects

D. Theoretical "evaluation" of a project before it has actually been done

E. A method to identify additional risks and risk categories on a project

F. A process for obtaining opinions or other input on the project from experts

G. A generic list of risk categories

H. A process of collecting and ranking risks contributed by a select group of participants

I. As a result of (X), (Y) may occur, which would/could/may lead to (Z)

Matching Game: Identify Risks

J. A meeting to come up with ideas or solve problems

K. A tool to evaluate the causes of risks

L. Determining specific risks by project and by activity

M. List of identified risks (threats and opportunities) for the project and other information added throughout the risk management process

N. Underlying risk

Answer Key

1.	L	8.	E
2.	G	9.	F
3.	I	10.	H
4.	N	11.	B
5.	K	12.	C
6.	J	13.	M
7.	D	14.	A

Questions for Discussion

1. What method or combination of methods for risk identification will you use for your real-world projects?

2. Why is it important to include end users in risk identification efforts?

3. Why is using a form to identify risks not always the best choice?

4. What is the best reason to use the Delphi technique?

5. Why should an affinity diagram should be used after the other methods of risk identification are completed?

6. How would your projects be different if you identified risks until it was stupid?

Adapt This to Your Real-World Projects

Identify Risks

Please visit the RMC Project Management Web site at www.rmcproject.com/risk to download the full version of these forms.

Steps to follow:
1. List as many risks on your project as you can. Try to use the cause-risk-effect format for each threat and opportunity.
2. List risks by activity.
3. Look at the list of risks in Appendix 2 and see if that list helps you identify additional risks for your project.
4. Use the list of risk categories in Appendix 2 to help you create a list of common risk categories for the types of projects you work on. Keep the list with you when you are identifying risks to stimulate discussion and to make certain all risks are identified. You will find a form entitled, "Common Categories of Risk for My Projects" at the end of this chapter.

Overall Project Opportunities	
Opportunity	Cause

Risk	Effect

Overall Project Threats	
Threat	Cause

Risk	Effect

Risks per Activity	
Activity	Cause

Risk	Effect

Common Categories of Risk on My Projects

Objectives of the Perform Qualitative Risk Analysis Process

Does it make sense to plan responses to all the risks from the Identify Risks process? No, because some of the risks identified are not very probable or, if they occur, will not have a great impact. The overall objective of the Perform Qualitative and Quantitative Risk Analysis processes is to determine which risks warrant a response. The specific objectives of Perform Qualitative Risk Analysis are to:

- *Subjectively* evaluate the probability and impact of each risk
- Create a shorter list of risks by determining the top or critical risks that you will quantify further and/or address in the Plan Risk Responses process
- Make a go/no-go decision (Having evaluated the risks, do we still want to do this project?)

The inputs to Perform Qualitative Risk Analysis include:

- Risk management plan
- Risk register (list of potential risks)
- Project scope statement
- Project type and an understanding of the work needed to complete the project
- Data about the risks to be used during this step to measure their precision
- Assumptions to test
- Scales for probability and impact (if they are standardized for your department or company)
- Historical records: How were similar risks qualified in the past?

Determine Additional Information Needed

There needs to be a real understanding of the risks in order to measure them in the Perform Qualitative Risk Analysis process. Otherwise it can feel as if this step involves asking questions, rather than subjectively measuring probability and impact. Before you start the Perform Qualitative Risk Analysis process, verify that the following work has been performed:

- Ask the experts and the customer any questions not answered in the project charter or earlier discussions
- Review data already supplied to the team in light of questions that arose during the Identify Risks process

Determine Frequency and Timing

If you have not used RMC Risk Notes (previously described) to identify risks, you may need to collect more information about when and how often a risk might occur before you can effectively qualify risks. When a risk might occur in the project life cycle, and how often, will help to determine its impact and your risk response. A risk that could occur later in the project should be rated higher than one that could occur earlier in the project, because the later the risk occurs, the greater the impact it will have on the project. A risk that could impact an important part of the project should be rated higher than one that could affect less important activities. A risk that might occur more than once may need the same response several times or a unique response for each occurrence.

Assumptions Testing

Before you can use the risk information collected, assumptions made when determining risks must be tested. Too many guesses make the data unreliable, thus adding risk to the project if these assumptions are wrong.

Imagine one of your stakeholders had assumed incorrectly that training the end users was part of the project, or a stakeholder assumed that the project work would not interfere with his or her daily work. Each instance of assumption, if wrong, could add risk or cause the related risk to have a greater probability or impact.

A project manager should look at the stability of each assumption (how realistic or valid is it?) and the consequences if the assumption is false. First, the project manager should make certain that assumptions have been satisfactorily identified in the Identify Risks process. *"What assumptions have been made?"* Then, if the project manager feels more work with assumptions is needed, a separate discussion with the risk team about the assumptions, stability, and consequences could be the start of the Perform Qualitative Risk Analysis process. The higher priority the project, the more certainty is needed.

In assumptions testing, the stability and consequences are rated from 1 to 10. A stability rating of 5 to 10 means the assumption is valid. A consequences rating of 5 to 10 means the assumption could have a large impact on the project. You can use this version or another scale or interpretation on your projects.

Assumptions Testing		
Assumption	Stability (1 to 10)	Consequences If False (1 to 10)
Project work will not interfere with stakeholder Morgan's daily work.	2	8

Data Quality Assessment

Beginning in the Perform Qualitative Risk Analysis process, the project team will be relying on the data about risks acquired in the Identify Risks process. It would therefore be wise to make sure the data to be used in qualitative risk analysis is precise and reliable. Before we start qualitative risk analysis, we need to ask ourselves, "How well understood is the risk?" This should include an analysis of the following to rate the precision of each risk:

- Extent of the understanding of the risk
- Amount of data available about the risk
- Reliability and integrity of the data

TRICKS OF THE TRADE® Use a Chart

This analysis could be accomplished by the use of a chart (see the following example) that uses a scale of 1 to 10 (or any other rating scale; I prefer a numerical scale since most people feel such a scale is easier to interpret and score). Determine if the entire team will rank each risk and compile the answers, or if you will do the work yourself. The choice depends on your understanding of the project and your professional experience. The higher priority the project, the more precise the data needs to be.

Data Quality Assessment Chart			
Risk	Extent of the Understanding of the Risk	Availability of Data about the Risk	Reliability of the Data
The XYZ system will arrive late, causing a two-week delay in the deliverable due date.	9	7	2
The software will not be compatible with the computer operating system, resulting in the need to select new software.	2	2	9

In this example, a decision has been made that any risks receiving a five or lower score in any area will be further investigated. Therefore, you, the risk team, and other stakeholders might be involved in additional expert interviews and data collection before detailed qualitative risk analysis is begun. Take this seriously, as data quality assessment will help make the rest of the risk management process flow more smoothly as well as decrease the number of risks.

Probability and Impact Scales

Once you are sure you have enough information about all the risks identified in the previous step, the probability and impact of each risk must be determined. Probability is the likelihood that a risk will occur. Impact is the effect the risk will have on the project if it occurs. For the purposes of the Perform Qualitative Risk Analysis process, probability and impact will be estimated subjectively, with the word "impact" encompassing all possible impacts.

If risk scales are not already standardized in your organization, you must decide which scales to use to determine probability and impact qualitatively. The following chart shows four possible choices of scales to use for probability and impact.

Probability and Impact Scales									
Option	Rating								
1	Very Low		Low		Moderate		High		Very High
2	.05		0.1		0.2		0.4		0.8
3	0.1		0.3		0.5		0.7		0.9
4	1	2	3	4	5	6	7	8	9	10

Remember that a 9 or 10 for probability is considered a fact. A risk with a probability of a 9 or 10 should be considered in developing the work breakdown structure and other parts of the project management plan.

Reducing Bias

It is important that all those who are evaluating the risk use a standard interpretation for their assessment of probability and impact, in order to achieve consistent evaluation of risk across multiple projects. Sometimes it is difficult for people who are evaluating risks to be objective. They may attempt to bias the results in one direction or another (motivational bias), or their evaluation may be biased due to a difference in perception (cognitive bias). Having a description for 1 to 10 in the matrix will help eliminate some of these biases, but the risk team should continue to look to expose biases throughout the life of the project.

> **Remember that probability rating cannot be more than 8 on a scale of 1 to 10, as a higher rating indicates that you are dealing with a fact, not a risk!**

The rating on any scale should be defined. Here is an example:

Probability										
Rating	1	2	3	4	5	6	7	8	9	10
Interpretation	Low		Medium		Medium-High		High		Fact	

Generally, the impact includes impacts to all the project objectives. A further interpretation of the impact rating follows:

Perform Qualitative Risk Analysis

Scale for Impact	
Rating	Interpretation
10	Project failure
9	Over budget by 40% or project delayed by 40%
8	Over budget by 30% to 40% or project delayed by 30% to 40%
7	Over budget by 20% to 30% or project delayed by 20% to 30%
6	Over budget by 10% to 20% or project delayed by 10% to 20%
5	Slightly over budget
4	Large reduction of time or cost reserves
3	Medium reduction of time or cost reserves
2	Small reduction of time or cost reserves
1	No real impact

Warning: High, Medium, and Low Scales

Based on extensive experience in teaching risk management and watching problems occur repeatedly, it's evident that many companies make a big mistake of using high, medium, and low to sort their risks.

Why is this a mistake? For even 30 risks, a high, medium, low range does not provide enough spread between each risk to sort the risks. Why bother? As tested with thousands of people in my risk management classes, if you use numbers (even though qualitative risk analysis is subjective), your scale is broader and you will have fewer ties and a clearer picture of which risks to carry forward. A broader range will also decrease the ambiguity that can arise from differing interpretations of the terms "high," "medium," and "low."

How to Determine Probability and Impact

Imagine that you have identified over 500 risks. You know you have to determine the probability and impact of each one. Many project managers pick a risk and ask the team to determine its probability. When a consensus is reached after about 10 minutes, they determine the impact. Now imagine the reaction of the team. They are realizing they will be there for hours in order to determine the probability and impact of all the risks and stop fully participating. Would you like to see a way to significantly shorten the duration of this effort? Here are several ways to do just that.

Choice 1: Explain the risk and impact to five people familiar with the project and/or the risk in question. Ask them for their opinion of the level of probability using the 1 to 10 scale. Of the five probability ratings you receive, discard the highest and lowest, and then average the remaining three ratings. Round off the answer to the nearest number ending in zero or five.

Choice 2: Have all the risks entered into a computerized spreadsheet and create a form. Have each person list the probability and impact of each risk using a predetermined scale. Then total the probabilities for each risk, and find the mean. This becomes the probability rating for the risk. Do the same for the impact, and for all the other risks. There is one caveat, however: this method can be tedious to the contributors. Thus, you may lose buy-in and productivity. There is another method that is also fast and yet keeps the interest of the participants. See the next choice.

TRICKS OF THE TRADE®

Choice 3: Here is a method (my favorite) for sorting a huge number of risks—fast. Using the specially formatted RMC Risk Notes described in the Identify Risks chapter makes this method even faster!

1. Create a six-foot by six-foot chart (1.83 meters by 1.83 meters) that looks like the following example. If you have many RMC Risk Notes to sort, you could create a separate chart to sort the opportunities.
2. Place the chart(s) on the floor. This location will make the chart(s) easier to reach and the process fun for the participants, thus increasing their participation and changing the pace and flow of your risk meeting—a true Trick of the Trade®.
3. Distribute the risks on the RMC Risk Notes to the team members who identified them and divide the risks identified by others evenly among the team members.
4. Have team members place their risks in the appropriate place on the chart (i.e., rate their probability and impact). With this method, 160 risks can be sorted in only 20 minutes.
5. You need to do more! Ratings done individually may not be accurate. Give each team member a different colored marker and ask them to look over all the risk ratings and mark the risks they feel need to be discussed, i.e., those ratings they disagree with. Interestingly, only a very small portion of the risk ratings will need to be discussed.
6. Discuss the risks that are marked and make adjustments.
7. Determine if any risks need additional information or clarification (as you did in data quality assessment), and eliminate any risks that are no longer considered valid risks.

8. Mark each RMC Risk Note with the probability and impact determined by the team so they can be moved and re-sorted in other ways throughout the risk process.

You have just performed qualitative risk analysis in record time. Can you see how this will speed up the process, keep everyone involved, and improve the quality of the results?

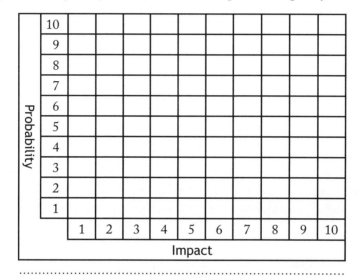

Determining Risk Ranking within the Project

Not all risks move forward in the risk management process, because some of them are improbable, and some will have very little impact. You will not have the time or money to deal with all the risks. Don't make the mistake of randomly selecting a specified number of risks to move forward. A better choice is to move risks forward depending on their ranking among all the risks.

The risk ranking is determined based on the risk scores (multiplying probability times impact) for each risk. Remember, it is not important if a risk is number two or three on the list. Many teams get carried away, taking the task of creating a prioritized list of risks too literally. This should not happen. It is only important to know which are the top risks that move forward and which are non-top risks that do not.

First determine the risk score for each activity, and then rank them.

Risk	Risk Score	Risk Ranking
A	56	1
B	30	5
C	35	3
D	12	6
E	5	7
F	42	2
G	32	4

Choice 1: In this choice, any risks with a risk score of a certain number (25, for instance; for scores of five on probability and five on impact) will move forward. If you and your company are less risk averse, you could choose any risks that have a risk score of 49 or higher (seven on probability and seven on impact) or some other combination.

Choice 2: Create or request a standard probability and impact matrix for all projects in your organization. Any risks that fall within the predetermined range are automatically moved forward. Those that fall into the middle area may be moved forward or just documented. A standard probability and impact matrix takes the form of a shaded chart. The probability and impact of each risk is looked up on the chart to determine if the risk moves forward in the risk process.

The next chart shows a probability and impact matrix adapted from a scale where choices of 1 to 10 can be selected for impact, and 1 to 8 for probability. A risk that falls into the white area would not move forward. A risk that falls into the middle, light gray area would be reviewed by the risk team and a determination made if the risk moves forward based on detailed knowledge of the project. A risk that falls into the dark gray area would definitely move forward in the risk management process.

Probability and Impact Matrix

Probability									
8	16	24	32	40	48	56	64	72	80
7	14	21	28	35	42	49	56	63	70
6	12	18	24	30	36	42	48	54	60
5	10	15	20	25	30	35	40	45	50
4	8	12	16	20	24	28	32	36	40
3	6	9	12	15	18	21	24	27	30
2	4	6	8	10	12	14	16	18	20
1	2	3	4	5	6	7	8	9	10
				Impact					

Key	
Risks to simply document (low risk)	
Risks you might decide to move into the Perform Quantitative Risk Analysis process and/or the Plan Risk Responses process (medium risk)	
Risks you should definitely move into the Perform Quantitative Risk Analysis process and/or the Plan Risk Responses process (high risk)	

TRICKS OF THE TRADE® Remember that if a risk has a probability rating of 9 or 10, it is not a risk, but a fact. These issues should be addressed as part of product or project scope, not as part of the risk management process.

Choice 3: Use the risk rating chart already created and eyeball which risks should move forward. This method is fast and uses the contribution of the group. It is freeform, meaning one does not use a standard probability and impact matrix to determine which risks move forward in the process and which do not. Therefore, the team can be flexible depending on the project, and its overall complexity and risk.

Look at the results on the following matrix. Almost always, you will see a definitive line or space that separates the top risks from the others.

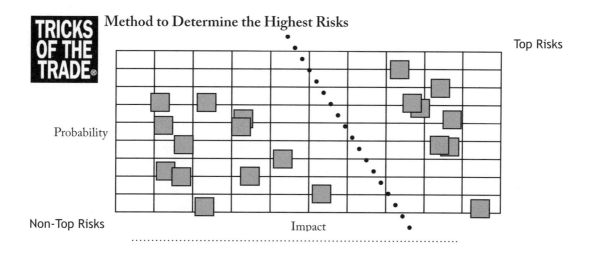

Method to Determine the Highest Risks

Top Risks

Probability

Non-Top Risks

Impact

Project Risk Threshold

A project risk threshold is the total amount of risk acceptable on the project and usually takes the form of a maximum project risk score on a predetermined scale (e.g., a risk score of no more than 50 on a scale of 1 to 80; a probability of no more than 5 times an impact of no more than 10). Remember that there can be different opinions on the risk threshold for the project from the customer and the project manager's management. The project must meet all risk thresholds.

Project Risk Score

To find a project's risk score, add the risk score for the individual risks on the project (risk score = probability times impact) and then divide that sum by the number of risks.

The project risk score is the standard by which the risk efforts are measured. There is a risk score for the project before risk response planning and another, lower score after risk response planning. The difference in scores shows the success of the risk response planning efforts. During risk monitoring and control, the project risk score is remeasured and maintained throughout the life of the project.

The following examples show how the project risk score is used.

"We are working on four projects with risk scores of 50 to 62, and we do not have the resources to manage another project at that level."

Or, *"We were very interested in completing this project but now that we have discovered that the project's risk score is the highest of any project we have attempted, we will not go forward because the potential benefit does not justify the risk."*

Or, *"The risk score for this project is 72. Management is willing to invest $100,000 more in the project if we can decrease the risk score to 60."*

TRICKS OF THE TRADE®

If You Do Not Have Historical Records

If you do not have historical project risk scores to compare against, consider the following options:

1. The department manager could create a checklist to calculate a high-level risk score for all similar, previously completed projects and then compare the high-level scores for each project to determine which are the ones with the greatest risk.
2. Determine the risk score for the project. Ask management if that level of risk is acceptable. If, yes, move on. If not, try to lower that number with risk response planning efforts. At the same time, you should start to collect risk scores for use on future projects.

Determining Risk Ranking Between Projects

A project's ranking as compared to other projects affects the project management plan! The project that has the highest risk ranking as compared to other projects should have the best project manager assigned to it. A high risk ranking might cause more experienced resources to be committed to the project and might get more management support.

The risk ranking of a project is based on its risk score, as compared to the risk scores of other projects.

Let's see an example. For this company, all risks with a risk score of 35 or higher move forward in the risk management process.

© 2010 RMC Publications, Inc. • (952) 846-4484 • info@rmcproject.com • www.rmcproject.com

Risk Score Form for XYZ					
Threats and Opportunities	Probability	Impact	Risk Score (P x I)	Risk Ranking within the Project	Calculation of Project Risk Score
1T	8	7	56	3	56
2T	6	5	30	Non-top risk	
3T	5	7	35	7	35
4T	3	4	12	Non-top risk	
5T	5	1	5	Non-top risk	
6T	6	7	42	5	42
7T	4	8	32	Non-top risk	
8T	7	7	49	4	49
9T	8	8	64	2	64
10T	3	3	9	Non-top risk	
11T	5	3	15	Non-top risk	
12T	8	9	72	1	72
1-0P	6	6	36	6	(36)
13T	3	8	24	Non-top risk	
Total Risk Score for the Project (282 divided by 7 risks)					**40.3**

Compare the risk score of this project to the risk scores of other projects in the company or department to get the risk ranking for the project.

Project Risk Ranks		
Project	Risk Score for Project	Risk Ranking Compared to Other Projects
XYZ	40.3	4
A	64.0	2
B	33.1	6
C	71.3	1
D	55.6	3
E	38.9	5
F	23.5	7

The result—Our project XYZ has a risk score of 40.3 and is number 4 in the ranking of risk scores for all projects in the company.

Look for Trends

Any trends in the number of risks identified, the number of high-scoring risks, or the interest and support of risk management by project stakeholders should be reported to management. As time passes and management better understands their role in risk management and the importance of risk management in general, this step will become an important feedback loop for management.

Go/No-Go Decision

Should we do this project? How risky is it compared to other projects? Here we see another reason so many people are starting to learn about risk management. A go/no-go decision can be made for the project based on the risk in the project, not just if it can meet the time and cost objectives!

Ask yourself:
- Is the project too risky to continue, compared to the potential benefits?
- Have risks been uncovered that could have a major impact on the project?

If so, management should be informed, a go/no-go decision made, and an exit strategy from the project planned if the decision is a "no-go." *"Now that we know this, do you still want to do the project?"*

A go/no-go decision can be made at any time during the project. However, this point is the first of several times this assessment would be made on a more formal basis.

Document the Results

What do you do with non-top risks (the ones that do not move forward in the risk management process)? Think about this: our major effort for risk identification occurs during project planning. You will not know the project as well during planning as you will during project executing. Some of the ratings for the risks will change when better or more complete information becomes available. Therefore, non-top risks are documented and revisited later in the Monitor and Control Risks process to confirm the risk ratings and risk scores.

The following is an example of such documentation. The source of the risk should be listed to make it easier to revisit the risk during the Monitor and Control Risks process with the person who identified it.

Non-Top Risks			Risk Rating		Risk Score		
Risk	Activity		Probability	Impact	P x I	Ranking	Source

Documentation also includes keeping records of the risks that will continue through the risk management process. The best way to do this without a lot of rework is to add to the risk register (as shown next).

Risk Register	Threats and Opportunities			Potential Risk Owner	Potential Responses	Triggers	Category	Risk Rating		Risk Score	Ranking
	Cause	Risk	Effect					P	I	P x I	
Overall Project Risks											
Risks per Activity											
A											
B											
C											
D											

Use care! All projects are different. If you think there should be other information recorded on your projects, change the form. You should always adapt any examples in this book to your real-world needs. Be careful not to get carried away. Ask yourself what information you really need to manage risks later in the project, to include in the project management plan, and to begin the creation of historical records.

 Consider assigning each risk a unique identification number to make it easier to track risks throughout the project management process.

 Move Risky Activities Forward

Imagine that an activity contains no major risks, but all the small risks add up to make the activity one of the riskiest to deal with. Wouldn't it be wise to move the riskiest activities forward in the risk management process in addition to the highest risks?

Risks that move forward include overall risks to the project as well as the riskiest activities.

An activity can be risky based on the number of risks it contains or its risk score. Such information will tell you:
- If you have any activities that stand out as being riskier than others
- Which activities must be included in risk response planning in addition to individual risks
- How to better assign resources
- Where, in addition to the critical path, you should focus your management attention

For example, in Project A, risks with risk scores of 50.0 or higher have been carried forward into the Plan Risk Responses process. The average number of risks per activity is three. Activity X in that project has only one risk carried forward into the Plan Risk Responses process; however, the activity contains a total of eight risks with the following scores:

Risks	Risk Score
Risk 1	50
Risk 2	22
Risk 3	13
Risk 4	18
Risk 5	45
Risk 6	33
Risk 7	44
Risk 8	35
Total Risk Score	**32.5**

This activity, and any like it, should be carried forward into the Plan Risk Responses process.

TRICKS OF THE TRADE® ## Move Common Causes of Risk Forward

In addition to sorting risks by activity, an even more sophisticated effort is to sort them by cause. If you use the cause-risk-effect format to write your risks, and then sort them by cause, you may discover that one activity, person, event, etc., is causing more than one risk. Therefore, not only the highest ranked risks and activities, but also the most common causes of risk, move forward in the risk management process.

> **Risks that move forward include common causes of risk.**

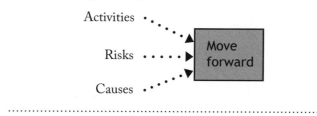

Common Causes of Risk		
Cause	Risk	Effect
The country's infrastructure is different than that of the home country	which means the equipment could be damaged from storms that would not be considered normal	resulting in a loss of equipment and possible delays to the project
The country's infrastructure is different than that of the home country	which could cause interruption of electrical power or brownouts for part of the day or year	resulting in possible project delays

There is no clear method to determine which causes move forward. You could select the causes with the most occurrences, ones with more than five occurrences, or any other such number. It is best to just see what you have and make a decision based on your understanding of the specific project you are working on.

Risk responses developed after consideration of all these factors will have a much greater impact on diminishing the overall risk picture.

Show Risky Activities on the Network Diagram

The project manager, the team, and others need to be aware of which activities require the most attention. Using the network diagram as a communication and/or management tool on your projects, show the riskiest activities by highlighting them in another color. Most software programs will allow you to do this in addition to coloring the critical path.

Note Path Convergence and Path Divergence

An activity may not seem risky on its own. However, when you take a look at a network diagram created during project management planning and see that many paths converge into that activity or diverge from that activity, then the risk of the central activity is greatly increased. All activities have uncertain outcomes. Watch for predecessor activities that affect the performance, and therefore the risk, of successor activities. A successor activity with two or more predecessor activities might have more risk than is apparent if you only look at that activity. For example, if you only look at the risks of activity G, without looking at the network diagram, you would not see the risk caused by the number of activities leading into it; activity G has more risk because of that convergence.

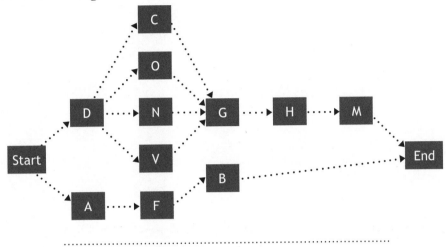

Build Historical Records

Building historical records is an important part of project risk management. You should record the results of the Perform Qualitative Risk Analysis process for use on future projects.

List the Activity Risk Score and Person Assigned on the Bar Chart

Have you thought about listing the risk score for each activity on the bar chart? This can be huge, because it keeps everyone focused on the riskier activities.

A bar chart shows the project schedule developed from the work breakdown structure, network diagram, and estimates. One of the tricks of risk management is to realize that simply because they have become known, many risks will not occur. Take advantage of this phenomenon by letting as many people as appropriate know the risks identified on your project by putting the risk score and the name of the resource assigned to each activity on the bar chart as shown next.

ID	Activity Name	Predecessors	Risk Score	Resource Names			September				October
					8/18	8/25	9/1	9/8	9/15	9/22	9/29
1	Start										
2	D	1	45	Elias							
3	A	1	33	Ben							
4	F	2, 3	10	Emily							
5	E	2	90	Rylee							
6	G	4, 5	22	Sydney							
7	B	4	112	Allison							
8	H	6	40	Luke							
9	C	8	45	Sara							
10	Finish	7, 9									

Determine If You Should Proceed to the Perform Quantitative Risk Analysis Process or to the Plan Risk Responses Process

Assuming you have made a decision to continue with the project, you must decide whether quantitative risk analysis is necessary for this project.

The Perform Quantitative Risk Analysis process is not as important as most people think it is. How much good would it be to concentrate on quantitative risk analysis if you do not have all risks identified? With that in mind, here are the guidelines. You must make your own decision!

Proceed to the Perform Quantitative Risk Analysis process if:
- You believe that you have identified "all" project risks
- It is worth the time and money on your project
- You have a very high-priority or visible project
- There is very little tolerance for cost or schedule overruns

Proceed to the Plan Risk Responses process if:
- You have a small budget or short length project
- You are new to risk management and have not perfected quantitative risk analysis

Steps of the Perform Qualitative Risk Analysis Process

1. Collect additional information you may need in order to evaluate the risks.
2. Determine if you will use risk owners now to help with qualifying risk or only assign risk owners later during the Plan Risk Responses process. This decision is made by preference, depending on the number of risks identified and how familiar the risk team is with the risks identified.
3. Look for and test any assumptions made in qualifying risks and look for any data that is biased (i.e., determine what assumptions have been made and how well the risk is understood).
4. Determine what scales of probability and impact to use and what methods of qualitative risk analysis to use, how they will be used, and who will be involved (if not already done in risk management planning).
5. DO IT. Determine probability, impact, limits, and timing for each risk (a prioritized list of risks).
6. Determine which risks, activities, and causes you will move forward in the risk management process (list of risks for additional analysis).
7. Determine the overall risk score and ranking for the project.
8. Document the risks.
9. Look for trends.
10. Make a go/no-go decision about the project.
11. Move on to the Perform Quantitative Risk Analysis process or directly into the Plan Risk Responses process.

Output of the Perform Qualitative Risk Analysis Process

The output of the Perform Qualitative Risk Analysis process is updates to the risk register. At this point in the risk management process, it is updated to add the results of the Perform Qualitative Risk Analysis process, including the following information.

Risk Register Updates

- **Risk ranking for the project compared to other projects:** As noted earlier in this chapter, qualitative risk analysis can lead to a number to be used to rank the project in comparison to others (e.g., this project has a risk score of 8.3). One of the impacts of the project risk score and risk ranking is that once you complete risk response planning, you can then redo qualitative risk analysis and PROVE the value of your efforts. You can report, "The project now has a risk score of 4.8." Think how this will help you prove the value of risk management!

- **List of prioritized risks and their probability and impact ratings**
- **Risks grouped by categories**
- **List of risks requiring additional analysis in the near term**
- **List of risks for additional analysis and response:** These are the risks that will move forward into quantitative risk analysis and/or response planning.
- **Watchlist (non-top risks):** These risks are documented for later review during the Monitor and Control Risks process.
- **Trends:** Qualitative risk analysis may be redone in planning (as previously explained) or while the project work is being done. The project manager should know if risk is increasing, decreasing, or staying the same, so that trends can be analyzed.
- **Go/no-go decision**

Qualitative risk analysis can also be used to:
- Compare the risk of the project to the overall risk of other projects
- Determine whether to proceed to the Perform Quantitative Risk Analysis process or the Plan Risk Responses process (depending on the needs of the project and the performing organization)

Chapter Summary

Key Concepts

- The Perform Qualitative Risk Analysis process involves taking an initial look at the identified risks to determine the top risks that you will quantify further and/or address in the Plan Risk Responses process.

- The probability and impact of risks are subjectively determined.

- An important part of this process is to assess the quality and reliability of the information you are working with.

- The risk ranking of the individual risks as compared to all other risks on the project is determined.

- The risk ranking of the project as compared to other projects is determined.

Key Terms

- Perform Qualitative Risk Analysis process

- Assumptions testing

- Data quality assessment

- Probability and impact scales

- Common causes of risk

- Go/no-go decision

- Bar chart

- List of risks to move forward

- Non-top risks

- Path convergence

- Motivational bias

- Cognitive bias

- Risk rating

- Risk ranking

- Risk score

- Project risk ranking

- Project risk score

Matching Game: Qualitative Risk Analysis

Instructions: Match the risk management key word to its definition.

Key Word

_____ **1.** Perform Qualitative Risk Analysis process

_____ **2.** Risk score

_____ **3.** Assumptions testing

_____ **4.** Motivational bias

_____ **5.** Probability and impact scales

_____ **6.** Risk ranking

_____ **7.** Common causes of risk

_____ **8.** Go/no-go decision

_____ **9.** Bar chart

_____ **10.** List of risks to move foward

_____ **11.** Path convergence

_____ **12.** Cognitive bias

_____ **13.** Data quality assessment

Definition

A. Instances where one activity, person, event, etc., is causing more than one risk

B. Method of determining probability and impact of identified risks

C. A chart showing activity information; in risk management it is modified to include the risk score and risk owner

D. "Is the project too risky to continue, compared to the potential benefits?"

E. Looking at the stability (validity) of each assumption and the consequences if each assumption is false

F. Risks that will be addressed in the Perform Quantitative Risk Analysis or Plan Risk Responses processes

G. Subjectively analyzing the risks obtained in the Identify Risks process and deciding which risks warrant a response; creating a "short list" of risks

H. Prioritization of risks based on risk scores

I. A numerical value of a risk calculated by mutiplying probability times impact.

J. Determining "How well understood is the risk?"

Matching Game: Qualitative Risk Analysis

K. As illustrated on a network diagram, many activities leading into a central activity

L. Bias due to a difference in perception

M. Intentionally biasing results in one direction or another

Answer Key

1.	G	8.	D
2.	I	9.	C
3.	E	10.	F
4.	M	11.	K
5.	B	12.	L
6.	H	13.	J
7.	A		

Questions for Discussion

1. What method or combination of methods for qualitative risk analysis will you use for your real-world projects?

2. What could happen if enough risks are not fully understood before beginning the Perform Qualitative Risk Analysis process?

3. Why are unknown assumptions a problem in risk management?

4. Why is it inappropriate to use high, medium, and low as the scale for qualitative risk analysis?

5. What should happen to non-critical risks?

6. Why is an activity more risky if multiple paths converge into it?

Adapt This to Your Real-World Projects

Qualitative Risk Analysis Templates

Please visit the RMC Project Management Web site at www.rmcproject.com/risk to download the full version of the following forms.

Assumptions Testing

"What assumptions have been made?" Before the project manager can use the risk information collected, assumptions made in determining risks must be tested. Too many unknown guesses make the data unreliable and risky. Additional risks are added to the project if these assumptions are wrong.

Use your own scale of interpretation, or use this one: A stability rating of 5 to 10 means the assumption is valid. A consequence rating of 5 to 10 means the assumption could have a large impact on the project.

Assumption	Stability	Consequences If False

Data Quality Assessment

Beginning in the Perform Qualitative Risk Analysis process, the project team will be relying on the data about risks acquired in the Identify Risks process. It would therefore be wise to make sure the data to be used in the Perform Qualitative Risk Analysis process is precise and reliable. We need to ask ourselves, "How well is the risk understood?"

Risk			Extent of the Understanding of the Risk
Cause	Risk	Effect	

Amount of Data Available About the Risk	Reliability of the Data

Perform Qualitative Risk Analysis

Qualitative Risk Analysis Form

Take the list of risks from the Identify Risks process and subjectively list the probability and impact. Then come up with the risk scores and risk ranking as described in this chapter.

Threats and Opportunities
Total Risk Score for the Project (the sum of the risk scores for each risk divided by the number of risks):

© 2010 RMC Publications, Inc. • (952) 846-4484 • info@rmcproject.com • www.rmcproject.com

Probability	Impact	Risk Score (P x I)	Risk Ranking within the Project	Calculation of Project Risk Score

Non-Top Risks Form

Document the non-top risks for your project for later review during the Monitor and Control Risks process.

Risk			Activity
Cause	Risk	Effect	

Risk Rating		Risk Score	Ranking	Source
Probability	Impact	P x I		

Notes

RMC Risk Notes and the six-foot by six-foot Risk Chart, as described in this chapter to sort the risks, may be purchased at www.rmcproject.com.

Perform Quantitative Risk Analysis

Objectives of the Perform Quantitative Risk Analysis Process

Are you worried about this topic? Don't be. If you have decided to move into the Perform Quantitative Risk Analysis process, the focus now changes to *numerically* analyzing the probability and impact of each risk and analyzing the extent of overall project risk. In simple terms, we are now looking for probabilities like 20 percent (rather than a probability risk rating of three) and impacts like two weeks or $30,000 (rather than an impact risk rating of eight). We drop the subjective risk score concept from qualitative risk analysis in favor of the more objective concept of expected monetary value. The evaluation is expanded to look at the specific time and cost impacts of each risk.

Quantitative risk analysis is an attempt to determine how much risk the project has, and where, so that you can spend your limited time and effort in the areas of greatest risk, to decrease the risk on the project. After you have planned responses, the Perform Quantitative Risk Analysis process can be redone to illustrate the benefits of the risk response efforts.

The Perform Quantitative Risk Analysis process can be thought of as an attempt to make more informed decisions about the amount of risk on the project than is possible with qualitative risk analysis. The amount of time and effort spent on the Perform Quantitative Risk Analysis process will improve the data used for decision making, but decisions are always made with incomplete data. Doing quantitative risk analysis at any level has a cost. The trick is to balance the amount of effort with the needs of the project. More time should be spent on the Perform Quantitative Risk Analysis process for complex projects and complex decisions. Less time should be spent on this process for short projects, less important projects, and projects that are less complex. Use your judgment on how much time should be spent here.

More detailed objectives of the Perform Quantitative Risk Analysis process include:
- Decide which risks warrant a response
- Objectively evaluate the probability and impact of each risk
- Determine the level of risk the project currently has and whether that level of risk is acceptable for the expected gain from the product of the project
- Determine how much the project will cost and how long it will take if no further risk management actions are taken to decrease project risk
- Determine which risks require response planning
- Determine the probability of achieving cost or schedule objectives for the project

In order to perform quantitative risk analysis well, the following inputs are needed:
- Risk management plan
- Risk register, which currently includes:
    - Prioritized risks from the Perform Qualitative Risk Analysis process
    - List of risks carried forward for additional analysis
- Historical records: how were similar risks quantified in the past
- Outputs from other parts of project planning, including the cost management plan, and schedule management plan

 The Perform Quantitative Risk Analysis Process Is NOT the Most Important Part of Risk Management

A question I am frequently asked before risk management classes is, "Are you going to cover quantification?" It seems like people are looking for a magic cure—something that will make all their troubles go away.

What good is quantifying risks if you have not identified as many specific risks as possible? Time spent in the Identify Risks process can yield more benefits than a quantitative assessment of risks.

Quantitative risk analysis is not always required in risk management.

Also keep in mind that many people hate numbers. Some quantification techniques are considered too "quantitative" for many stakeholders, thus turning them off to risk management as a whole. There are also those who are terrified of dealing with probabilities and statistics. Be careful how much you expect to gain from the Perform Quantitative Risk Analysis process.

....

Probability and Impact

Good quantitative risk analysis makes use of probabilities, but do not get turned off yet! Let's make it easy.

Many people in RMC risk management classes ask, "How do you come up with probability and impact ratings?" especially when we get to the topic of the Perform Quantitative Risk Analysis process.

To make decisions based on 100 percent objective data, you would need to have a perfect understanding of the situation and complete information. Conversely, you could base a decision on 100 percent subjective data, which would rely on intuition and guessing without any evidence or support. Most decisions are made with data that falls somewhere in between. Obviously, it would be better to have objective data. But such data would be impossible to achieve in the real world and extremely expensive if it were possible to collect it.

Even subjective data can lead to better analysis and decision making than you would get from not doing risk management at all. The best you can do is to invest the most appropriate amount of time and effort in collecting the most accurate data available to help make better decisions.

Some of the ways to come up with quantified probabilities and impacts are similar to those discussed in the Perform Qualitative Risk Analysis chapter, but with quantitative analysis, you calculate a cost or time (or customer satisfaction, quality, or other) impact and a percentage for probability.

Some of the best ways to quantitatively come up with probabilities and impacts are:
- **Guess at a percentage of probability, or a dollar or time impact using subjective judgment:** This concept is described next.
- **Calculate the actual cost and/or time impact:** Note that there is no such thing as an exact probability.

- **Use historical records:** What were the time, cost, and probability single value estimates or distributions on other projects?
- **Use the Delphi technique:** This technique was described in the Identify Risks chapter. In this case, the probability and impact single values, distributions, or ranges are determined for each risk and consensus is achieved.
- **Conduct interviews:** This technique was described in the Identify Risks chapter and is further described below.

Yes, it is okay to guess probability and impact in the Perform Quantitative Risk Analysis process. Though the impact can often be based on a calculated estimate (a guess like two weeks or US $34,000), the probability is often a more subjective guess (e.g., I have worked on similar activities before and I guess this risk is 20 percent probable). It would be better to be objective, but that is not always possible.

It is okay to guess at the probability and impact!

The key to decreasing the limitations of subjective evaluations is to:

- Estimate something small (e.g., the estimate for an activity or work package instead of a larger piece of work).
- Give as much detail as possible to the person(s) performing the evaluation.

To quantify risks through interviews, separate interviews with many different people are held for each risk. Interviewing to quantitatively determine probability and impact is a time-consuming activity. Experienced project managers may choose to combine this interview with the expert interview conducted during the Identify Risks process, but be wary. You will inevitably spend time collecting probabilities and impacts for risks that do not make it past qualitative risk analysis. If you do use interviewing, follow the rules for expert interviews discussed in the Identify Risks chapter. Remember: to get a clearer picture of the risk, ask for a range, not a single estimate.

As you get more familiar with statistics, you might begin to study more advanced topics such as objectivity, bias, beliefs, and perception errors. There is always more to learn if you want to improve your risk interview skills.

Another very advanced topic in risk management is to begin to look at other impacts in addition to time and cost. What about impacts to other project constraints? Are impacts to quality or customer satisfaction less important? Though they may be hard to measure, they are not less important to an advanced, project-management literate company.

Expected Monetary Value of Risks

In the real world, not all negative or positive events that could happen will happen. The concept of expected monetary value is used to determine what the overall probable circumstance will be as a result of the events.

Expected monetary value is the probability weighted average of all possible outcomes and is calculated as EMV = P x I. It helps determine which risks need the most attention and should therefore be moved into the Plan Risk Responses process.

Expected monetary value, as used here, is the sum of all quantitative probabilities times their impacts. Since opportunities are benefits or savings, they are subtracted from the expected monetary value of the threats to come up with the total expected monetary value of the risks.

The following is a standard form for quantitative risk analysis.

Quantitative Risk Analysis Form					
Risk	Activity	Probability	Cost Impact	Expected Monetary Value of the Cost	Risk Moved into Plan Risk Responses?
14	B	30.00%	$66,000	$19,800	Yes
13	C	50.00%	$39,000	$19,500	Yes
12	B	50.00%	$22.000	$11,000	Yes
8	A	75.00%	$12,000	$9,000	Yes
1	A	30.00%	$20,000	$6,000	Yes
20	B	30.00%	$8,000	$2,400	No
21	B	25.00%	$9,000	$2,250	No
10	E	80.00%	$1,900	$1,520	No
18	F	30.00%	$4,300	$1,290	No
7	A	10.00%	$11,000	$1,100	No
4	C	25.00%	$4,000	$1,000	No
5	B	5.00%	$15,000	$750	No
19	B	15.00%	$5,000	$750	No
17	C	20.00%	$3,200	$640	No

Quantitative Risk Analysis Form					
Risk	Activity	Probability	Cost Impact	Expected Monetary Value of the Cost	Risk Moved into Plan Risk Responses?
16	B	10.00%	$5,900	$590	No
9	D	25.00%	$1,200	$300	No
3	D	5.00%	$5,000	$250	No
11	F	60.00%	($1,800)	($1,080)	No
2	B	10.00%	($22,000)	($2,200)	No
6	E	15.00%	($35,000)	($5,250)	Yes
15	A	15.00%	($86,000)	($12,900)	Yes
Total expected monetary value of the cost of threats and opportunities				**$56,710**	

In the preceding example, it had been decided that any risks with an expected monetary value of $2,500 or higher would move into the Plan Risk Responses process. Notice how fast and easy this calculation is. Such a calculation could also be done for time.

Don't forget to move risky activities forward into risk response planning!

Do not forget to identify and consider high-risk work packages and activities as well. In order to know which activities have the highest risk when planning responses, let's look at the same data sorted by activity.

Quantitative Risk Analysis Form						
Risk	Activity	Probability	Cost Impact	Expected Monetary Value of the Cost	Risk Moved into Plan Risk Responses?	Activity Moved into Plan Risk Responses?
8	A	75.00%	$12,000	$9,000	Yes	
1	A	30.00%	$20,000	$6,000	Yes	
7	A	10.00%	$11,000	$1,100	No	
15	A	15.00%	($86,000)	($12,900)	Yes	
	A Total			$3,200		No

© 2010 RMC Publications, Inc. • (952) 846-4484 • info@rmcproject.com • www.rmcproject.com

Quantitative Risk Analysis Form						
Risk	Activity	Probability	Cost Impact	Expected Monetary Value of the Cost	Risk Moved into Plan Risk Responses?	Activity Moved into Plan Risk Responses?
14	B	30.00%	$66,000	$19,800	Yes	
12	B	50.00%	$22,000	$11,000	Yes	
5	B	5.00%	$15,000	$750	No	
16	B	10.00%	$5,900	$590	No	
2	B	10.00%	($22,300)	($2,200)	No	
19	B	15.00%	$5,000	$750	No	
20	B	30.00%	$8,000	$2,400	No	
21	B	25.00%	$9,000	$2,250	No	
	B Total			$35,000		Yes
13	C	50.00%	$39,000	$19,500	Yes	
4	C	25.00%	$4,000	$1,000	No	
17	C	20.00%	$3,200	$640	No	
	C Total			$21,140		Yes
9	D	25.00%	$1,200	$300	No	
3	D	5.00%	$5,000	$250	No	
	D Total			$550		No
10	E	80.00%	$1,900	$1,520	Yes	
6	E	15.00%	($35,000)	($5,250)	Yes	
	E Total			($3,730)		No
18	F	30.00%	$4,300	$1,290	Yes	
11	F	60.00%	($1,080)	($1,080)	Yes	
	F Total			$210		No
Total expected monetary value of the cost of threats and opportunities				**$56,710**		

The previous chart shows you that activities B and C have the most cost risk on the project. These activities should also move into the Plan Risk Responses process. Notice that activity B has many risks that individually would not have been moved to the Plan Risk Responses process? They may not be large risks, but they contribute to the activity having the most risk. The risk of the activity can be decreased by eliminating or decreasing the probability of some of its associated risks.

Document the Non-Top Risks

One of the mistakes often made in risk management is to forget to document the risks that do not move forward in the risk process so that these risks can be revisited later during risk reviews. It is possible that some of the risks with low probabilities or impacts may have been evaluated incorrectly or new information may come to light.

Risk Exposure

Determine the Level of Risk the Project Currently Has

We looked at individual risks, and then risks by work package and activity. Now we need to look at the overall risk in the project so that we can determine whether the expected monetary value of the project (the risk exposure) is within the threshold set by management. Of course, the risks listed are not all definitely going to happen because they are not 100 percent probable. If they were 100 percent probable, they would not be risks! We need to forecast the effect of those risks on the project. Expected monetary value of the project is one of the ways to forecast the project risk exposure.

Expected Monetary Value of the Project

Determine Project Cost and Length if No Further Risk Management Actions Are Taken

We can try to plan responses to certain risks in the Plan Risk Responses process and then redo this analysis to see how much we have decreased the risk of the project. This cycle is repeated until the expected monetary value of time is within the schedule requirements of the project and the expected monetary value of cost is within the cost requirements of the project. If no requirements exist, the cycle stops when the risk is acceptable compared to the benefits received for completing the project.

Using expected monetary value is fast and easy. Let me explain how to do it with a new example. Do you want to get the most value out of this book? Try to complete the exercises on your own before you look at the answers.

● ● ● ● **Exercise 1** You are planning the manufacture of a new product. Your project estimate results in a project cost of US $600,000. In addition, your analysis has come up with the following:

A. A 5 percent probability of a delay in receiving parts with a cost to the project of $75,000

B. A 55 percent probability that the parts will be $60,000 cheaper than expected

C. A 75 percent probability that two parts will not fit together when installed, resulting in an extra $100,000 cost

D. A 5 percent probability that the manufacture may be simpler than expected, resulting in a $25,000 savings

E. A 15 percent probability of a design defect causing $8,000 of rework

Question 1: What is the expected monetary value of the cost of these threats and opportunities?

● ● ● ● **Answer**

Risk	Calculation	Expected Monetary Value of the Cost
A	0.05 times $75,000	$3,750
B	0.55 times $60,000	($33,000)
C	0.75 times $100,000	$75,000
D	0.05 times $25,000	($1,250)
E	0.15 times $8,000	$1,200
Total		$45,700

What does this number $45,700 mean, and what do we do with it? Let's look at the next example to see the answer in action.

Question 2: Assuming that these are the only risks on the project:

1. What is the best case cost (only good things happen)?
2. With no further risk analysis, how much will management expect the project to cost?
3. What is the expected monetary value of the project?
4. What is the worst case cost (only bad things happen)?

Perform Quantitative Risk Analysis

● ● ● ● **Answer**

	Question	Calculation	Answer
1	Best case	$600,000 - ($60,000 + $25,000)	$515,000
2	Sponsor's or customers' expectations		$600,000
3	Expected monetary value (the best guess as to where you will actually end up)	$600,000 + 45,700	$645,700
4	Worst case	$600,000 + 75,000 + 100,000 + 8,000	$783,000

This means that without analyzing risks, a person could say that the project budget should be $600,000. But in reality, the estimates for the project are not deterministic; they have a range of probabilities based on the uncertainties of the project. Therefore, if we take the uncertainties into account, it is probable that the project cost could range from $515,000 to $783,000. You might ask yourself if those uncertainties are more than can be tolerated. Is the $783,000 beyond the cost risk tolerance for the project? If yes, the Plan Risk Responses process should be done to deal with or eliminate some threats impacting costs as well as to increase opportunities. This calculation should be redone and the process repeated until the project is below the cost risk tolerance.

Notice that the expected monetary value of the project just described is not as high as the worst-case scenario. It is common practice to use the expected monetary value of the project to forecast potential project costs because it is considered the only unbiased predictor and the best single value estimate for forecasting. Therefore, if no further risk management actions are taken to decrease the project threats, or to increase opportunities, the project should be thought to cost $645,700.

> **Expected monetary value of the project is one of the tools to forecast how much the project will cost or how long it will take.**

Did you miss something that was hinted at but not directly stated? Let me rephrase. Using risk management, you can PROVE that schedule or cost objectives set by management or the customer are

172

unrealistic! Imagine that management has said that the project must be completed for less than $620,000. The previous chart shows that this is unlikely with the current state of risk on the project. Something has to be done. Risks must be eliminated or reduced or some other actions taken (see the Plan Risk Responses chapter), or budget constraints must be changed, such as increasing the budget to at least $645,700. Management might not like it, but this is a statement of fact. Something must give! You cannot do a $645,700 project for $620,000. Now at least you and your management can know what you are getting into before the project begins.

If you think that was exciting, you should see the next section of this chapter. But first, let's look at another example.

● ● ● ● **Exercise 2** You are planning the manufacture of a new product. Your project estimate results in a net project cost of US $400,000 and 224 days. In addition, your analysis has come up with the following (keep in mind that the real world will probably have many more risks than the five listed here):

A. There is a 5 percent probability of a stakeholder making a major change to the project, costing the project $75,000 and a 14-delay.

B. There is a 15 percent probability of gaining a new, valuable resource, making the project $30,000 cheaper than expected and saving 28 days.

C. There is a 75 percent probability that the software will be delayed in its release from the vendor, resulting in an extra $3,000 labor expense and a 56-day delay.

D. There is a 5 percent probability that the coding may be simpler than expected, resulting in a $2,500 savings and a savings of 14 days.

E. There is a 15 percent probability of a major bug causing $8,000 of rework and a 21-day delay.

Question: What is the expected monetary value of the cost of these risks? What is the expected monetary value of the time of these risks?

Perform Quantitative Risk Analysis

● ● ● ● **Answer**

Risk	Calculation	Expected Monetary Value of the Cost
A	0.05 times $75,000	$3,750
B	0.15 times $30,000	($4,500)
C	0.75 times $3,000	$2,250
D	0.05 times $2,500	($125)
E	0.15 times $8,000	$1,200
		$2,575

Risk	Calculation	Expected Monetary Value of the Time
A	0.05 times 14 days	0.7
B	0.15 times 28 days	(4.2)
C	0.75 times 56 days	42
D	0.05 times 14 days	(0.7)
E	0.15 times 21 days	3.15
		40.95 days

Question: Assuming that these are the only risks on the project:

1. What is the best case (only good things happen)?
2. With no further analysis, how much will management expect the project to cost (without a risk analysis)?
3. What is the expected monetary value of the project?
4. What is the worst case (only bad things happen)?

● ● ● ● **Answer**

	Question	Calculation	Answer
1	Best case	$400,000 - $30,000 - $2,500	$367,500
2	Sponsor's or customer's expectations		$400,000
3	Expected monetary value (the best guess as to where you will actually end up)	$400,000 + $2,575	$402,575
4	Worst case	$400,000 + $75,000 + $3,000 + $8,000	$486,000

	Question	Calculation	Answer
1	Best case	224 – 28 – 14	182 days
2	Sponsor's or customer's expectations		224 days
3	Expected monetary value (the best guess as to where you will actually end up)	224 + 40.95	264.95 days
4	Worst case	224 + 14 + 56 + 21	315 days

Do you see how much more information you have in order to really understand the uncertainties in the project?

Monte Carlo Simulation
Determine Project Cost and Length if No Further Risk Management Actions Are Taken

Remember that statistics class you wish you never took? Well, it can be useful in the Perform Quantitative Risk Analysis process. But since most projects do not need in-depth quantitative analysis, I will keep this section simple and easy to understand.

If asked for the probability or impact, you could respond with a single number. That estimate is said to be deterministic (based on a single value; the information is taken as fact or certain). Yet for most risks, the probability of occurrence is uncertain and is actually a continuous range of probabilities (e.g., there is a 20 percent probability that the cost impact of the risk will be $30,000, a 30 percent probability that it will be $38,000, and so on). Therefore, instead of a fixed, certain estimate, probabilistic methods determine distributions, or ranges, to give a comprehensive picture of the possible uncertainties.

Let's use an example to help you understand. Suppose I were to ask someone to estimate the effort of an activity. They might tell me 33 hours, thereby implying certainty. In projects, there is little certainty and most estimates are not 100 percent accurate. Now, let's suppose I were to ask instead for their pessimistic, optimistic, and most likely estimates of the duration and they were to say that the optimistic estimate is 30 hours, pessimistic estimate is 41 hours, and most likely estimate is 33 hours. Graphically, this can be illustrated as follows.

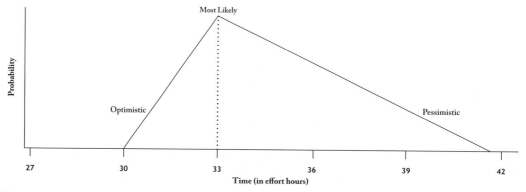

This estimate is saying that there is some probability that the duration could be anywhere from 30 to 41 hours. Therefore, the estimate is really a continuous probability distribution, or range of possibilities, not just three estimates. Doesn't this type of estimate tell you more about the uncertainties in the estimate? Wouldn't this be a more valuable estimate?

The wider the range (or its standard deviation), the more uncertainty exists in the estimate. The previous diagram shows a particular range of probabilities. It is called a triangular distribution because, obviously, it looks like a triangle, but also because the most likely estimate is not in the middle of the other two.

> Monte Carlo simulation can be used to determine how much the project will cost or how long it will take.

Monte Carlo simulation is used when there are continuous probability distribution iterations performed to calculate the possible impact on project objectives. Monte Carlo simulations can be done with just a calculator, but the number of calculations can be staggering. Therefore, most people use some form of computer software to do Monte Carlo simulations. With this in mind, let me give you an overview of how they work.

First, you will need the software, estimates (three time estimates for each activity, or a continuous probability distribution for each activity), and a network diagram. The software uses a random sampling process to pick up one time estimate for each activity and determine the project length and critical path. It will then redo the simulation five hundred or more times in order to run a probability distribution like the following diagram. It uses a random sampling process to select one of the possible estimates for time (or cost) for each activity from the available probability distribution.

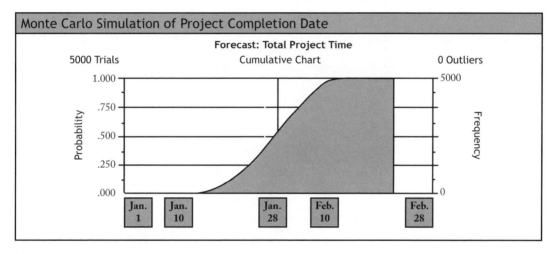

This probability distribution shows the probability of completing the project within a range of possible dates. The same can be done for cost. Read on.

Determine the Probability of Achieving Total Cost or Completion Date Objectives for the Project

Let's assume that your manager has stated that the project must be completed by January 28 with a budget of $47,500. Looking at the probability distribution, you can see that there is only about a 55 percent probability of completing the project by January 28, illustrating that the project is risky. At this point, to be 100 percent certain of completing the project on time, you would commit to a completion date of February 28. Most companies choose a 90 percent probable date.

You can prove to the sponsor or the customer that the date or cost they have given you to complete the project is unrealistic! *"We only have a 55 percent probability of completing the project by January 28, and I can prove it!"* Risk management (and project management, for that matter) is not a chore; it is a way to focus our efforts to know in advance the probable outcome of our projects.

If the January 28 date cannot change, the Plan Risk Responses process can help to decrease the probability of the specific risks identified in the Identify Risks process. A Monte Carlo simulation would then be rerun in order to determine the risk that remains.

A Monte Carlo simulation for total project cost might provide the following probability distribution.

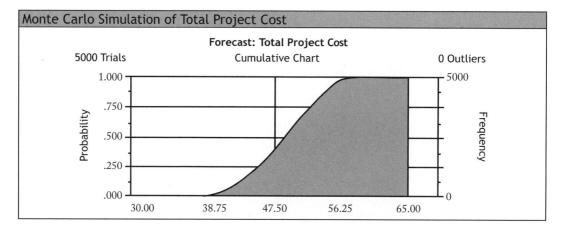

According to the probability distribution, there is only about a 45 percent chance that the total cost for the project meets the $47,500 project requirement.

Other outputs of Monte Carlo simulations include:
- The probability of completing the project on any specific day, or for any specific amount of cost
- The probability of any activity actually being on the critical path

Monte Carlo is often mistakenly considered to be the entire risk management process. Watch what you read in other publications! Notice that Monte Carlo does not help you identify specific risks for which responses can be planned, or that can be eliminated. It does, however, translate uncertainties into impacts to the total project.

The Monte Carlo simulation technique has the following advantages:
- Helps to determine the overall risk of meeting required project time or cost
- Does not weigh estimates toward the most likely estimate as do some other estimating methods
- Helps identify early in the project if time or cost changes are necessary
- Helps determine the most realistic length of time the project will take
- Provides an overall view of the amount of time or cost contingency needed
- Indicates what activities might have the highest probability of becoming critical activities, allowing better management and oversight
- Provides a vehicle for improved project planning

The Monte Carlo simulation technique has the following disadvantages:
- ONLY evaluates overall (not detailed) project risk, time, and cost necessary to manage the project
- Many people do not realize that specific risks must be identified as part of risk management in addition to Monte Carlo simulations
- Requires the purchase of Monte Carlo software, Microsoft Project, or add-ins to a spreadsheet

Remember, no matter what name this software is given, it is not risk management software. Do not rely on software to tell you what to do for risk management! The software available generally only provides calculations, not all the functions to be performed for risk management. Yet, with this in mind, the time saved and the value of the information may make investing in Monte Carlo software worthwhile.

Decision Tree

Decision trees are models of real situations and are used to see the potential impacts of decisions by taking into account the associated risks, probabilities, and impacts.

- A decision tree takes into account future events in trying to make a decision today.
- It calculates the expected monetary value (probability times impact) in more complex situations than the expected monetary value examples previously presented.
- It involves mutual exclusivity (two events are said to be mutually exclusive if they cannot both occur in a single trial).

Some examples of decision trees have the costs occurring only at the end of the project, while others have costs occurring in the middle of or early in the project. Because a decision tree models all the possible choices to resolve an issue, costs can appear anywhere in the diagram, not just the end.

The following exercise shows a picture of a decision tree. The box represents a decision to be made and the circles represent what can happen as a result of the decision.

● ● ● ● **Exercise** A company is trying to determine if prototyping is worthwhile on the project. They have come up with the following impacts (see the diagram) of whether the equipment works or fails. Based on the information provided in the diagram, what is the expected monetary value of your decision?

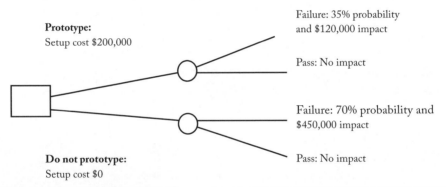

Prototype	
Do Not Prototype	

● ● ● ● **Answer** If you just look at the setup cost of prototyping, it would seem like an unwise decision to spend money on prototyping. However, the analysis proves differently. Taking into account only one future event, the decision is that it would be cheaper to do the prototyping. The answer is $242,000, which is the expected monetary value of the decision to prototype.

Prototype	35% x $120,000 = $42,000
Do Not Prototype	70% x $450,000 = $315,000

If you cannot afford more software, or you have small projects, try using any existing computer spreadsheet. Some will do Monte Carlo simulations, though doing so is cumbersome.

© 2010 RMC Publications, Inc. • (952) 846-4484 • info@rmcproject.com • www.rmcproject.com

Failure Modes and Effects Analysis

Failure Modes and Effects Analysis (FMEA), also known as fault tree analysis, is described in the Identify Risks chapter. This technique can also be used in the Perform Quantitative Risk Analysis process.

Trends in Risk as the Perform Quantitative Risk Analysis Process Is Repeated Throughout the Life of the Project

As previously stated, the Perform Quantitative Risk Analysis process will be repeated during project planning in order to determine the level of project risk after risk responses have been determined. It can also be repeated throughout the life of the project in order to reestimate the risk on the project. In addition, the Perform Quantitative Risk Analysis process should be done whenever there is a change in the project to determine the risk impact of the change on the project as a whole.

Tricks for Quantifying Risks

- Make sure you have clearly defined activities and risks so the probability and impact can be calculated!
- Remember to analyze opportunities separately from threats so they both get adequate attention.
- Use a combination of methods for identifying probability and impact to get truthful estimates.
- Build historical information about the risks and their probability and impact for use on future projects.
- List the total expected monetary value of threats and opportunities for each activity and the person assigned to each activity on the bar chart.

Steps of the Perform Quantitative Risk Analysis Process

1. Determine what methods of quantitative risk analysis to use, how they will be used, and who will be involved (if not already done in the Plan Risk Management process).
2. Determine the quantified probability and impact of each risk using one of the choices provided.

3. Determine which risks warrant a response in the Plan Risk Responses process.
4. Determine which activities include risks that warrant a response in the Plan Risk Responses process.
5. Determine the level of risk the project currently has.
6. Determine how much the project will cost and how long the project will take if no further risk management actions are taken to decrease the project risk.
7. Determine the probability of achieving the cost or schedule objectives for the project.

Outputs of the Perform Quantitative Risk Analysis Process

As with the Perform Qualitative Risk Analysis process, the output of the Perform Quantitative Risk Analysis process is updates to the risk register. It is updated to add the results of this process, including the following information.

Risk Register Updates

- **Prioritized list of quantified risks:** This list identifies the risks that are most likely to cause trouble, to affect the critical path, or that need the most contingency reserve.
- **Amount of contingency time and cost reserves needed:** For example, *"The project requires an additional $50,000 and two months of time to accommodate the risks on the project."*
- **Possible realistic and achievable completion dates and project costs, with confidence levels, versus the time and cost objectives for the project:** For example, *"We are 95 percent confident that we can complete this project on May 25th for $989,000."*
- **The quantified probability of meeting project objectives:** For example, *"We only have an 80 percent chance of completing the project within the six months required by the customer."* Or, *"We only have a 75 percent chance of completing the project within the $800,000 budget."*
- **Trends:** As the Perform Quantitative Risk Analysis process is repeated during project planning and when changes are proposed, changes to the overall risk of the project can be tracked and trends can be seen.

Chapter Summary

Key Concepts

- Determine whether the Perform Quantitative Risk Analysis is worth the time and effort for your project.

- The focus of the Perform Quantitative Risk Analysis process is numerically analyzing the probability and impact of each risk.

- Use various methods to quantitatively assess probability and impact.

- Monte Carlo simulation cannot replace the entire risk management process.

- Expected monetary value of an individual risk is probability times impact, and expected monetary value (the risk exposure) of a project is the sum of all those probabilities and impacts.

- You can PROVE how likely you are to complete the project by any date or cost BEFORE you start the project.

- You can predict the most probable time and cost for the project BEFORE you start the project.

- Quantitative risk analysis should be repeated after the Plan Risk Responses process to determine if the lower amount of risk in the project is within the acceptable project time and cost requirements.

- Non-top risks should be documented for review during the Monitor and Control Risks process.

Key Terms

- Perform Quantitative Risk Analysis process
- Expected monetary value
- Monte Carlo simulation

- Continuous probability distributions
- Risk exposure
- Decision tree

Matching Game: Quantitative Risk Analysis

Instructions: Match the risk management key word to its definition.

Key Word

_____ **1.** Perform Quantitative Risk Analysis process

_____ **2.** Expected monetary value

_____ **3.** Monte Carlo simulation

_____ **4.** Risk exposure

_____ **5.** Decision tree

Definition

A. The probability weighted average of all possible outcomes, calculated by summing all the quantitative probabilities times impact for risks on the project

B. Computerized method of estimating that simulates the project to determine time or cost estimates based on probability distributions

C. Numerically analyzing the probability and impact of risks obtained in the Identify Risks process and analyzing the extent of overall project risk

D. The level of the risk on a project

E. A model of a situation used to see the potential impacts of decisions by taking into account associated risks, probabilities, and impacts

Answer Key

1.	C	4.	D
2.	A	5.	E
3.	B		

Perform Quantitative Risk Analysis

Questions for Discussion

1. What is the difference between the Perform Qualitative Risk Analysis and the Perform Quantitative Risk Analysis processes?

2. Under what circumstances should quantitative risk analysis be used?

3. What method or combination of methods for quantitative risk analysis will you use for your real-world projects?

4. Explain when and why guessing is acceptable, as long as proper project management techniques have been used.

5. Why would a probability distribution be of value in the Perform Quantitative Risk Analysis process?

6. Explain why a detailed list of specific risks is need for risk management in addition to a Monte Carlo simulation.

Adapt This to Your Real-World Projects

Quantitative Risk Analysis Template

Please visit the RMC Project Management Web site at www.rmcproject.com/risk to download the full version of the following form.

Steps to follow:

1. Take your risks from the Perform Qualitative Risk Analysis process and numerically determine the probability and impact of the time and cost of each risk.
2. Determine the expected monetary value of the project.

Risk			Activity
Cause	Risk	Effect	

Time Probability	Time Impact	Time Expected Monetary Value (P x I)	Cost Probability	Cost Impact	Cost Expected Monetary Value (P x I)	Move into Plan Risk Responses?

Notes

Objective of the Plan Risk Responses Process

The objective of the Plan Risk Responses process is to determine what can be done to reduce the overall risk of the project by decreasing the probability and impact of threats and increasing the probability and impact of opportunities. This information is documented in the risk register. You should:

- Include in the analysis activities with the highest risk scores, the most common causes of risk, and any individual activities with high risk scores
- Use risk owners in the process

Whereas the Identify Risks process uses experience, and the Perform Qualitative and Quantitative Risk Analysis processes use analytical and mathematical skills, this step uses creativity.

 Look for a Change in Team Dynamics

Something unusual often happens during the Plan Risk Responses process. Plan Risk Responses is a creative exercise and creative people will enjoy this part of risk management. Those who have been the quietest or participated least in the process until this point because they are not comfortable with calculations may now propose creative ideas regarding what can be done about the risk.

Project planning (of which risk is a part) decreases project risk! Any decrease in project risk causes a decrease in project schedule and/or cost! This is one of the key reasons that risk management is becoming more popular. Everyone likes to save time and money before project executing even begins.

The inputs to the Plan Risk Responses process include:
- Risk management plan
- Risk register, which includes:
  - List of prioritized risks
  - Ranking of the project risks
  - Risk scores and expected monetary values of top risks
  - Potential risk owners
  - Watchlist
- Forecast of potential schedule and costs for the project
- Monte Carlo Analysis probability of achieving the project objectives
- Historical records about risk responses from past projects and common risk causes
- Risk thresholds

What Approach Will You Use?

A great project manager thinks through the Plan Risk Responses process before beginning. Ask yourself questions such as, *"How much time should be spent? Should risk responses be developed as a group or by e-mail? Should this process be done first with the other stakeholders and then with the risk team, as was done in the Identify Risks process?"* There are an infinite number of options, but thinking about a particular project's needs, the resources available, and the priority of the project to the company will help you make the proper decisions. The approach used for the Plan Risk Responses process should be part of the risk management plan you created in the Plan Risk Management process.

For a small project (whatever your company considers small), you might consider holding a meeting, in person or virtually, with the project team and the stakeholders affected by the risks. They will form the risk team. Then brainstorm prevention and ways to deal with each risk. This meeting could take only 30 minutes to plan responses.

For medium and large projects, you might organize the risks into categories or groups of risks relating to separate functional groups, and then meet with or assign someone from the risk team to meet with the stakeholders from those areas to plan responses. The risk team will meet after the departmental meetings to compile ideas generated from the departments and finish planning responses to all risks.

See the sample risk management plan in the Plan Risk Management chapter for more ideas.

Risks that do not arise from within the project (e.g., risks that are caused by other projects, other departments, or customer requirements) may not be within the project manager's or the project team's control. Such risks need to be identified and quantified, if possible. In such cases, you will need to seek management's active involvement in risk response planning. For example, a deliverable from another project could be delayed, causing a delay to your project. Management will need to moderate such multi-project risks to determine the actions to be taken on each project.

Options for the Plan Risk Responses Process

You can use the following lists of options for threats and opportunities to make sure all risk responses are considered. The lists do not need to be shown to the team, as needless arguments about which option a strategy falls into can occur. Simply make sure all possible options are explored.

Options for risk response planning are generally referred to, in their entirety, as risk response strategies.

Risk response strategies for threats include:
- **Avoid:** Eliminate the threat of a risk by eliminating the cause
- **Mitigate** (Control): Reduce the expected monetary value of a risk by reducing its impact or probability of occurrence.
- **Transfer** (Allocate): Assign the risk to someone else by subcontracting or buying insurance.
- **Accept:** Acceptance can be passive ("If it happens, it happens") or active (create a contingency plan). This is a response strategy for both threats and opportunities.

Note: In some parts of the world, these choices have slightly different labels—for example: Tolerate, Terminate, Transfer, and Treat. The previous list (Avoid, Mitigate, Transfer, Accept) is the current standard for risk.

Plan Risk Responses

Risk response strategies for opportunities include:

- **Exploit** (instead of avoidance): Increase the opportunity by making the cause more probable.
- **Enhance** (instead of mitigation): Increase the expected time, quality, or monetary value of a risk by increasing its probability or impact of occurrence.
- **Share** (instead of transfer or allocate): Retain appropriate opportunities or parts of opportunities instead of attempting to transfer them to others.
- **Accept:** As noted in the previous list, acceptance can be passive ("If it happens, it happens") or active (create a contingency plan). This is a response strategy for both threats and opportunities.

When selecting risk response strategies, it is important to remember:

- Strategies must be timely.
- The effort selected must be appropriate to the severity of the risk—avoid spending more money preventing the risk than the impact of the risk would cost if it occurred.
- One response can be used to address more than one risk.
- Involve the team, other stakeholders, and experts in selecting a strategy.

Let's expand on this with an example (and have a little fun while we are at it).

Example: Suppose that your project is to design a new piece of equipment that will be used to test water temperature and current flow in the ocean. The project requirements call for the equipment to be tested prior to its delivery. There can be many risks, but how about this one: Sharks live in this part of the ocean and could attack the testers while they are testing the newly designed equipment, which could cause injury to the testers, resulting in project delay and increased costs.

How could we **avoid** this threat? Eliminating the threat could involve removing the activity, resource, or other negative risk-generating cause. Can you think of a way to eliminate the threat of a shark attack? One solution would be to kill all the sharks. Or we could take a humane and environmentally friendly approach. How about getting approval to change requirements by deleting the testing activity from the project?

Notice that we are looking at causes here. If risks are identified using the cause-risk-effect format, many risks can be eliminated when one cause is removed. The first option— killing all the sharks—may simply prevent the sharks from disturbing the testing, or it may decrease the time it takes to perform the testing since the threat will be gone.

How could we **mitigate** this threat? To mitigate is the most commonly chosen option, as the others are often not practical. Make sure that you do not choose it simply because it is most common, however. The options for decreasing the probability of a threat (or increasing the probability of an opportunity) are evaluated separately from the options for affecting the impact. Can you think of options that will mitigate the probability, but only the probability, of a shark attack? Think before you read on.

Options to mitigate the probability:
- Feed the sharks elsewhere.
- Spray shark repellent.
- Study the habits of the sharks to see where they go at certain times of the day, and then perform the test when the sharks are elsewhere.
- Test in a pool of salt water instead of in the ocean.
- Find ways to perform the testing faster.
- Have fake people in the water to distract a shark if it comes.
- Hire a shark expert to perform the testing.

Can you think of an option that would mitigate the impact, but only the impact, so that the project will not be hurt as much if the risk occurs? Think before you read on.

Options to mitigate the impact:
- Test in a shark cage.
- Have the testers wear shark suits.
- Have the testers carry weapons or spear guns.

Looking at probability and impact separately is not a requirement, but it is good exercise to try since it will result in more ideas.

Encourage All Contributions

You may have noticed that some of these options seem ridiculous. As in any ideation or brainstorming session, ridiculous ideas can lead to realistic ones. Therefore, ridiculous ideas should be encouraged during the brainstorming session.

TRICKS OF THE TRADE®

Solicit Expert Opinions

Naturally, expert opinions would be required to identify options (know any shark experts?) and to make the most realistic selection based on the needs of the project. A shark expert (I get all kinds in my classes) told me that feeding the sharks elsewhere means that they will have to swim through your testing area to get to the food and may eat the testers along the way. For more real-world options, consider the following possibilities:

- Change the approach to completing an activity.
- Prototype.
- Use less complex processes.
- Delete activities.
- Add time.
- Increase redundancy.
- Add or change resources or suppliers.
- Use more experienced people or suppliers.
- Outsource.
- Postpone activities until later in the schedule to decrease probability.
- Schedule activities earlier to decrease impact.
- Have the customer perform the activity.
- Increase communication in specific ways.

....

How could we **accept** this threat? To accept this risk (as for many risks) is simply to say, "If it happens, it happens." This may be chosen when there are no possible contingencies for a risk, the other options create too many new risks (secondary risks), or the options are too costly or time consuming. The risk team must thoroughly evaluate all options to ensure that acceptance is the best strategy. If adequate risk management is not done, the risk team, by default, accepts all the risks.

How could we **transfer** this threat? Think before you read the following options.

- Have your manager do the testing. (I cannot help adding some humor. Do you really mind?)
- Hire a shark expert to perform the testing. (Some ideas can qualify in more than one option.)
- Outsource the testing to a company more experienced with sharks.

- Purchase shark attack insurance (assuming there is such a thing).
- Purchase liability insurance .

Now let's focus on opportunities. Here is the scenario again:

Suppose that your project is to design a new piece of equipment that will be used to test water temperature and current flow in the ocean. The project requirements call for the equipment to be tested prior to its delivery. There can be many risks, but how about this one: Sharks live in this part of the ocean and could attack the testers while they are testing the newly designed equipment, which could cause injury to the testers, resulting in project delay and increased costs.

What is the opportunity?

Because there are so many sharks in the ocean and this equipment will need to be installed and maintained by people when it is in the ocean, we could design it to also test for sharks in the vicinity of the equipment and thus make the equipment more valuable to those who purchase it.

How could we **exploit** this opportunity?

- Since we are designing the equipment from scratch, we could design the equipment to also test for tsunamis and thus have a greater market for the equipment.

How could we **enhance** this opportunity?

- Research how far away from the equipment the sharks need to be to be detected.
- Determine what the equipment will do when a shark is detected.
- Ask the customer about other ways the equipment could be more valuable to them.

How could we **share** this opportunity?

- Allocate ownership of the opportunity to a third party that is best able to achieve the opportunity.
- Outsource the design of the shark detecting feature to a more experienced company familiar with and experienced working with sharks.

How could we **accept** this opportunity?

- If people want to buy the equipment, we might add the shark-testing capability later.
- If we add the capability and the customer finds it more valuable, then they'll find it more valuable.

Plan Risk Responses Forms for Threats and Opportunities

You may wish to use forms similar to the examples shown next when planning risk responses. The forms are useful to facilitate planning and help the risk team make sure they have identified all the options before selecting the option that best helps to decrease the threat or increase the opportunity. One or more choices may be selected for each risk.

Risk Responses Form for Threats						
Top Threats	Ideas to Avoid the Threat	Ideas to Mitigate the Probability	Ideas to Mitigate the Impact	Ideas to Accept the Threat	Ideas to Transfer the Threat	Choice(s) Selected

The results:
- Risks are eliminated.
- Risks drop out of the list of top risks.
- The project management plan is tweaked (changed) to implement the options selected.
- Residual threats are determined.

Risk Responses Form for Opportunities					
Top Opportunities	Ideas to Exploit the Opportunity	Ideas to Enhance the Opportunity	Ideas to Accept the Opportunity	Ideas to Share the Opportunity	Choice(s) Selected

The results:

- Opportunities are utilized.
- The project management plan is tweaked (changed) to implement the options selected.
- Residual opportunities are determined.

Let me put it in real-world project terms. Some threats can be eliminated, and some opportunities can be increased by changing the project management plan! As shown below, if threats are eliminated and opportunities are increased, the time and cost for the project can be decreased in planning!

Original Budget		Budget after Risk Management	
Activity	Cost Estimate	Activity	Cost Estimate
1	$300,000	1	$100,000
2	$900,000	2	$700,000
3	$2,400,000	3	$2,000,000

Update the Project Management Plan

As you may have already determined, the Plan Risk Responses process will result in work packages being changed, added to, or removed from the work breakdown structure, and personnel may be reassigned. Project planning is iterative! Remember, risk can affect any of the following components of a project management plan:

- Project definition/scope statement
- Work breakdown structure
- Network diagram

- Schedule
- Risk analysis
- Budget
- Assumptions
- Management plans (quality, procurement, cost, time, human resource, communications, etc.)

Once the draft project management plan is updated, see if you have met the project objectives. If not, continue risk response planning until the project meets these objectives by using one or more of the following options, or terminate the project.

Risk response planning results in a revised project management plan!

Some of the following choices relate to risk and some to other parts of project management. Decreasing risk affects cost (and other areas of the project), but cutting cost (or other areas of the project) could also add risk.

If the cost is too high, you could:
- Use less expensive people with the same skill set.
- Cut scope of work.
- Use less expensive equipment with the same capability.
- Decrease quality.
- Change the schedule.
- Decrease profit (where applicable).
- Outsource part of the work to a less expensive source.
- Move some of the work back to the customer (where applicable).
- Eliminate risks in estimates and reestimate.

If the schedule is too long, you could:
- Change the desired schedule end date.
- Prove the end date is not realistic based on the details (and risk) of the project.
- Cut activities on the critical path.
- Fast track: Have more activities done in parallel. (Note: This will add risk to the project even as it decreases the project length.)
- Crash: Make better use of resources, add resources, or move resources to different activities.
- Eliminate risks and reestimate.

Did you notice that the options of planning to work overtime, cutting 10 percent off the time or cost estimate for activities, or just living with it are not listed? These actions are unethical because they do not deal with the problem; they just waste company resources that would not be needed if effective project management was done.

It can be a real juggling act to achieve a final project management plan that is bought-into, approved, realistic, and formal, but such a plan is necessary to effectively manage a project.

Go/No-Go Decision

If all the options still don't work to meet the project objectives, management may choose to cancel the project.

Residual Risks

You can spend a great deal of effort eliminating as much risk on the project as possible. A decision needs to be made when risk response planning should stop. Risks that remain after the Plan Risk Responses process are called residual risks. These are the risks for which contingency plans and fallback plans are created.

Residual risks also include those risks that are passively accepted—risks that you cannot do anything about or that you decide not to do anything about. Residual risks must be clearly communicated to management.

Risk Owner: Who Will Be Involved?

Think back to the helicopter story at the beginning of this book. Who called the helicopter? If you remember the details, you (the project manager) were talking to your boss and the buyer's project manager when the helicopter arrived. You did not call the helicopter. Someone was assigned to watch over the risk. It was this person—the risk owner—who called the helicopter.

Most people become risk owners because of unique expertise with the issues relating to the risk, or because they have some responsibility or control over the risk. Risk owners could have valuable insight into qualitative and quantitative risk analysis, as well as response planning and risk management.

The project manager assigns a risk owner to watch for triggers and manage the risk response if the risk occurs. A risk owner is a stakeholder who could also be a project team or risk team member with particular knowledge about a risk or expertise in handling the risk (or the work to which the risk relates). The risk owner will be involved in helping to create the contingency or fallback plans for his or her assigned risk and then be responsible for carrying out the plans.

Identification of potential risk owners was recommended in the Identify Risks process. In the Plan Risk Responses process, these assignments must be finalized. A clear assignment of risks to risk owners is important to ensure that the most appropriate risk responses are planned and that such plans are promptly and completely carried out.

Risk Action Owners

Think for a moment about a large project where many of the risks can have serious consequences. In such cases, the risk owner may have other people working with him or her to manage the risk. Such an individual is called the risk action owner. This person will implement preapproved risk responses, leaving the risk owner with the responsibility of ensuring that the risk response is effective.

Imagine your projects now. What happens when a major problem arises? Do you frantically contact people to arrange a meeting to determine the best way to deal with the problem and create a workaround? Most project managers do. But think about this—for every second the meeting is being planned, project time and costs are being impacted because of the problem. Is this what a great project manager should be doing? Read on.

Let me show you one of the reasons risk management has such an impact on projects and is in such demand by the best project managers. Let's revisit the scenario above, but in a new way. When a problem arises, chances are that the problem has been identified as a risk and there is a plan for it. The risk owner takes action, no meetings are necessary, and the impact to the project is minimized. WOW! Can you imagine how much time this would save? Can you imagine how many meetings would no longer be necessary? This is why the best project managers in the world are on vacation during the beginning of project executing. There is nothing for them to do! Everything is organized, all problems that need to be planned for are planned for, and work to deal with the problems is assigned to risk owners. Now you are seeing the power of risk management.

An activity may have many risks and many risk owners. The activity owner may be the risk owner, but not always. An assignment as a risk owner is different than an activity assignment. A risk owner is not held at fault if the risk occurs. Instead, he or she is accountable for managing the risk if it does occur. The risk owner's effectiveness is monitored and reported through risk audits during the Monitor and Control Risks process.

Contingency Planning

Planned actions to be taken if it the threat or opportunity happens are called contingency plans.

In our helicopter story, there was a plan for what to do if rain fell within a certain specification (more than three inches of rain in a two-day period during installation of the structural steel). The plan called for a helicopter to use its blades to blow the rain off the construction site. Not only did they have a plan, but the contract to hire the helicopter was already signed and the helicopter pilot knew what to do and why. This is a contingency plan.

In this story, the risk owner knew what to do and could take action without a meeting and without needing to ask for permission. The project manager could state, almost offhandedly, to the sponsor and the buyer's project manager that "the helicopter will be here in a moment" because the project manager knew there was a contingency plan and a risk owner. The risk owner knew why the effort needed to be made and the relevance of the effort to the project.

To continue our other example, let's say that the shark attack occurs. What would be an appropriate contingency plan? Can you think of one or many actions that should be planned in advance? Think before you read on.

Plan Risk Responses

How about the following?

- Call for emergency medical help. The contact number for emergency medical assistance has been found in advance, and is posted at the testing site, and the medical team has been advised that you are working in a shark-infested area and may require assistance (mitigate the impact).
- Wait three days for the sharks to leave the area (the length of time recommended by the shark expert), and then continue testing (mitigate the probability).
- Have time allocated in the project manager's schedule to visit the injured person(s) in the hospital (mitigate the impact).

Ideas from many response options can be chosen to work together.

Fallback Planning

What happens if the contingency plan does not work? Remember we are talking about risks with large impacts on the project. Risk management involves creating plans in case the contingency plans fail. These are called fallback plans.

Let's take the helicopter story. What happens if the helicopter does not succeed in blowing enough water off the construction site? Well, there was a plan for that also; they had a fallback plan in case the contingency plan did not succeed.

In this case, the risk owner was also assigned to see if the required amount of rain was removed by the helicopter. If it was not, the risk owner was to direct two individuals waiting nearby to roll out a sponge-like carpet to absorb the remaining water. The carpet could not be used for all of the water (in place of the helicopter), but it could remove the small amount of remaining water that was hindering construction. Again, no more problem!

In our shark story, depending on the contingency plan selected, the fallback plans could include:

- Contact the insurance company to inform them of the accident.
- Eliminate further testing.
- Tell another person to immediately get in the water and continue testing.

Ideas from many response options can be chosen to work together.

Triggers

A trigger is an early warning sign that tells risk owners and project managers that an accepted risk has occurred or is about to occur and, therefore, when to implement contingency or fallback plans. You may have begun identifying triggers in the Identify Risks process, but they must be documented as part of the Plan Risk Responses process.

How did the risk owner know when to call the helicopter? Was it when the rain began? Well, it can always rain, but rain was not the risk; a previously determined amount of rain was. The risk owner was assigned to measure the rain and when the specific measure of rain was reached, he knew who to call and had the telephone number to call them.

 Determining Triggers

To determine triggers, the team, you, and your risk owners should consider the answers to the following questions for each residual risk:
  • What will happen just before this risk occurs?
• What can we measure to discover that the risk is about to occur?
• How will we know right away when the risk occurs?

Triggers should be listed in the risk response plans.

Check for Other Impacts before Making a Selection—Secondary Risks

A secondary risk is a risk that is generated by a response strategy to another risk. In other words, the response to a risk can create another risk. Risk response plans should include addressing secondary risks. Secondary risks should be qualified and/or quantified, and responses should be planned. A secondary risk should not have a greater impact than the initial risk from which it was derived.

In our helicopter story, the hiring of the helicopter mitigated the risk of a certain amount of rain in a certain time period, but couldn't hiring a helicopter and using it in such a way cause more risk? They were ready for that also. The helicopter could crash into the building, or the wind caused by the helicopter's rotors could damage something else in the construction area. These are secondary risks, which the risk owner was also watching for. Everything that might be expected to be impacted by the wind from the helicopter was tied down or protected. The risk owner was watching the helicopter's proximity to the building and using predetermined signals to the helicopter pilot in case he got too close.

Secondary risks can be found by comparing the responses for each risk against every other strategy, as illustrated in the following diagram.

Secondary Risk Chart

	Risk 1	Risk 2	Risk 3
Strategy for Risk 1		O	-
Strategy for Risk 2	O		-
Strategy for Risk 3	+	+	

Key	
Not applicable	
No effect	O
Negative effect	-
Positive effect	+

The secondary risks should be included in risk response planning. For those secondary risks that remain, contingency plans, fallback plans, and triggers should also be identified. In our shark example, a decision to perform the test faster may lead to secondary risks as follows:

- Because we could be testing too quickly, one of the tests could be skipped, resulting in the need for an additional test and incurring the additional cost of the test.
- The fake people we use to sidetrack the sharks while the testers get out of the water could blow up when the sharks bite them, which could result in the flying pieces injuring others nearby.
- The testers could accidentally shoot each other instead of the shark with their spear guns, resulting in unanticipated injuries and costs.

Contingency planning for these secondary risks might include:

- Have testers practice completing the test in a swimming pool to prove that they can meet the time required (mitigate the probability).
- If a shark attacks the fake people, have the risk owner immediately remind everyone to get undercover (mitigate the probability).
- Test the fake people for how they will explode when bitten (mitigate the impact).

- Eliminate the testing (avoid).
- Train the testers in the use of spear guns and warn them of the danger of shooting the wrong thing (mitigate the probability).
- Hire a spear gun trainer that carries insurance for injuries (transfer).
- Accept the risk (accept).

If the contingency plans do not work, the following are possible fallback plans:
- Go back and do the test.
- Have medical staff on board to treat people injured by flying parts.
- Have medical staff on board trained in dealing with spear gun injuries.
- Eliminate testing (avoid).
- Accept the fact that an additional test will be needed (accept).
- Test in a pool even though it will not provide the close simulation preferred (mitigate the impact).
- Call for emergency medical help. Find the contact number for emergency medical assistance in advance, post it at the testing site, and advise the medical team that you are working in a shark-infested area and may require assistance (mitigate the impact).

Notice how one fallback or contingency plan can be used to deal with more than one risk.

Do Your Contingency Plans and Fallback Plans Have a Greater Impact than the Risks?

This might be silly to even mention, but some project managers and risk teams create too many time-consuming or expensive plans that actually have a worse effect on the project than the risks. Be sure your risk team does not make this error.

Create Reserves

If what we have described is not exciting enough and has not provided you with major insights, this will. I have already said that risk management can decrease project cost and time. Let's finish the topic by discussing how to derive a finalized schedule and budget (part of schedule development and cost budgeting).

Nothing in life is 100 percent probable. Why then total the estimates for each activity and commit to finishing the project for that total time or cost? How accurate do you think that estimate will be? As discussed in the inputs section of this book, it is only 5 percent to 15 percent likely to be accurate. Yet a project manager should be held to the project schedule and budget. What is missing? Reserves.

A reserve is an amount of time and/or cost added to the project to account for—you guessed it—risks. There are two types of reserves: contingency reserves (to deal with the known unknowns, i.e., the identified residual risks that remain after risk response planning) and management reserves (to deal with unknown unknowns, i.e., risks that have not been identified).

Project schedule = critical path duration + contingency reserve + management reserve

Note: Definitions for types of reserves vary widely, and there is no clear standard. These are the most common.

A reserve is not a "pad." A pad is hidden; a reserve is not. Adding a reserve is required in project management and is part of a certified project manager's professional responsibility to include in projects. Many people say the first thing management will do is to cut the reserves from the budget, on the legitimate grounds that if they are there, they will be spent. They should be! Reserves are like activities; they are required in order to describe the full time or cost of the project.

Imagine that one of the following problems occurs on your project.

- Due to loss of personnel, critical components of the project were delayed and not completed to meet quality assurance tests.
- Due to bad source data, additional work had to be done to clean up the data, which delayed the project and caused additional unplanned work.
- Due to new technology with new resource skill set requirements to support the new system, additional support staff was required, causing an increase in project cost.

These are all bad situations, but there is something that was missed. These situations should have been identified as potential risks, and responses should have been planned for these risks or reserves should have been established to accommodate these risks.

The management reserve is usually a percentage of the total project cost and usually falls between 2 and 15 percent, depending on the contingency reserve method used, how much effort has gone into risk management, and preference.

The following are methods to calculate reserves and primarily focus on contingency reserves.

Reserve Method 1: 10 Percent

Add a percent of the project time and cost as a reserve (e.g., a total of 10 percent) for both contingency reserve and management reserve. This is not a favored method because it is not based on the risks of the project.

Reserve Method 2: Guess

Guess the appropriate amount of time and cost contingency reserve based on the number and severity of the risks, and add it to the time and costs to create the final project schedule and budget. Add a separate management reserve based on percentage of project costs (e.g., 5 percent).

Reserves created in this manner are better than no reserves at all. As we have seen, a project has almost no probability of being completed within the time and cost estimates for all the activities. Uncertainties always exist. However, these reserves are not defensible if questioned by management.

Reserve Method 3: Expected Monetary Value

If risks are analyzed quantitatively (as in the following charts), take the total cost of all activities (total direct cost plus overhead costs and profit margin). Then find the expected monetary value of the risks to create a contingency reserve. Add 5 percent for a management reserve (or some other number). The total is the project budget.

This is the preferred method. As it is a realistic, objective measure, it has the greatest impact on decreasing project risk (and thus cost and schedule). It also provides the project manager with the greatest understanding of the project details so he or she knows where to focus efforts during project completion.

> **Project budget =**
> **Cost of the activities +**
> **contingency reserve (based on the expected monetary value of the cost of risks) +**
> **management reserve**

Do you recall the exercises from the last chapter? Let's take another look at Exercise #1:

You are planning the manufacture of a new product. Your project estimate results in a project cost of US $600,000. In addition, your analysis has come up with the following:
A. A 5 percent probability of a delay in receiving parts with a cost to the project of $75,000
B. A 55 percent probability that the parts will be $60,000 cheaper than expected
C. A 75 percent probability that two parts will not fit together when installed, resulting in an extra $100,000 cost
D. A 5 percent probability that the manufacture may be simpler than expected, resulting in a $25,000 savings
E. A 15 percent probability of a design defect causing $8,000 of rework

Using the data from the exercise, we ended up with the following information regarding cost.

Risk	Calculation	Expected Monetary Value of the Cost
A	0.05 times $75,000	$3,750
B	0.55 times $60,000	($33,000)
C	0.75 times $100,000	$75,000
D	0.05 times $25,000	($1,250)
E	0.15 times $8,000	$1,200
Total		**$45,700**
Best case		$515,000
Sponsor's or customer's expectations		$600,000
Expected monetary value		$645,700
Worst case		$783,000

Management is expecting the project to cost US $600,000 based on the costs of the activities. You should present the estimate as a range, acknowledging the uncertainties of the project. It could cost as much as $783,000 or as little as $515,000. The expected cost is $645,700, requiring a contingency reserve for known unknowns of $45,700.

Let's try it again with Exercise #2.

© 2010 RMC Publications, Inc. • (952) 846-4484 • info@rmcproject.com • www.rmcproject.com

You are planning the manufacture of a new product. Your project estimate results in a net project cost of US $400,000 and 224 days. In addition, your analysis has come up with the following:

A. There is a 5 percent probability of a stakeholder making a major change to the project, costing the project $75,000 and a 14-day delay.

B. There is a 15 percent probability of gaining a new, valuable resource, making the project $30,000 cheaper than expected and saving 28 days.

C. There is a 75 percent probability that the software will be delayed in its release from the vendor, resulting in an extra $3,000 labor expense and a 56-day delay.

D. There is a 5 percent probability that the coding may be simpler than expected, resulting in a $2,500 savings and a savings of 14 days.

E. There is a 15 percent probability of a major bug causing $8,000 of rework and a 21-day delay.

Using the data from the exercise, we ended up with the following information regarding time (see the following chart). Management is expecting the project to take 224 days based on the time estimates for the activities. This estimate has very little probability of actually occurring. The project could take as few as 182 days and as many as 315 days. The expected duration is 264.95 days, requiring a contingency reserve for known unknowns of 40.95 days.

Risk	Calculation	Expected Monetary Value of the Time
A	0.05 times 14 days	0.7
B	0.15 times 28 days	(4.2)
C	0.75 times 56 days	42
D	0.05 times 14 days	(0.7)
E	0.15 times 21 days	3.15
Total		**40.95 days**
Best case		182 days
Sponsor's or customer's expectations		224 days
Expected monetary value		264.95 days
Worst case		315 days

Note: The previous examples are simple ones designed to show how to calculate reserves, but in reality, you should have many more risks included in your analysis. If your project really ends up with only a few risks after the Perform Qualitative and Quantitative Risk Analysis processes, you should not rely on expected monetary value to determine the contingency reserve. One common choice is to create a contingency reserve based on having all the threats occur in their entirety. In the case of Example 1, this would mean a contingency cost reserve of $183,000 ($783,000 minus $600,000). The management reserve is up to you.

Reserve Method 4: Monte Carlo Simulation

Based on the results of the Monte Carlo simulation described in chapter 6, the total reserves for time could be the difference between the project schedule estimate after risk response planning and the 100 percent likely (or 80 or 90 percent likely) schedule found by redoing the Monte Carlo schedule simulation of the project. Some people pick the 80 or 90 percent probable schedule depending on how safe management wants or needs the estimate to be. The total reserves for cost would be the difference between the project cost estimate after risk response planning and the 100 percent (or 80 or 90 percent) likely cost found by redoing the Monte Carlo cost simulation of the project.

Follow these steps to create a contingency reserve using Monte Carlo:
- Determine the acceptable probability (e.g., 80 percent, 90 percent).
- Refer to the Monte Carlo simulations to see the time and cost associated with that probability.
- That amount will be the project budget or schedule length.
- Deduct the schedule or cost length from the total activity-based schedule or cost estimate created during project planning.
- The difference is the contingency reserve.

Be warned! This is NOT a preferred method to determine reserves! Monte Carlo simulation is only as good as the work breakdown structure, the network diagram, and estimates it is based on. Using Monte Carlo simulation alone does not provide the project manager with a detailed understanding of the specific risks on the project that will be needed for day-to-day project management. Team involvement is required to ensure that all the work is identified and sequenced properly, risks are identified and understood by activity, and realistic schedule and cost estimates created.

If you like to be more analytical, or if you think that such a probabilistic analysis might sway your management to accept how long or how much the project will take to complete, I suggest that you first do detailed calculations using Reserve Method 3 and then use the Monte Carlo method as a sanity check.

Redo the Perform Qualitative and/or Quantitative Risk Analysis Processes

The following charts show you how the Plan Risk Responses process can change the project cost and time. The first example is for projects where quantitative risk analysis has not been done. The second is for projects where quantitative risk analysis has been done.

Qualitative Risk Analysis Update					
Estimate: _____		Time: _____		Cost: _____	
Risks	Risk		P	I	Risk Score
Project Risk Score					
Response Strategy					
New Project Risk Score					
New Estimate	Time _____		Cost _____		

Key	
P	Probability
I	Impact
Risk Score	P x I

Quantitative Risk Analysis Update				
Estimate: _____ Time: _____ Cost: _____				
Risks	Risk	P	I	EMV
Project EMV				
Response Strategy				
New Project EMV				
New Estimate	Time _____		Cost _____	

Key	
P	Probability
I	Impact
EMV	Expected monetary value

Now here is a completed example of an activity estimating form.

Activity Estimating Form					
Original estimate				13 days	$275,000
Risk identification, and qualitative and quantitative risk analysis result in:					
Original risks	Probability	Impact		Expected monetary value	
		Time in days	Cost in $	Time in days	Cost in $
Shark attack	60%	12	$140,000	7.2	$84,000
Boat breaks	55%	2	$90,000	1.1	$49,500
Expected monetary value of risks				8.3	$133,500
Estimate for the activity to be performed				4.7	$141,500
Total expected monetary value of the activity before planning risk responses				13	$275,000

Activity Estimating Form				
The Plan Risk Responses process results in:				
Responses to the risks	Shark expert hired; team instructed in shark behavior		Time in days	Cost in $
			.5	$21,000
New activities added	Newer boat rented; common spare parts available		.5	$11,000
Total added for risk responses			1	$32,000
New ratings for risks	Probability	Impact	EMV	
		Time	Cost in $	Time in days	Cost in $
Shark attack	25%	12	$140,000	3	$35,000
Boat breaks	10%	.5	$90,000	.05	$9,000
Expected monetary value of risks after planning risk responses			3.05	$44,000
Estimate for the activity to be performed			4.7	$141,500
Final activity estimate ($44,000 + $141,500 = $185,500); (3.05 + 4.7 = 7.75)			7.75	$185,500
Savings due to risk management: 13 – (7.75 + 1) = 4.25 days; $275,000 – ($185,500 + $32,000) = $57,500)			4.25	$57,500

As shown in the preceding chart, the original time estimate for the activity was 13 days and the original cost estimate was $275,000. Top risks were identified and were included in the original estimates. Risk responses decreased the risk, saving 4.25 days and $57,500.

How far should you decrease the risk on the project? How much is it worth to the project to decrease risk further?

TRICKS OF THE TRADE®

Prepare Management and the Customer

When the project is first assigned to you, inform management and the customer that you will analyze the risks of the project and let them know the results. This will begin to prepare them for when you meet with them to describe the risk of the project and the scope, cost, schedule, quality, resources, and customer satisfaction options for decreasing the risk.

....

Document Risk Responses in the Risk Register

Recall that in the Identify Risks process, a risk register for the project was created. In the Perform Qualitative and Quantitative Risk Analysis processes, additional information was added to the register. By the time the Plan Risk Responses process begins, the risk register includes the following information:

- Description of risks
- The activities they relate to
- Potential risk owners, risk responses, and triggers
- The final probability and impact rating of each risk
- The risk's ranking among the remaining risks on the project

The Plan Risk Responses process uses that information collected throughout the project and adds the following information to the risk register:

- Finalized triggers for each risk
- Response plans for each risk
- Contingency and fallback plans for each risk
- Triggers for contingency plans and fallback plans
- Finalized risk owners (persons assigned to each risk)
- List of non-top risks for future reference that will be monitored throughout the project
- If quantitative risk analysis has been done, quantitative probabilities, impacts, and expected monetary values of time and cost can be included
- You may also choose to add other information specific to your project

Risk Register											
	Threats and Opportunities			Risk Owner	Response	Triggers	Category	Risk Rating		Risk Score	
	Cause	Risk	Effect					P	I	P x I	
Overall Project Risks											
Risks per Activity											
A											
B											
C											
D											

Risk Register (Continued)				
Ranking	Contingency Plan	Trigger	Fallback Plan	Trigger

The risk register will be used for meetings with management, to get reserves accepted, and to make a go/no-go decision. You will also use it to manage the project during the Monitor and Control Risks process. It will be updated based on risks that occur or do not occur and the success of the planned responses. New risks can still be added and tracked in this document.

Note that non-top risks do not have risk owners. The project manager is responsible to monitor these. The following format can be used to document non-top risks.

Non-Top Risks						
Risk	Activity	P	I	Risk Score	Ranking	Source

Proving the Value of Risk Management and Getting Reserves Accepted

If management will not accept reserves, many people resort to just disguising them by adding an activity to the network diagram such as "clean up" or "final documentation." I strongly encourage you to consider other options.

One of the questions I am frequently asked during my speaking engagements is, "How do I get support for risk management (or project management) within my company?" This is an important question, but not one that can be fully addressed here. In short, however, those attending my senior management classes tell me the secret is to "Prove it works!"

Haven't we already shown that risk management can decrease the cost and schedule of projects dramatically while still in planning? Why not inform management of these facts?

For most people, numbers more clearly show proof. So provide numbers! The following chart proves, without a doubt, the benefit of risk management.

Original Budget		Budget after Risk Management	
Activity	Cost Estimate	Activity	Cost Estimate
1	$300,000	1	$100,000
2	$900,000	2	$700,000
3	$2,400,000	3	$2,000,000
		Reserve	$300,000
Total Cost Estimate	$3,600,000	Revised Cost Estimate	$3,100,000

Risks Removed

There is a cost to risk responses. Someone had to pay for the helicopter and the time to sign the contract for using it. But that should not be a deterrent to gaining support for risk management. How can you not get support for risk management (or project management) when you are able to say, *"We originally estimated the project at $300,000. Because of our risk efforts, we were able to reduce the total cost of the project to $263,000."*

If none of the options presented help gain approval for the contingency reserve, there is another idea. Point out the Monte Carlo simulation results to management and show how those results support the need for some reserve. *"So you think the reserve of 12 days is too high because it results in a project completion date of December 10? At only an 80 percent confidence level, the Monte Carlo simulation suggests that a date of December 7 is realistic."*

The point of these exercises is to work with management, not against them. The more detailed information management has about risks, the more they can effectively support the project and fulfill their management role.

Go/No-Go Decision

Check with management and the other project stakeholders to make sure the risk response plans are viable and to make another go/no-go decision on the project. Canceling a project makes sense if the risk is too high or the cost too great. The concept of canceling a project based on its level of risk has not yet filtered into common project management practice.

Ask yourself and others:
- Are we able to meet the project objectives?
- Is the cost of responding to the risk worth the value received from the project?
- Now that we know this, do we still want to do the project?

Contracts

The term "contract," as used here, refers to any legal agreement for the purchase or sale of goods and services. It may include purchase orders, service agreements, or contracts.

Risk management may help the risk team determine that it would be less risky to transfer one or many risks to another company through contracting. Perhaps another company can do the work faster, has more efficient equipment, or has more experience, resulting in a less risky activity and lower cost or time.

Risk management will also help determine what terms and conditions to put into contracts to decrease project threats, to increase opportunities, and to adequately distribute risk between the buyer and seller. A contract should not be created without a risk analysis.

Proposals and Bids: Seller's Point of View

In many organizations, a proposal or bid is prepared by salespeople, without project management input. What is wrong with this picture? The sales and sales management bear no responsibility for doing the work, only for getting the contract. They do not have the skill set to create a proposal that reflects the project management process. Therefore, what is sent to the buyer is a proposal not estimated using project management techniques. That proposal cannot be used to help management or to control the project. A better method would involve the project manager and create estimates using historical records, a charter, work breakdown structure, estimating techniques, and an analysis of risk to estimate the project. The estimates should then be formatted by activity so that the total cost by activity can be managed and the project controlled to those estimates during project's executing.

Here is a revelation for some people: the same process for creating a project management plan described in the Inputs to Risk Management chapter of this book (project charter, scope, team, work breakdown structure, work breakdown structure dictionary, network diagram, estimating, and risk) should be followed by sellers to respond to requests for proposals or bids, but on a high-level basis! Proposal costs must include risk. Therefore, project management input is critical in order to create a valid proposal that is truly reflective of time, cost, risk, etc., and that can help management control the project.

Proposals and Bids: Buyer's Point of View

If you are a buyer of services, why would you ever consider hiring a company that did not know about risk management? This would mean their proposal or bid is probably based on old-fashioned guessing or some high-level metrics, not the kind of planning that will make you confident they have the project management ability to control the project and certainly not enough planning to ensure that their cost is realistic for the work needed on the project.

Buyers should ask the seller for a high-level work breakdown structure and risks on the project. Consider finding another company to work with if the seller does not know about work breakdown structures, risk management, and project management.

What do you do when the proposed contract price is too high, or the schedule is too long? Many inexperienced negotiators and project managers would negotiate overhead rates and profit margins. Why not address risks? Many of the risks on the project can be eliminated if the buyer and seller work together. Some risks caused by the buyer, seller, or activities on the project may be eliminated, thus decreasing project time and cost in a practical manner without having to resort to reducing overhead rates and profit margins.

Insurance Purchased

When risks of fire, theft, or other areas for which insurance is available are identified, the risk response may be to purchase insurance. This is transference, as someone else will be responsible if the risk happens. This is also a mitigation choice because the complete impact is not removed. If a fire occurs, the damage cost would be covered by insurance, but such things as project delays would not.

Tricks for the Plan Risk Responses Process

TRICKS OF THE TRADE® ### Are You Ready to Plan Responses?

If you find you need to collect or clarify project information during this step (e.g., *"Is it true that we cannot change the layout of the floor plan?"* or *"In our previous meeting, you mentioned a problem with the customer's telecommunication network. It seems that I need more information on what you see."*), it means the earlier steps of risk management were not completed well. The large percentage of the information needed to handle risk response planning should be available by the time you reach this step.

TRICKS OF THE TRADE® ### Do Not Just Pick the First Choice Presented

Remember, the objective of the Plan Risk Responses process is to decrease the overall project risk. Because many people do not realize this, they rush this process by choosing the first sound idea generated instead of looking at all the options before making a decision. The result is a poor decision and the selection of an option that may not positively impact risk as much as other options.

TRICKS OF THE TRADE® ### Do Risk Response Planning in a Group

Risk response planning is an exercise in creativity. Many risk teams forget that creativity can be enhanced by doing risk response planning in a group, using brainstorming techniques to increase the number of ideas generated. Some teams ignore other stakeholders in risk response planning and thus do not make use of the ideas from those who might have the most to contribute about a risk that may affect them.

TRICKS OF THE TRADE® ### Let the Risk Team Know the Process

Because many risk teams have not performed risk management before, it is helpful to let them know what the risk management (and project management) process is in advance of performing it. In this way, they will be prepared for each step of the risk process and more ready to contribute. For the Plan Risk Responses process, it is important for the risk team to understand that risk response plans may result in changes to the project management plan currently under development (in other words, such plans may impact the work breakdown structure, network diagram, human resource plan, etc.).

....

Outputs of the Plan Risk Responses Process

The following are outputs of the Plan Risk Responses process.

Risk Register Updates

The risk register is updated to add the results of risk response planning, including:

- **Residual risks:** These are the risks that remain after risk response planning, including those that have been accepted and for which contingency plans and fallback plans can be created. Residual risks should be properly documented and reviewed throughout the project to see if their ranking has changed.
- **Contingency plans:** Contingency plans are plans describing the specific actions that will be taken if the opportunity or threat occurs.
- **Risk owners:** Each risk must be assigned to someone who may help develop the risk response and who will be assigned to carry out the risk response or "own" the risk. The risk owner can be a stakeholder other than a team member.
- **Secondary risks:** Frequently, what is done to respond to one risk will cause other risks to occur. For example, if a portion of the project work is outsourced to a seller because the project team does not have the expertise to complete the work efficiently, there will be a secondary risk of the seller going out of business. This was not a risk to the project prior to outsourcing.
- **Risk triggers:** The early warning signs (indirect manifestations of actual risk events) for each risk on a project should be identified to know when to take action.
- **Contracts:** A project manager must be involved before a contract is signed. Before the contract is finalized, the project manager should complete a risk analysis and include contract terms and conditions required to mitigate or allocate threats and to enhance opportunities.
- **Fallback plans:** These are specific actions that will be taken if the contingency plan is not effective.
- **Reserves (contingency):** Having reserves for schedule and cost is a required part of project management. You cannot come up with a schedule or budget for the project without them.

Project Management Plan Updates

The efforts spent in risk management will result in changes to the project management plan. Work packages or activities could be added, removed, or assigned to different resources. Thus, planning is an iterative process. Spend a minute now thinking about how risk response planning could change the schedule, cost, quality, and procurement management plans, as well as the human resource plan, the work breakdown structure, and the time and cost baselines for the project. This is critical for understanding the impact of risk management in the real world, especially if you don't currently do risk management.

Project Document Updates

The other documents and plans a project manager has created to help manage the project may also change. Can you imagine how risk response planning might affect the roles and responsibilities on a project, your stakeholder management strategy, and your quality metrics?

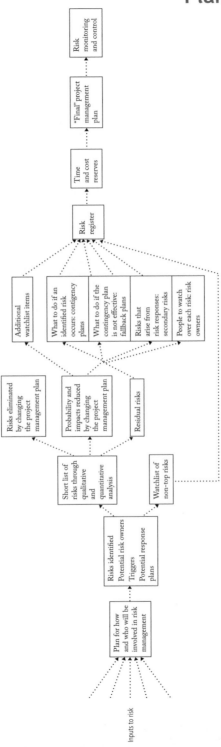

Chapter Summary

Key Concepts

- The objective of the Plan Risk Responses process is to determine what you can do to reduce the overall risk of the project by decreasing the probability and impact of negative risks (threats) and increasing the probability and impact of positive risks (opportunities).

- Strategies are agreed upon in advance by all parties.

- Risk responses, contingency plans, and fallback plans are selected.

- Risks are assigned to individuals or groups to watch for the risks and take responsibility for implementing the planned risk responses.

- Strategies are reviewed over the life of the project for appropriateness as more information about the project becomes known.

Key Terms

- Plan Risk Responses process
- Exploit
- Enhance
- Share
- Accept
- Avoid
- Mitigate

- Transfer
- Mitigate the probability
- Mitigate the impact
- Residual risks
- Secondary risks
- Trigger
- Risk response plans
- Contingency plan

- Fallback plan
- Reserve
- Management reserve
- Contingency reserve
- Insurance
- Contract
- Risk owner
- Risk action owner

Matching Game: Plan Risk Responses

Instructions: Match the risk management key word to its definition.

Key Word

_____ **1.** Plan Risk Responses process

_____ **2.** Exploit

_____ **3.** Contingency plan

_____ **4.** Trigger

_____ **5.** Avoid

_____ **6.** Risk action owner

_____ **7.** Accept

_____ **8.** Transfer

_____ **9.** Enhance

_____ **10.** Share

_____ **11.** Residual risks

_____ **12.** Risk owner

_____ **13.** Reserve

_____ **14.** Management reserve

_____ **15.** Contingency reserve

_____ **16.** Contract

_____ **17.** Insurance

_____ **18.** Secondary risks

_____ **19.** Fallback plan

_____ **20.** Mitigate

_____ **21.** Risk action owner

Definition

A. Risks that are generated by a response to another risk

B. Eliminate the threat of a risk by eliminating the cause

C. Do nothing—"If it happens, it happens," or create a contingency plan

D. Retain appropriate opportunities or parts of opportunities instead of attempts to transfer them to others

Matching Game: Plan Risk Responses

E. Increase the expected time, quality, or monetary value of a risk by increasing its probability or impact of occurrence

F. Increase the opportunity by making the cause more probable

G. Assigns the liability for a risk to someone else

H. An amount of time and/or cost added to the project to account for risks

I. A legal agreement for the purchase or sale of goods and services

J. An amount of time and/or cost added to the project to deal with known unknowns, i.e., identified risks

K. Determining what can be done to reduce the overall risk of the project by decreasing the probability and impact of threats and increasing the probability and impact of opportunities

L. Planned actions to be taken if the risk happens and contingency plans are not effective

M. Risks that remain after risk response planning

N. Assign the risk to someone else by subcontracting or buying insurance

O. Planned actions to be taken if the risk happens

P. Reduce the expected monetary value of a risk by reducing its impact or probability of occurrence

Q. An amount of time and/or cost added to the project to deal with unknown unknowns, i.e., risks that have not been identified

R. The person assigned by the project manager to watch for triggers and manage the risk response if the risk occurs

S. Early warning sign that a risk has occurred or is about to occur

T. The person assigned by the risk owner to implement approved risk responses

U. The person assigned by the risk owner to implement preapproved risk responses

Plan Risk Responses

Matching Game: Plan Risk Responses

Answer Key

1.	K	12.	R
2.	F	13.	H
3.	O	14.	Q
4.	S	15.	J
5.	B	16.	I
6.	T	17.	G
7.	C	18.	A
8.	N	19.	L
9.	E	20.	P
10.	D	21.	U
11.	M		

Questions for Discussion

1. What method or combination of methods for risk response planning will you use for your real-world projects?

2. Why do you need to know the forecast of the potential schedule and costs for the project before you can properly complete risk response planning?

3. What should be done if the probability of meeting the desired schedule or desired cost is unacceptable?

4. How are contingency plans different than fallback plans?

5. Why is it important to prove the value of risk management?

6. What is the preferred method of calculating a contingency reserve?

7. How is a management reserve different than a contingency reserve?

Adapt This to Your Real-World Projects

Plan Risk Responses

Please visit the RMC Project Management Web site at www.rmcproject.com/risk to download the full version of the following forms.

Steps to follow:
1. For each top opportunity on your project, determine what you are going to do to increase the opportunity or its probability or impact.
2. For each top threat on your project, determine what you are going to do to eliminate the risk or reduce the probability or impact.
3. Identify triggers, and create contingency plans and fallback plans for the residual risks on your real-world project.

Plan Risk Responses

Top Opportunities Form		
Top Opportunities	Ideas for Exploiting	Ideas for Enhancing the Probability

Ideas for Enhancing the Impact	Ideas for Sharing	Choice(s) Selected

Risk Response Form for Opportunities							
Opportunities				Rating		Score	
Cause	Risk	Effect	Activity	P	I	P x I	Ranking

Trigger	Contingency Plan	Trigger	Fallback Plan	Risk Owner

Plan Risk Responses

Top Threats Form		
Top Threats	Ideas for Avoidance	Ideas for Mitigating the Probability

Ideas for Mitigating the Impact	Ideas for Transferring	Choice(s) Selected

Risk Response Form for Threats								
Threats					Rating		Score	
Cause	Risk	Effect	Activity		P	I	P x I	Ranking

	Trigger	Contingency Plan	Trigger	Fallback Plan	Risk Owner

Notes

CHAPTER 8

Monitor and Control Risks

Objectives of the Monitor and Control Risks Process

How about getting some rewards for your efforts? During the Monitor and Control Risks process, the benefits of the previous processes are realized by the project manager and the team. If you have spent the appropriate amount of time with the appropriate stakeholders and have performed good project management (particularly in creating a work breakdown structure and getting good estimates), this step will be substantially easier. If not, you will spend plenty of time dealing with problems that could have been avoided. There will be rework and overtime, as well as damage to your reputation, as too many things will go wrong that you did not prepare for.

There are many objectives of the Monitor and Control Risks process. On a high-level basis, the objectives of this process are to:
- Implement the risk response plans, ensure compliance, and manage progress
- Manage the contingency and management reserves
- Create workarounds
- Control the project risk
- Refine and update the risk register
- Perform additional risk identification, qualitative and quantitative risk analysis, and risk response planning
- Reestimate the project
- Keep stakeholders informed about the status of risks on the project—communicate about risks

- Create lessons learned
- Evaluate the risk impact of scope, schedule, cost, and other change requests

Many project managers neither understand nor perform control. This step is important in order to make sure the benefits of earlier steps are realized. Let me rephrase the objectives as simple phrases you can remember for the Monitor and Control Risks process but also for project control in general.

- Implement
- Manage progress
- Communicate
- Ensure compliance
- Reassess
- Refine
- Add new risks
- Reestimate the project
- Measure
- Take corrective action
- Evaluate the effectiveness of corrective action

To achieve the benefits of risk management, it is important to have the following inputs before beginning the Monitor and Control Risks process:
- Risk register, which now includes:
  - Risks
  - Risk response plans
  - Risk owners
  - Triggers
  - Contracts
  - Watchlist
  - Time and cost reserves
- Risk management plan
- Work results
- Project communications
- Risk events
- Project changes
- Additional risks that have been identified as the project progresses

Implement the Risk Response Plans, Ensure Compliance, and Manage Progress

During the Monitor and Control Risks process, risk owners will respond to risk triggers by implementing contingency plans and fallback plans, if needed. The project manager should make sure the contingency plans and fallback plans are understood and complied with. Unauthorized changes to these plans have the same impact to the project as other unauthorized project changes and should therefore be avoided.

Management during these activities requires the same monitoring, motivating, assisting, coaching, and other management activities that are required for managing the project as a whole.

Manage the Highest Risk Path, Not Just the Critical Path

Most project managers know that they need to keep an eye on the critical path and that a problem with an activity on the critical path requires immediate attention. Why not also determine the path through the network diagram that has the highest risk score? The activities on this path may not occur immediately after one another as do those in the critical path, but the path with the highest risk score should be managed as closely as the critical path.

During the Monitor and Control Risks process (or the executing and monitoring and controlling processes of the project), the huge impact of risk management activities will be dramatically felt.

Imagine a 90 percent decrease in problems!
Imagine the time impacts of fewer problems!

With risk management, up to 90 percent of all project problems are prevented, thus saving a phenomenal amount of time while the project is being completed. This creates a major improvement in project performance and project success.

Imagine also what happens on real projects when there is a major problem. Most people cringe. If the project made good use of risk management, they would not worry as much. Chances are the problem would have been identified and a plan would already be in place.

This may be the most important thing you read in this book. If you do risk management, people will fight to work on your projects because your projects will be in control!

Manage the Contingency and Management Reserves

You worked hard to set up the reserves and get approval. During project executing and monitoring and controlling, you will manage, use, and protect these reserves.

Remember that the contingency reserve is to accommodate the known unknowns for the project. This means that it should ONLY be used for identified risks that actually take place.

The management reserve is for unknown unknowns—risks that have not been identified. There are no standards for how contingency or management reserves are used. Some people believe that management reserves should only be used by management, and may be used for any changes. I cannot support this view. The entire reserve (and the project) must be controlled by the project manager. The management reserve should be used for unknown unknown risks that occur related to the baseline scope of work. Any change to the baseline scope of work requires a change to the project and thus a change order with additional reserves.

Let's look at a few examples. Don't worry if you do not agree. We could argue this forever. This is my opinion; there are no standards.

Reserve Management

Situation	Change Order Outside the Scope	Contingency Reserve/Known Unknowns	Management Reserve/Unknown Unknowns
The project has identified a risk that a deliverable will be late, causing US $20,000 in costs. The risk occurs.		√	

Situation	Change Order Outside the Scope	Contingency Reserve/Known Unknowns	Management Reserve/Unknown Unknowns
During the middle of the project, management determines that the project must be completed three weeks earlier than planned.		√ If this occurrence had been identified as a risk	√ If this occurrence had not been identified as a risk
Management wants to add additional scope of work.	√		
A risk was identified but its probability and impact could not be determined. The risk occurs.			√

Everyone will want to make use of the "free" time or cost available on the project. This can become a problem, as the project manager is held accountable for completing the project in accordance with the approved project management plan (plus approved change orders). If the reserve runs out, you must adjust somewhere else in the project to meet the project requirements, including completion date and project cost. Careful management of the reserves, as well as the project, is key to completing the project within the requirements.

TRICKS OF THE TRADE® Be Sure the Stakeholders Understand Reserves

When the project work is underway is no time to be describing to the project stakeholders the concept of reserves, how they are calculated, and what they are to be used for. This important activity should have occurred before the Monitor and Control Risks process. Such an explanation helps the stakeholders realize that reserves are not a pad (an unsupportable addition to the project cost or budget) and they cannot easily make use of the cost or time in the reserves. Having made this clear, you should have fewer attempts to access the reserves for inappropriate uses during project executing.

Create Workarounds

Though the title "workarounds" might be new to you, the subject matter should not be. A workaround is an unplanned response to an unidentified risk that occurs.

Workarounds are reactive; project management is supposed to be proactive. Project managers should be spending much more time executing contingency and fallback plans then creating workarounds.

The need for a high number of workarounds on a project indicates a lack of adequate project planning and a project that is in trouble! Risk management greatly decreases the need for workarounds.

Many studies say that it is between 75 to 100 times more expensive to fix a problem than to prevent it. Think about how much more time and money you would have available if you identified and planned for most of the things that go wrong on a project!

In our helicopter story, a workaround would have been needed if the risk of more than three inches of rain in a two-day period during installation of the structural steel had not been identified and the rain occurred. It would also have been needed if there was no contingency plan to hire the helicopter or no fallback plan to use the sponge carpet. A workaround would also have been needed if the carpet did not work or if the helicopter's efforts resulted in an unexpected event.

 What Is the Difference Between a Risk and an Issue?

An issue is an unforeseen, minor problem that has occurred. It may be handled by listing it on a project action item list and managing it, or by creating a workaround. Each time an issue occurs, the best project managers will ask themselves questions such as:

- If we missed this problem during planning, what else did we miss?
- Is this problem an indication of a deeper root cause that might affect the project later?
- Is this problem an indication of a risk?

Control the Project Risk

During project monitoring and controlling, you must have a plan to measure against, make measurements of performance, and then take corrective action to bring performance back in line with the plan.

This sounds good, but believe it or not, too many project managers do not have a proper project management plan to measure against, or do not know that they have to measure performance.

One way to measure the status of the project is to include the evaluation of risks. You might check:

- The number of identified risks that were not in the original risk evaluation
- The number of workarounds needed

Let's look at two more scientific ways to measure performance.

Risk Review

A risk review is a way to control risks and manage changes. It can also be the vehicle for identifying new risks and making sure everyone understands the contingency and fallback plans. Risk reviews take place during regularly scheduled meetings with the risk owners and project team and may also include the other stakeholders. Risk reviews look forward in time to what should happen for risk. These meetings can be the primary way to manage risk on the project.

In our helicopter story, the risk of more than three inches of rain in a two-day period during installation of the structural steel was reviewed before the installation of the structural steel to determine if the risk was still valid and the planned responses were still appropriate.

 The following are the types of questions that can be asked during a risk review:

- What additional risks have you uncovered since the last meeting?
- Which of the triggers that we have identified no longer seem appropriate?
- Which of the risk response plans that we have created seem to need more development?
- If you could change one thing about the risks of this project, what would it be?

- Have we discovered anyone who has additional insight into our major risks?
- Activity X is our riskiest activity. John, that activity is assigned to you. From 1 to 10 (10 being the most comfortable), how comfortable are you that we can complete the activity as planned? Is there extra assistance or information that would make the activity easier for you?
- We were not satisfied with our contingency plan for risk Y. Has anyone come up with new ideas since our last meeting?
- Now that we are three months into this project, let's look at the order of our top risks and see if we are still in agreement on which are top and which are not, and the order of the top risks. Which of our residual risks do you think needs a different risk impact or probability rating?
- Risk Z has been triggered and our plans put into place. However, turnaround time by the engineering department was much faster than expected. Let's look at the other risks we have identified that involve the engineering department and make sure we incorporate this new information into the contingency and fallback plans.

TRICKS OF THE TRADE® ### Be Alert for Indications of Unidentified Risks

No matter how well risk management is done, there will always be risks that are not uncovered until project execution. Imagine a situation where one of the project team members keeps showing up late for team meetings. Two others are constantly arguing. These are not insignificant situations, but indications of unidentified risks (if not already planned for in the risk register). These situations should be included in risk reviews.

TRICKS OF THE TRADE® ### Use a Risk Review Board to Perform a Risk Review

To be most effective, a risk review board should include people who have not been part of the risk management process for the project to date. Representatives of management, program or portfolio managers, and other project managers may be involved to gain additional perspectives on the project and its risks. This board does not generally include the project manager of the project being reviewed.

If well managed, risk reviews will result in:
- Additional risk response planning ideas
- Changing the order of the top risks
- Revisiting non-top risks to see if the ranking of non-top (or even top) risks needs to change
- Adjusting to the severity of actual risks
- Determining if assumptions are still valid
- Looking for any unexpected effects or consequences of risks
- Monitoring residual risks
- Reviewing all workaround situations to see if they provide insight into the existence of additional risks
- Making changes to the project management plan when new risk responses are developed

Measuring Performance through Risk Audits

A risk audit takes another look at what the project team has done for risk management and whether it has worked.

Many people ask about what is the difference between a risk review and a risk audit. The best way to understand this difference is to remember that risk audits look backward in time to what has occurred, while risk reviews look forward in time to what should happen.

A risk audit includes:
- Reviewing if the right risk owners have been assigned to each risk
- Determining if the risk owners are effective
- Examining and documenting the effectiveness of contingency plans and fallback plans

On critical projects, a risk audit could be done before the project management plan is approved. However, risk audits are more commonly done during the execution of the project. As a result of a risk audit, corrective action may be taken. Risk owners might be changed, or contingency and fallback plans for risks might be adjusted.

A risk audit may be done by the project manager alone, by the project manager and the team, by an outside "risk audit" group (to help eliminate biases), or as part of a full-scale project management audit. It might include conversations with risk owners or simply measuring the results of risk actions taken and then reporting on the resolution of the risk. Once the analysis is completed, corrective action is taken and the effectiveness of the corrective action is measured. Results of the risk audit are used in the project and also become a part of historical records. They can then be used as lessons learned for future projects.

Earned Value Analysis

Earned value analysis is used to quantitatively measure and monitor overall project performance against the project baseline. It entails an analysis of the value to the company of the cost and time put into a project and makes use of actual project information to measure cost and schedule performance. Some of the key indicators are listed on the following chart.

Name of Indicator	Number derived by calculating the formula	This indicator means:	Interpretation
Cost Performance Index (CPI)	0.89	I am only getting 89 cents out of every dollar invested into this project.	A CPI of less than one means a bad situation.
	1.3	I am getting 1.3 dollars out of every dollar I put into this project.	A CPI of one or greater means a good situation.
Schedule Performance Index (SPI)	0.85	I am only progressing at 85% of the rate originally planned.	A CPI of less than one means a bad situation.
	1.25	I am progressing at 125% of the rate originally planned.	A CPI of one or greater means a good situation.

Name of Indicator	Number derived by calculating the formula	This indicator means:	Interpretation
Estimate at Completion (EAC)	$495,000	As of now, how much do we think the project will cost?	This forecast can be used to compare to earlier cost estimates to the actual cost when the project is over to assess performance.

CPI and SPI are measures of project performance. An SPI of 0.85 implies that the project is only progressing at 85 percent of the rate originally planned. Project management would include a detailed evaluation of what specific activities took longer than planned and what can be done to correct the situation. Plans would be implemented, and the project manager would determine the SPI again to see if the situation had been corrected.

To correct such a situation, the project schedule is reestimated during project executing. In this case, it is determined that the project is currently three weeks late. Corrective action is needed, and that action can have only minimal impact to project cost.

In the following charts, the left-hand column represents the activities that are on the critical path. The project team has determined options for shortening the length of each critical path activity in order to meet the new deadline. Options selected for the previous situation could include changing resources to someone who can complete the activity faster or cutting part of the scope of an activity and thus saving time. However, saving time does not happen in a vacuum. The effect on the other project constraints must also be considered.

Looking at the chart, which activity would you choose to save three weeks?

Activity	Duration (in weeks)	Crash Duration (in weeks)	Time Savings (in weeks)	Cost	Crash Cost	Extra Cost
D	6	4	2	$10,000	$14,000	$4,000
E	7	5	2	$17,000	$27,000	$10,000
G	5	4	1	$15,000	$16,000	$1,000
H	7	6	1	$8,000	$10,000	$2,000
C	8	5	3	$12,000	$21,000	$9,000

The answer would be to choose the options for activities D and G because they have the least impact on cost.

Now let's add a column for risk impact. A 10 is a high impact and a 1 is a low impact. Now which activity or activities would you choose to save three weeks?

Activity	Duration (in weeks)	Crash Duration (in weeks)	Time Savings (in weeks)	Cost	Crash Cost	Extra Cost	Risk Impact
D	6	4	2	$10,000	$14,000	$4,000	9
E	7	5	2	$17,000	$27,000	$10,000	2
G	5	4	1	$15,000	$16,000	$1,000	3
H	7	6	1	$8,000	$10,000	$2,000	9
C	8	5	3	$12,000	$21,000	$9,000	0

See how your answer is different when the risk column is added! Choosing activities D and G is shown to have an extremely high impact on the risk of the project. Looking at other options, you cannot choose activity H because of its high risk impact. Though the answer depends on the specifics of your project, with the information provided here, you are most likely to select activity C, the choice with the lowest overall impact to risk.

Imagine the same chart completed with a column for the other project constraints. Now you are seeing what a true analysis of options for adjusting a project should include.

Refine and Update Risk Responses

The project management plan and risk response plans should be refined and updated throughout the life of the project. As the project progresses, the project team will become more familiar with the project and thus be able to determine that the risk score or the number of unidentified risks may be a warning sign. Additional risks identified and a large number of project changes are also warning signs. (See also the reasons for reestimating the project listed later in this chapter.) Such situations require reassessing or changing the project management plan and the risk register.

> **Risk should be the #1 topic at each team meeting!**

Risk ratings, prioritization of risks, contingency plans, and fallback plans may change during the life of the project, requiring updates and refinements to the risk register.

Technical Performance Measurement

Every project has technical requirements that must be met. Examples include strength of concrete, measurable wind resistance of a building, meeting functionality requirements, strength of the plastic used in a product, or shelf life.

When actual results of technical performance deviate from the project baseline, the Identify Risks, Perform Qualitative Risk Analysis, Perform Quantitative Risk Analysis, and Plan Risk Responses processes should be updated while fixing the problem. Such deviations imply a risk to achieving the project's scope. Keep in mind the project constraints. A change in the cost performance could potentially impact the quality, customer satisfaction, or schedule of the project.

> **Risks should be evaluated for the impact to all of the project constraints.**

Look for Risks During the Verify Scope Process

The Verify Scope process is when the project manager reviews the deliverables for compliance with the requirements, meets with the customer, and tries to get formal approval in the form of a sign-off on the deliverable.

Additional risks and more accurate risk ratings for risks can also be obtained while meeting with the customer during the Verify Scope process. As the scope of various deliverables is verified throughout the project, you can ask questions about the customer, how the project fits into the customer's department (or company) priorities, anything new in the department (or company), and any other technical and managerial topics that you can reasonably think of. The following are examples of questions to ask:

- How has the response been within your department (or company) to our last deliverable?
- What problems did you have with using/implementing our last deliverable?
- What should be done differently with future deliverables?
- If we could do the last deliverable over again, what would you suggest we do differently?
- How many changes to the scope of work on this project are currently under discussion? (Asking "how many" instead of "what changes" provides a better response.)
- You helped us identify a risk to the Z component. Do you have any more information about that component now that some weeks have gone by?
- Here is a current list of the major risks for the project. What is missing? Do you still think they are in the proper order from highest risk score to lowest? (This list may only be the risks the customer has identified, rather than all the project risks. The full list may contain some risks that remain confidential, and are accessible only to the project team.)

Be prepared with questions appropriate to the project before a scope verification meeting.

Risk Reassessment
Additional Risk Identification, Qualitative Risk Analysis, Quantitative Risk Analysis, and Risk Response Planning

An interesting aspect of risk monitoring and control is that it also involves risk identification, qualitative risk analysis, quantitative risk analysis (if needed), and risk response planning. Can you think of a reason why this might be?

There are two major times when a risk reassessment might occur: when new risks are identified and when changes occur on the project. New risks can be identified during risk reviews, by holding additional brainstorming or risk identification sessions, in project meetings, by watching what is going on, and through any project activity. It is the project manager's role to look for new risks and to schedule additional risk identification sessions as required, based on the specific needs of the project.

No matter how well risk management is completed, unidentified risks and project changes will still occur. This does not mean that changes occur in isolation from risk management. Integrated change control is a term that implies that any change to scope, time, cost, resources, quality, or risk (any part of the project) should be evaluated for any impact on other parts of the project. A change to the quality level desired for the project will most likely have an impact on the risk of the project by adding new risks and changing the ratings and rankings of existing ones. A change to the scope will change the risks. A change to the cost...you get the picture.

Therefore, keep looking for risks when any changes are made on the project. Then qualitatively (and possibly quantitatively) assess the risk in conjunction with already identified risks. Plan responses if necessary, and update the risk register. If you lose control of risks or ignore risks during execution and control of the project, you will sacrifice the benefits gained by previous risk activities. That is an asset you don't want to lose.

Reestimating the Project

Activity estimates and project estimates are just that—estimates. Estimates can change based on more complete knowledge of the work needed to be done on activities, other project changes, and changes in risk to the project. Take this seriously! Activity and project estimates should be updated and revised over the life of the project to make sure the project requirements can be met. A project manager does not take a "wait and see" attitude, but more of a "prove we can make it" attitude toward meeting the project requirements. Not meeting the requirements means the project manager has failed and that company or client resources have been unethically wasted. It is that serious.

What might necessitate reestimating? Instances relating to risk management include, but are not limited to:

- When new risks are identified
- When new risk ratings for probability or impact are determined for existing risks
- When the prioritization of risks changes
- To accommodate the time and cost for workarounds

- When any refinement or reassessing of the risk response plans is done
- When reserves are used faster than expected
- When the project has had many changes
- When the project has never been done before
- When there is little confidence in the project management plan
- When a new project manager takes over a project
- When many unidentified risks occur

To reestimate the project, you could start from scratch, create a completely new work breakdown structure, ask each person completing a project activity to reestimate the activity, and continue with the full planning process. You could also just reestimate the activities that have been affected and determine the effect on the whole project. In any case, do not forget to adjust the project (e.g., crashing, fast tracking, cutting scope) to meet the project requirements.

Communicating About Risk

Imagine you are a stakeholder. You have a lot of your own work to do when, suddenly, a project manager shows up to tell you that the network computer system you were going to work with will be down that day because of project work. This is not a good situation, yet it happens all the time. A great project manager will keep the stakeholders up to date on the status of the project.

Even better yet, the project manager should have previously identified the stakeholders and determined their needs, including what each stakeholder needs to know about the project to better integrate the project into their everyday work. The project manager could then regularly provide required information to the stakeholders. Can you see the improved cooperation, improved performance, and more successful project that are the result of this practice?

Risks should be treated like activities; they are part of the project and can impact the project if they happen. Risks can be communicated to stakeholders using the following methods:

- Project management plan
- Project monthly reports
- Activity status reports
- Bar charts

- Communication with other projects
- Risk register
- Activity estimating form

The project management plan could include a statement such as the following when it addresses risk. With such a statement, how can you not get support for risk management?

"The original expected monetary value of the risk of this project was $45,700. Actions we have taken to respond to the risks have cost $1,700 and resulted in an expected monetary value of $21,600. The savings due to risk management have so far been $22,400 for this project."

TRICKS OF THE TRADE® Decrease Risks by Communicating Them

Simply naming the top risks in a report substantially decreases the probability of their occurrence! Including risk information in the monthly project report keeps focus on the risks. Everyone will know about the risks and everyone will be watching out for them. If you were to add the sources of the risks, then more focus would be placed in the appropriate place. This trick is enhanced if you include a discussion of risks, how they were derived, and their impact in the kickoff meeting that takes place at the end of project planning.

Monthly Project Status Report		
Project: _____ Project #: _____ PM: _____		
Sponsor: _____ Completion Date: _____ As of Date: _____		

Status

| Cost _____ |
| Schedule _____ |
| Scope _____ |
| Quality _____ |
| Risk _____ |
| Resources _____ |
| Customer Satisfaction _____ |

Plan vs. Actual

Accomplishments

Work for Next Month

Exceptions to Plans

Issues/Problems

Milestone chart

Activity 1 ▲

Activity 2 ▲——▲

Activity 3 ▲——▲

Risks

Sources

SIGNED:

Above is a sample monthly status report form to adapt to your projects.

Notice two things: First, this report is not an output of "project management" software. Second, it includes a listing of the current top risks on the project. The status of risk, as well as cost, schedule, etc., can be indicated with the following code:

Red	Problem
Yellow	Danger
Green	Good

If we are going to include risk in the monthly report, we will also need to accumulate information about risks to put into that report. Do not just think about holding a meeting. Rather, basic status should be collected by e-mail or a form using the following as a template. So what is the result of this practice? Better information is collected, and there is more time in team meetings for real work to be done, such as working to decrease project risk.

Activity Status Form		
Project: _____ Activity Number:_____ Person Assigned: _____		
Date: _____		
Exceptions to plan (if any):		
Status: How much has been done (in hours)?		
How much is left to do (in hours)?		
Problems/Issues		
Risks: List any new risks List changes to existing risks		
Signed:		

TRICKS OF THE TRADE®

Use the Bar Chart

What about using a Bar chart for communicating risks? Include the risk score and the risk owner as text columns in the bar chart. This will maintain focus on risk and on the activities that need more assistance. Therefore, a functional manager may be less likely to arbitrarily move resources or change the scope of a risky activity.

A discussion of bar charts should also come with a warning. Years of dealing with management and other stakeholders in training sessions have led me to discover something important. Bar charts scare people. Yes, it is true. People do not know how they are developed and do not believe that they are realistic representations of the schedule. Bar charts also seem too much like micromanagement for those people not trained in project management. Bar charts should only be used by management and other stakeholders trained in using them.

TRICKS OF THE TRADE® ## Communicate with Other Project Managers

Few projects exist in isolation. In many cases, concurrent projects make use of the same resources and thus are in competition with each other. There is a positive side to this. Experiences on one project can make another project better. A great project manager will notice what is going on with other projects and have a formal or informal communication plan with other project managers to share lessons learned. So, for example, a project manager might be told, "I understand you are concerned about delay caused by a slow turnaround from the accounting department on one of your deliverables. We are also working with that department on a project and have had excellent cooperation."

Get to know other projects and project managers. Review their list of risks and contingency and fallback plans and share information with them. Such sharing of lessons learned could be facilitated by a project management office, if one exists, or by informal coordination meetings between project managers. The more cooperation you can encourage, the better your reputation will be and the more effective you can be on your own projects.

A Risk Reserve Report

A risk reserve report keeps a running balance of the remaining reserve and helps the project manager control the reserve. It is used like a checkbook or a savings account would be. Money is added when activities are completed cheaper or faster, and money is deducted when it is used for risks. A risk reserve report may look something like the following:

Cost Risk Reserve Report

Reserve used for:	Used Contingency Reserve	Used Management Reserve	Contingency Balance ($21,600 at start)	Management Balance ($5,000 at start)
A	$2,000		$19,600	$5,000
B	$8,000		$11,600	$5,000
C		$600	$11,600	$4,400

The same type of report can be done for time.

Lessons Learned

Lessons learned should include an evaluation of risk.

A lessons learned evaluation looks at what went right and wrong with the project and what should be done differently next time. At a minimum, the project manager creates lessons learned as a personal record, including productivity rates and other data for use on future projects. Better yet, this documentation is created by the whole project team. Best yet, it is created by the team and put into a corporate historical database that is available to all project teams.

The purpose of lessons learned documentation is to:
- Prevent the same problems from occurring on project after project
- Continuously improve the project management process
- Save money and time on future projects

Unfortunately, many people who complete lessons learned miss something; they only focus on technical lessons learned (for instance, we should have used this brand of equipment rather than that one). A real lessons learned evaluation looks at three areas:
- **Project management:** Relating to the process of project management (including the work breakdown structure, communication planning, the network diagram, risk, etc.)
- **Management:** Relating to communication, facilitation, leadership, and other management topics
- **Technical:** Relating to the process of completing the technical work

For risk management, lessons learned also include an evaluation of how the risk effort was handled and how it can be improved next time. Here's an example:

Lessons Learned Form
Project Management—Including Risk Management
Management
Technical

Promote Lessons Learned

One way to acquire lessons learned is to promote them. Imagine at some organizational meeting one of the top managers mentioning, "You would not believe what we have discovered!" Do this once and everyone will want to be the person who provided the great new idea for the next meeting.

Risk management is essentially an optimistic activity, even when it is addressing threats to the project. It is about taking control and being in command. When this attitude is held by the project manager, more lessons learned will be created. Some project managers even include prizes for the best lessons learned submitted by their teams in the reward system for their projects.

Summary of the Tricks of the Trade® for the Monitor and Control Risks Process

- Risks should be the number one topic (meaning first and most important) for project meetings. Ask: "Are there any changes to the risks we have? Are there any new risks? Are any changes needed to our contingency plans?"
- Instruct stakeholders in the function and use of reserves before they try to use them.

- Get in the habit of asking yourself, "If we missed this problem, what else did we miss?"
- Realize that all the risks will not have been identified and keep looking for risks.
- Look for risks during the Verify Scope process and any other interactions with the customer.
- Watch actions during project execution to uncover more risks.
- Periodically reassess the entire risk plan.
- Watch for low-ranking risks that become more important.
- Continually communicate with stakeholders.
- Remember, the more you keep risks visible, the less likely they are to occur.
- Include top risks, responsibility, and the risks' status in every monthly status report.
- During project monitoring and controlling, bar charts are often used to show project status. Include the risk score and responsibility as text columns in this chart.
- Discover what is happening with other projects to help identify or clarify risks on your project.
- Include an evaluation of risk management on the project in the lessons learned.

Activities in the Monitor and Control Risks Process

The following activities are part of the Monitor and Control Risks process:
- Managing the risk management plan and risk response plans
- Watching for triggers (events that show that a risk is about to occur or has occurred)
- Keeping track of the identified risks
- Managing the reserves
- Ensuring the execution of the risk management plan and risk response plans
- Dealing with risks that were not identified
- Performing workarounds (in other words, dealing with problems)
- Performing risk audits
- Performing risk reviews
- Coming up with additional risk response planning ideas
- Taking corrective action to adjust to the severity of actual risks
- Revisiting non-top risks to see if the rankings of non-top (or even top) risks need to change, or if risk responses need to be determined
- Collecting and communicating risk status
- Communicating with stakeholders about risks

- Determining if assumptions are still valid
- Looking for any unexpected effects or consequences of risk events
- Monitoring residual risks
- Identifying new risks
- Reviewing all workaround situations to see if they provide insight into the existence of additional risks
- Updating the risk register
- Making changes to the project management plan when new risk responses are developed
- Creating a database of risk data that may be used throughout the organization on other projects
- Recording results of team meetings and other meetings
- Reviewing results from other projects not yet formalized into lessons learned
- Reevaluating risk identification and qualitative and quantitative risk analysis when the project deviates from the baseline

Outputs of the Monitor and Control Risks Process

The following are the outputs of the Monitor and Control Risks process.

Risk Register Updates

The risk register is updated with the following information as a result of this process:
- Outcomes of the risk reassessments and risk audits
- Updates to previous parts of risk management, including the identification of new risks
- Closing of risks that are no longer applicable
- Details of what happened when risks occurred
- Lessons learned

Change Requests, Including Recommended Corrective and Preventive Actions

The Monitor and Control Risks process will uncover changes needed to the project.

Project Management Plan Updates

The Monitor and Control Risks process can result in updates to the schedule, cost, quality, and procurement management plans, as well as the human resource plan, the WBS, and the time and cost baselines for the project.

Project Document Updates

The Monitor and Control Risks process might also affect the roles and responsibilities on a project, the stakeholder management strategy, and the quality metrics.

Organizational Process Assets Updates

The Monitor and Control Risks process will lead to the creation of risk templates, such as a risk register including project risks and risk responses, checklists, and other data to be used as historical records for future projects.

Chapter Summary

Key Concepts

- The objective of the Monitor and Control Risks process is to manage the project according to the risk management plan and the risk response plans recorded in the risk register.

- The Monitor and Control Risks process involves the following activities:

    - Monitor

    - Ensure compliance

    - Measure

    - Take corrective action

    - Evaluate effectiveness

    - Reassess

    - Refine

- Contingency and management reserves must be controlled, not just used for any need that arises.

- Do not assume all the risks have been identified in the Identify Risks process.

- Risk management should be one of the most important topics at each team meeting.

- Workarounds should be less frequent than implementing risk response plans.

- Taking corrective action involves taking measures of performance, taking action, and evaluating the effectiveness of the corrective action.

- The more you communicate about risks, the less likely they are to occur.

- Remember to communicate with stakeholders.

- Prove the effectiveness of risk management by showing and reporting results.

- Risk response audits help you to determine lessons learned.

Chapter Summary

Key Terms

- Monitor and Control Risks process
- Monitor
- Ensure compliance
- Respond to triggers
- Manage reserves
- Workarounds
- Measure
- Earned value analysis
- Corrective action

- Evaluate the effectiveness
- Reestimate
- Refine
- Risk review
- Technical performance measurement
- Risk reassessment
- Risk audit
- Risk reserve report

Matching Game: Monitor and Control Risks

Instructions: Match the risk management key word to its definition.

Key Word

_____ **1.** Monitor and Control Risks
  process

_____ **2.** Monitor

_____ **3.** Ensure compliance

_____ **4.** Manage reserves

_____ **5.** Workarounds

_____ **6.** Risk audit

_____ **7.** Earned value analysis

_____ **8.** Corrective action

_____ **9.** Evaluate the effectiveness

_____ **10.** Risk reassessment

_____ **11.** Risk review

_____ **12.** Technical performance
  measurement

Definition

A. Analysis of what the project team has planned for risk management to determine whether it is still appropriate

B. Control the appropriate use of reserves

C. Analysis of what the project team has done for risk management to determine whether it has worked

D. Changes implemented in order to bring performance back in line with the project management plan

E. A method to quantitatively measure and monitor overall project performance against the project baseline

F. Making sure policies, procedures, and plans are being followed

G. Implementing the risk response plans as risks occur, looking for risk triggers, identifying new risks, and evaluating the effectiveness of risk responses

H. Looking for new risks when changes are made on the project

Matching Game: Monitor and Control Risks

I. Oversee project performance and activities

J. Measurement of factors such as strength of concrete, measurable wind resistance of a building, meeting functionality requirements, strength of the plastic used in a product, etc., to identify deviations from the plan

K. Measure to determine the results of actions taken

L. Unplanned responses to unidentified risks that occur

Answer Key

1.	G	7.	E
2.	I	8.	D
3.	F	9.	K
4.	B	10.	H
5.	L	11.	A
6.	C	12.	J

Questions for Discussion

1. What method or combination of methods will you use in the Monitor and Control Risks process on your real-world projects?

2. What ways can you use risk management results to gain support for risk management efforts in the company?

3. What is the first step to be taken when a risk trigger occurs?

4. What should happen if fallback plans are not effective?

5. What should be done when the frequency of workarounds is greater than the frequency of implementing contingency and fallback plans?

6. Why does publishing identified risks in monthly reports often decrease the probability of a risk occurring?

Adapt This to Your Real-World Projects

Monitor and Control Risks

Please visit the RMC Project Management Web site at www.rmcproject.com/risk to download the full version of the following forms.

Cost Risk Reserve Report	
Reserve Used For:	Used Contingency Reserve

Used Management Reserve	Contingency Balance ($_____ at start)	Management Balance ($_____ at start)

Time Risk Reserve Report	
Reserve Used For:	Used Contingency Reserve

Used Management Reserve	Contingency Balance (_____ at start)	Management Balance (_____ at start)

Notes

Risk Governance

The work of risk governance extends throughout the project. Risk governance involves oversight of the entire risk management process, making sure the risk management activities are consistent, and that they are continuously improved throughout the organization. Governance is a matter of not starting from scratch on each project, but rather from benefiting from the successes and failures of projects that have gone before yours.

Roles and Responsibilities for Risk Governance

The responsibility for risk governance may fall to the project manager, the project management office (PMO), the risk management department, or management of the organization. There may even be a risk management governance body set up within the organization, as described later in this chapter.

The project manager should understand and be trained in risk management, and manage the project's risk management process. This might involve determining how risk management will be handled for the project and how that effort will meet any company policies and procedures for risk management.

A program manager (if one exists) in the organization would be involved in overseeing the risk management function for all the projects in the program. This includes making sure all parties are trained in risk management as well as project management, coordinating risk management efforts throughout the program, and making sure that the risk management effort is appropriate for the size and importance of the projects.

The PMO might create some policies and procedures for risk management and serve as a governance body overseeing all projects, including how the projects manage risks.

Since risk management is such an important topic, company management may also be involved in the project, helping to identify risks and making decisions on the amount of acceptable risk in the project.

Standards, Policies, Procedures, and Practices

Some of the standards, policies, and procedures that might be set up for all projects include:

- Organizational risk tolerances and thresholds
- Methods to use to identify risks
- Definitions of impact ratings to be used in the Perform Qualitative Risk Analysis process
- Standard probability and impact matrix

Policies and procedures could also cover such topics as how sponsors should participate in risk management activities, who should be trained in risk management (e.g., all project managers and risk owners), how often risks should be reviewed on projects, and any other policies relating to risk that are deemed valuable.

These organizational standards and policies are updated based on lessons learned from applying these standards and policies on other projects. This is critical information for the project manager to uncover at the beginning of the Plan Risk Management process, as it will influence how he or she approaches any project within the organization.

Risk governance involves not only creating such policies relating to risk management, but also making sure that projects are planned using relevant risk policies and standards. Then while the project is underway, risk governance involves making sure the project actually follows the policies. Such policies and best practices are designed to improve risk management effectiveness. They may be enforced by the project manager, PMO, or the management of the organization if a risk governance body does not exist.

Lessons Learned Management

Another function of governance is to ensure that lessons learned related to risk management are captured on all projects and then made available for use on other projects. Lessons learned support the practice of continuous improvement within an organization. Imagine being able to see all the risks that similar projects within the organization have had! Wouldn't this help to eliminate issues like the same problem occurring over and over again within an organization? Organizations would grow and evolve much more quickly and have fewer growing pains. People would be able to focus their knowledge and expertise toward pushing the boundaries of what is possible while completing the project instead of dealing with the same problems that other projects faced.

As we discussed in the Monitor and Control Risks chapter of this book, lessons learned should include:

- What went right?
- What went wrong?
- What would be done differently if the project could be done again?

Lessons learned are created by the project manager and involve the input of the team and stakeholders. They are created throughout the life of the project and are finalized at project end. Lessons learned may be sent to other project managers or departments that might benefit from them as they are created, instead of waiting until the project is closed out.

Creation of Metrics

Metrics are standards of performance that, once evaluated, tell how work is performing against the plan. Risk governance involves the creation of metrics for risk management activities in the organization.

Project managers will have a performance measurement baseline for the project that includes broad requirements for scope, time, and cost. On most projects, this baseline is measured infrequently, leaving the project manager unsure of the real status of the project between performance measurements. This is why metrics are valuable—to provide an additional measure of progress and to warn of potential problems.

Project managers may individually be able to determine some metrics for their projects, but they usually end up basing these metrics on their own beliefs and attitudes. For example, a project manager might think that nine unidentified risks are acceptable, or that having the team arguing constantly is acceptable.

The role of governance in risk management is to identify acceptable measurements of risk management success to be used on projects. Some examples of risk related metrics are:

- Risk management activities should take up 1/8 of the project planning time.
- Projects that have more than five major unidentified risks occur must be replanned.

These metrics can then become the baseline for risk management performance on projects throughout the organization. So instead of just hoping things are going well, or having to deal with big problems when measurement time comes, project managers can determine project performance using established standard metrics and know how things are progressing against the plan. Instead of having to guess which metrics have meaning on the project, they can use ones provided by risk governance.

There is another advantage of having standard metrics. Metrics make it possible to measure the performance of one project (and dare I say, one project manager) against others. Projects are hugely important to organizations, and the day will come when a project manager's performance will be able to be quantitatively measured against another. The rewards for great project management will then be given to the best project managers.

Helping to Monitor Risk Response Plans

Risk governance also involves using metrics in developing risk response plans and then monitoring performance of the project against the risk management plan and the risk response plans recorded in the risk register.

The Value of Risk Governance

Let me tell you a short story to help you see the value of risk governance. Recently I was presenting a workshop on risk management to about 900 people when someone asked me about politics. It seems that the political atmosphere in his company was adding a lot of risk to his projects. This is clearly an organization that would benefit from having a governing body that oversees risk management. The governing body would be able to see the overall impact to the organization of politics-related risks, and therefore take action to make organizational changes.

The project manager could then bring concerns about company culture or company systems to the attention of the risk governance body to explore the overall effect on the organization, rather than the project manager trying to make an organizational change based on the effect on just one project.

As you read this, you might think a risk governance body is far from what you will ever see in your organization. Think again. Since the first edition of this book was published, more and more organizations around the world have used it as their basic risk management reference. Therefore, more and more organizations are using the tricks of the trade and general advice this book provides from projects around the world. So perhaps it won't be such a long time before your organization realizes the benefits of a risk governing body.

If a project can make or break a department or even a company's future, and if a project can cause a negative impact of hundreds of times its planned cost to companies, then it will not be long before organizations take a more proactive role in managing the risk in projects.

Since projects have such a huge potential for negative or positive impact, many companies even have teams of auditors who will conduct the risk audit on a project to make sure that the project manager and the project team have identified all the risks, that adequate plans are in place, and that risk owners understand their roles in preventing and dealing with threats and maximizing potential opportunities.

As project managers progress in their careers, they can move up into the roles of program or portfolio managers, but with this chapter, I am also suggesting a new role. A project manager can move up into a risk governance position within the company, thus securing the assets of the organization against unnecessary expenditure.

The Future of Risk Governance

Risk governance practices bring to the table a more comprehensive picture of what other projects have faced and what risk response plans have worked the best on other projects. Risk governance may be a new idea, but it is one that holds promise for the future of project managers and projects worldwide.

Chapter Summary

Key Concepts

- Risk governance involves making sure risk management activities are effective, consistent, and continuously improved

- The project manager, PMO, or company management may be responsible for risk governance

- Risk governance includes:

  - Standards, policies, procedures, and practices

  - Lessons learned management

  - Creation of metrics

  - Monitoring and controlling risks

Key Terms

- Risk governance

- Governance body

- Standards, policies, procedures, and practices

- Lessons learned management

- Metrics

Matching Game: Risk Governance

Instructions: Match the risk management key word to its definition.

Key Word

_____ **1.** Risk governance

_____ **3.** Metrics

_____ **2.** Lessons learned management

Definition

A. Standards of performance that, once evaluated, tell how work is performing against the plan

C. Oversight of the entire risk management process

B. Ensuring that lessons learned are captured on all projects and made available for use on other projects

Answer Key

1. C   3. A

2. B

Questions for Discussion

1. What is the role of a risk governance body?

2. Who is responsible for risk governance in your organization?

3. What is the value of risk governance?

Notes

When you are ready, please turn to page 321 to take the Final Exam. See how much knowledge you have gained.

When you are ready, please turn to page 321 to take the Final Exam.

Taking the Risk Management Professional (PMI-RMP®) Certification Exam

CHAPTER 10

Why Take the PMI-RMP Exam?

First, think about what is risk management. Professional project risk management includes finding and addressing things that can hurt the project and therefore cause delay and added cost. It also includes finding and utilizing ways to increase the value of the project.

Now, think about being able to tell your manager that you have received an international certification in preventing things that can cause delay and added cost on projects, and actually increasing the value of projects while saving time and cost. Wouldn't this make you more valuable to your organization? Wouldn't this make you a candidate to gain a new position, a raise or promotion, or even keep your position when others do not?

The PMI-RMP certification is about setting yourself apart. Obtaining the PMI-RMP certification puts you ahead of the certified and non-certified project managers without this new credential. The question is, why wouldn't you take the PMI-RMP certification exam?

Let me make this an even a better opportunity for you. The PMI-RMP exam is not exceptionally difficult. I know of many people who already follow proper project management practices, and who understand the material in this book, that took some practice exams and then passed the exam. Passing the PMI-RMP exam should not take you a huge amount of effort if you already know project management.

Taking the Risk Management Professional (PMI-RMP®) Certification Exam

Qualifying to Take the Exam

To take this exam, you must meet requirements as outlined by PMI (the Project Management Institute). The current requirements are described in the following chart.

Education	Project Risk Experience	Project Risk Management Education
High School diploma, associate's degree, or global equivalent	At least 4,500 hours in the specialized area of professional project risk management in the past five consecutive years	40 contact hours of formal education in the specialized area of project risk management
or		
Bachelor's degree or global equivalent	At least 3,000 hours spent in the specialized area of professional project risk management in the past five consecutive years	30 contact hours of formal education in the specialized area of project risk management

Applying to Take the Exam

You must submit an application to PMI to take this exam. Applications may be submitted by mail or online. Submit online if at all possible, since PMI's response time is faster for electronic submissions. You will receive a notice authorizing you to schedule your exam. You may be subject to an audit of your application, however. Be aware that an audit will delay your approval to take the exam.

The exam is usually offered on a computer at designated testing sites, but it might be different depending on the country you are in. Your authorization notice will give you specific instructions. PMI is quickly moving to offer computerized testing around the world in many languages.

ONCE YOU RECEIVE YOUR AUTHORIZATION NOTICE, YOU MUST PASS THE EXAM WITHIN ONE YEAR!

In some instances, testing centers may not have openings for several weeks. It is recommended that you schedule your exam at least six weeks in advance of your preferred test date and at least three months before the end of your eligibility period. The examination eligibility period (the period of time during which you are able to test) is one year. The eligibility period starts on the day your application was approved. You may take the examination up to three times within this one-year eligibility period should you not pass on the first attempt.

What Is the PMI-RMP Exam Like?

The PMI-RMP exam includes 170 multiple-choice questions with four answer choices per question. The exam must be completed in three-and-a-half hours. Twenty of the 170 exam questions are "prerelease questions," meaning they are not included in your score for the exam. These questions will be randomly placed throughout the exam. You will not know which ones are which. They will be used by PMI to validate the questions for future inclusion in the master database. Your score will be calculated based on your response to the remaining 150 questions. PMI does not disclose the passing score for this exam, but states that the passing score for all PMI credential examinations is determined by sound psychometric analysis.

The questions are randomly generated from a database containing hundreds of questions. The questions may jump from topic to topic and cover multiple topics in a single question. You get one point for each correct answer. There is no penalty for wrong answers.

The score sheet that you will receive when you pass the examination breaks risk management down into the following domains: Risk Communication, Risk Analysis, Risk Response Planning, and Risk Governance. Your score sheet will rank you as Proficient, Moderately Proficient, or Below Proficient in each of the four domains of risk management. The following chart indicates the percentage of scored questions currently on the exam in each domain:

Domain	Percentage of Questions
Risk Communication	27%
Risk Analysis	30%
Risk Response Planning	26%
Risk Governance	17%

PMI occasionally makes changes to many aspects of its exams, including qualification requirements, the application process, the passing score, and the breakdown of questions in each domain. For the latest information, please visit www.pmi.org and read your authorization notice carefully. Any differences between what is listed here and what is communicated by PMI should be resolved in favor of PMI's information.

Although the exam is scored by domains, that is not an effective way to organize a book designed to help you learn risk management or to pass the PMI-RMP exam. We have therefore chosen to organize this book according to the detailed process of risk management. I believe that organizing the book this way will help you better understand each part of the process and help you answer more questions correctly on the exam. The following shows how the chapters of this book map to the score sheet you will receive.

Domain	Risk Management Processes/Chapter(s)
Risk Communication	Throughout
Risk Analysis	Plan Risk Management
	Identify Risks
	Perform Qualitative Risk Analysis
	Perform Quantitative Risk Analysis
	Monitor and Control Risks
Risk Response Planning	Plan Risk Responses
Risk Governance	Throughout
	Monitor and Control Risks
	Risk Governance

Risk Communication

Project managers spend approximately 90 percent of their time communicating. The topic of risk communication extends throughout the entire risk management process, and therefore, throughout this book. Communication of risk management efforts is included in the communications management plan, and impacted by the type of organization in which the project is being performed. Major risk areas requiring attention to communication include: when the charter is created and authorized, during the Identify Risks process, when unexpected risks arise, and as risk responses are planned and implemented. Keep the concept of communication in the front of your mind as you read each chapter of this book.

Risk Analysis

Risks are analyzed at a high level at the onset of the project. As discussed in the Identify Risks chapter, further analysis may be documented as risks are identified and added to the risk register. A majority of the risk analysis effort on a project occurs during the Perform Qualitative Risk Analysis and Perform Quantitative Risk Analysis processes. The effectiveness of risk responses is analyzed in the Monitor and Control Risks process.

Risk Response Planning

Potential risk responses may be documented as risks are identified. However, the majority of this work occurs in the Plan Risk Responses process on a project. This process addresses both threats and opportunities, as well as secondary risks, residual risks, and contingency and fallback plans. In this process, reserves are created.

Risk Governance

Risk governance is another topic that extends throughout the entire risk management process. Although it is subtly referenced in other chapters of this book, an entire chapter is devoted to this topic. Much of what occurs in risk management, including creating and enforcing risk standards, policies and procedures, and using historical lessons learned in improving risk efforts on projects, is influenced by the organization's approach to risk governance.

For many people, the most difficult risk management processes on the exam are Plan Risk Management and Monitor and Control Risks.

Be aware of the following for the exam:
- The PMI-RMP exam tests knowledge, application, and analysis. This makes the exam more than a test of memory. You must know how to apply the information in this book and be able to analyze situations involving this information. Do not expect the exam to have all straightforward, definition-type questions.
- It is important to realize that the PMI-RMP exam deals with real-world use of project risk management, and includes "What would you do in this situation?" questions (situational questions). These questions are extremely difficult if you have not used project risk management tools in the real world or if your project risk

management efforts include common errors. You have to have been there to pass the exam.

- Most acronyms will be spelled out (e.g., the exam will use the full term "work breakdown structure" rather than "WBS").

Some of the questions are situational, ambiguous, and wordy. Some questions may even seem like they have two right answers. Be prepared for the following types of questions so you will not waste time or be caught off guard when you are taking the exam.

1. **Situational questions:** These questions require you to have experience applying risk management in situations in the real world.

   Question: You receive notification that a major item you are purchasing for a project will be delayed. What is the BEST thing to do?

   A. Ignore it; it will go away.
   B. Notify your boss.
   C. Let the customer know about it, and talk over options.
   D. Meet with the team and identify alternatives.

   Answer: D

2. **Questions with two or more right answers:** Questions that appear to have two, three, or even four right answers are a major complaint from many test takers. Many questions will list choices that all could reasonably be done, or that less experienced or less qualified project managers are likely to choose. Experienced project managers have less trouble with this than people with limited experience and knowledge of project management.

   As you go through questions and review the answers in this book and in Rita Mulcahy's *PM FASTrack® Exam Simulation Software* for the PMI-RMP Exam, look for instances where you think there are more than one right answer and try to figure out why you think so. I have intentionally put questions like these into my products for PMI-RMP exam preparation.

   Let's look again at the previous question. Couldn't we really do all of the choices? The right answer is certainly D, but isn't it also correct to tell the customer? Yes, but that is not the first thing to do. Essentially this question is really saying, "What is the BEST thing to do next?"

3. **Questions with extraneous information:** It is very important to realize that not all information included in a question will be relevant. In the following question, the numbers are extraneous.

Question: Experience shows that each time you double the production of doors, unit costs decrease by 10 percent. Based on this, the company determines that production of 3,000 doors should cost $21,000. This case illustrates:

A. Learning cycle.
B. Law of diminishing returns.
C. 80/20 rule.
D. Parametric cost estimating.

Answer: D

Some questions on the PMI-RMP exam will be longer than this one. But not all the information presented will be required to answer the question. For example, imagine I changed the previous question to be wordier. It might read as follows:

Your company is a major manufacturer of doors, and has received numerous awards for quality. As the head of the manufacturing department, you have 230 people reporting to you on 23 different projects. Experience shows that each time you double the production of doors, unit costs decrease by 10 percent. Based on this, the company determines that production of 3,000 doors should cost $21,000. This case illustrates…

Can you see how the additional data does not add any value to the question? The data is a distracter. On the exam, you may see whole paragraphs of data that are not needed to answer the question. The trick is to look at each question to determine "What is this question asking about?" rather than getting lost in all the information provided. Do not get upset if you have difficulty with these long, wordy questions. Just mark them and come back to them later. If you know what to expect, you will not be upset or lose confidence when you see these questions.

4. **Questions using made-up terms:** Many people taking the exam expect that all the terms used as choices should mean something. They do not! There are often made-up terms used on the exam. Perhaps the question writer needed another choice, or perhaps the made-up terms are added to trick those who do not know the answer. If you consider yourself well trained and see a term you do not know on the exam, chances are it is not the right answer. For example:

Question: A form of project organization where power is evenly shared between the functional manager and the project manager is called:

A. A tight matrix.
B. A weak matrix.
C. A balanced matrix.
D. A strong matrix.

Answer: C

In this question, choice A, tight matrix, is not a real project management term.

5. **Questions where understanding is important:** First look at the following question.

Question: The process of decomposing deliverables into smaller, more manageable components is complete when:

A. Project justification has been established.
B. Change requests have occurred.
C. Cost and duration estimates can be developed for each work element at this detail.
D. Each work element is found in the WBS dictionary.

Answer: C

In order to answer this question, you must understand all the terms. Memorization is not enough!

6. **Questions with a new approach to a known topic:** There will be many instances where you understand the topic, but have never thought about it in the way the question describes. Some people say that most of the questions on the exam test them in this way. For example:

© 2010 RMC Publications, Inc. • (952) 846-4484 • info@rmcproject.com • www.rmcproject.com

Question: In a matrix organization, information dissemination is MOST likely to be effective when:

A. Information flows both horizontally and vertically.
B. The communication flows are kept simple.
C. There is an inherent logic in the type of matrix chosen.
D. Project managers and functional managers socialize.

Answer: A

7. **Questions with more than one item in each choice:** See the following example.

Question: The seller on the project has presented the project manager with a formal notification that the seller has been damaged by the buyer's activities. The seller claims that the buyer's slow response to sending the seller approvals has delayed the project, and has caused the seller unexpected expense. The FIRST things the project manager should do are:

A. Collect all relevant data, send the data to the company attorney, and consult with the attorney about legal actions.
B. Review the contract for specific agreed-upon terms that relate to the issue, see if there is a clear response, and consult an attorney if needed.
C. Review the statement of work for requirements, send a receipt of claim response, and meet to resolve the issue without resorting to legal action if possible.
D. Hold a meeting with the team to review why the acceptances have been late, make a list of the specific reasons, and resolve those reasons.

Answer: B

These questions can seem hard until you learn a secret: use the process of elimination on one item at a time. Consider the first item listed in each choice and eliminate the choices that contain an implausible first item. Then look at the second item in each choice and eliminate any implausible choices. Keep going until you have only one choice remaining.

Watch out, sometimes the items in each choice show a flow or process. See the example below:

Question: When managing a project, which of the following is the BEST order to deal with problems that arise?

A. Go to the team, go to management, go to resource managers
B. Go to resource managers, go to management, go to the customer
C. Handle it yourself, go to the customer, go to management
D. Resolve problems with resources you control, go to the resource manager, go to the customer

Answer: D

In this case, you would need to look at each choice independently to see if the process is correct.

8. **Excessively wordy questions:** Instead of saying "the project is behind schedule," the exam might use wordier phrasing, such as "the project float was zero and has recently gone to negative 2." Instead of saying "The team is not reporting properly," the exam could say "The team has lost sight of the communications management plan." The first step in answering many questions is to determine what the question is asking, and then to translate the wordy phrasing. If you are a non-English speaker, this becomes a huge problem, but it remains difficult for even native English speakers. Just take your time, and practice reading wordy questions before you take the exam.

How to Study for the PMI-RMP Exam

If you do not yet have the 30 to 40 risk-management-specific training hours required to apply for the PMI-RMP exam, your study plan should look like this:

1. Review any previous basic project management and risk management-related training you have taken.
2. Check the RMC website for e-Learning, live online, and classroom-based risk management training courses (multiple options available).
3. Use this book as your primary text for preparing for the exam, and specifically work on gaps in your existing risk management knowledge.
4. Briefly review PMI's *Practice Standard for Risk Management*.

5. Use Rita Mulcahy's *PM FASTrack® Exam Simulation Software for the PMI-RMP Exam* to familiarize yourself with the exam environment and test your existing risk management knowledge.
6. Take the exam.

If you have already met your training requirement for 30 or 40 hours of risk management related training:

1. Review any previous basic project management and risk management-related training you have taken in the past.
2. Check the RMC website for additional risk management-related study materials and products (multiple options available).
3. Use this book as your primary text for preparing for the exam, and specifically work on gaps in your existing Risk Management knowledge.
4. Consider purchasing RMC's online class titled Common Risk Management Errors That Can Ruin Your Career to uncover some things about risk management that you might have missed.
5. Briefly review PMI's *Practice Standard for Risk Management*.
6. Use Rita Mulcahy's *PM FASTrack® Exam Simulation Software for the PMI-RMP Exam* to familiarize yourself with the exam environment and test your existing risk management knowledge.
7. Take the exam.

Note that these products and courses are available on our Web site, www.rmcproject.com.

Before taking the exam, you should be familiar with all the risk management processes, what happens when, what tools and techniques are used in each, and the value of each process. The Identify Risks, Perform Qualitative Risk Analysis, Perform Quantitative Risk Analysis, and Plan Risk Responses processes are generally easy to understand by just reading about them in this book. They are also easier on the exam. The harder processes to understand for the exam are Plan Risk Management and Monitor and Control Risks. The exam focuses on these processes. The questions are extremely hard to answer if you have not "been there." If you have less experience with risk management than you would like, make sure you take the time to think through each of the risk management processes. Imagine doing each one, and imagine what problems you could run into in the real world while performing them. Then think about how you could overcome those problems.

Project Management Training

Many of those who fail the exam did not have adequate project management training. Don't make this mistake. If you need additional training, consider taking RMC's Project Management Tricks of the Trade® class.

Before You Take the Exam

Many people fail the exam because their preparation was faulty. You do not need to make that mistake. Read the following slowly and honestly assess how each item applies to you.

1. Be familiar with the types of questions you can expect on the exam including questions that are very wordy and questions that you can not even figure out what is being asked. Be prepared so that you do not get annoyed or worse yet, doubt your abilities during the exam.

2. Practice being able to pick an answer from what appears to be two or three "right" answers.

3. Decide in advance what notes you will write down when you are given a piece of scrap paper at the actual exam. You can use it as a download sheet for formulas or gaps in your risk management knowledge.

4. Deal with your stress BEFORE you take the exam. There is a free tip for nervous test takers on our Web site, www.rmcproject.com.

5. Plan and use your strategy for taking the exam. This may mean, "I will take a 10-minute break after every 50 questions because I get tired quickly," or "I will answer all the questions as quickly as possible and then take a break and review my answers."

6. Visit the exam site before your exam date to determine how long it will take to get there and to see what the testing room looks like. This is particularly helpful if you are a nervous test taker.

7. Do not expect the exam site to be quiet. People have had someone taking an exam that required intensive typing, and thus more noise, right next to them. Many testing sites will have earplugs or headsets available.

8. Do not overstudy. Getting completely comfortable with all the material in this book is just not possible. It is not worth studying for hundreds of hours.

9. Take the night off before the exam to do something relaxing and get a little extra sleep. DO NOT STUDY! You will need time to process all you have learned so you can remember it when you take the exam.

Tricks for Taking the PMI-RMP Exam

It's the big day! Get excited. You know you can pass! Here are some tips for taking the exam.

1. You must bring your authorization letter from PMI to the test site, as well as two forms of ID with exactly the same name you entered on the exam application.

2. Bring snacks! Bring lunch! You will not be able to bring snacks into the exam room, but having them stored close by will allow you to get access to them to stop hunger pains.

3. You will be given scratch paper and pencils (and possibly even earplugs or a headset) and have the chance to do a 15-minute computer tutorial, if your exam is given on computer, to become familiar with the computer and its commands. NOTE: The testing center will require you to exchange your used scratch paper if you need more during the exam.

4. During the 15-minute tutorial, you may wish to create your "download sheet" by writing down anything you were having trouble remembering. This will free up your mind to handle questions once the information you are concerned about is written down.

5. Some test sites provide physical calculators. At other locations, the calculators are online or on the computer and appear with every question that requires a calculation.

6. When you take the exam, you will see one question on the screen at a time. You can answer a question and/or mark it to return to it later. You will be able to move back and forth throughout the exam.

7. The exam does not adapt to your answers. This means that 170 questions are selected when your exam starts, and those 170 do not change.

8. Use deep breathing techniques to help relax. This is particularly helpful if you are very nervous before or during the exam and when you notice yourself reading the same question two or three times. Breathing techniques might include just deep breathing five times, to provide more oxygen to your brain.

9. Smile when taking the exam. Smiling relieves stress and makes you feel more confident.

10. Use all the exam time. Do not leave early unless you have reviewed each question twice.

11. Remember your own unique test taking quirks and how you plan to deal with them while taking the exam.

12. Control the exam; do not let it control you. How would you feel if you read the first question and had no idea of the answer? The second question? And the third question? This can happen because you are just not ready to answer questions and your level of stress is not allowing you to think. So what do you do? If you do not immediately know the answer to the question, use the Mark for Review function and come back to it later. This will mean that your first pass through the exam will generally be quick.

13. Control your frustration and maintain focus on each question. You might very well dislike or disagree with some of the questions on this exam. You might also be surprised at how many questions you mark for review. If you are still thinking about question 20 when you reach question 120, there will have been 100 questions that you have not looked at closely enough.

14. Answer each question from PMI's perspective, not the perspective you have acquired from your real-world or life experience. If approaching it from PMI's perspective does not give you an answer, rely on your training, and, lastly, your real-world experience.

15. Determine what your answer should be before you look at the choices provided.

16. One of the main reasons people answer incorrectly is because they do not read all four choices. Do not make the same mistake! Practice reading the questions and all four choices when you take the practice exams. It is best to practice reading the choices backwards (choice D first, then C, etc.). This will help you select the BEST answer.

17. Practice quickly eliminating answers that are highly implausible. Many questions have only two plausible options and two obviously incorrect options.

18. There may be more than one "correct" answer to each question, but only one "BEST" answer. Practice looking for the BEST answer.

19. Be alert to the fact that the answer to one question is sometimes given away in another question. Write down things that you do not understand as you take the exam. Use any extra time at the end of the exam to go back to these questions.

20. Attempts have been made to keep all choices the same length. Therefore, do not follow the old rule that the longest answer is the right one.

21. A concerted effort has been made to use "distracters"—choices that distract you from the correct answer. These are plausible choices that less knowledgeable people will pick. Distracters make it appear as though some questions have two or more right answers. To many people, it seems as though there are only shades of differences between the choices. Look for this type of question as you take practice exams.

22. Look for words like "first," "last," "next," "best," "never," "always," "except," "not," "most likely," "less likely," "primary," "initial," "most," etc. Make certain you clearly

© 2010 RMC Publications, Inc. • (952) 846-4484 • info@rmcproject.com • www.rmcproject.com

read the question, and take note of these words, or you will answer the question incorrectly! There are many questions that require you to really understand the process of project management and its real-world application.

23. Watch out for choices that are true statements but do not answer the question.

24. Watch out for choices that contain common risk management errors. They are intentionally there to determine if you really know risk management. Therefore, you may not know that you answered a question incorrectly! Look for errors in your knowledge and experience as you go through this book.

25. Options that represent broad, sweeping generalizations tend to be incorrect, so be alert for "always," "never," "must," "completely," and so forth. Alternatively, choices that represent carefully qualified statements tend to be correct, so be alert for words such as "often," "sometimes," "perhaps," "may," and "generally."

26. When a question asks you to fill in a blank space, the correct answer may not be grammatically correct when inserted in the sentence.

27. Look for the "rah, rah" answer (e.g., "Risk management is so important," "A project can not be successful without risk management").

28. You will have multiple chances to indicate that you have completed the exam. The exam will not be scored until you indicate that you are ready, or your time is up. You will receive a printed summary of your test results. If you pass, the computer will print out a certificate, and you will officially be certified. If you do not pass, PMI will send you information on retaking the exam. You will have to pay an additional fee to retake the exam.

29. A lot of the reason people get questions wrong on the exam is that they do not realize the following:

- "Rules" are meant to be broken. Rules such as what to do when can change depending on the situation. This drives people crazy who expect the exam to just test facts. You need to be able to read and understand the situations on the exam and then be able to figure out the best thing to do IN THAT SITUATION. Most of the questions are situational, and many people are just not prepared.

- Assume proper risk management was done. For example, assume that there is a risk management plan and company standards for risk management, even if the question does not say so.

- Notice where you are in the story. If the situation described in the question is taking place in planning, your answer may be different than if it occurred in execution.

30. Assume that you are managing a large project when you take the exam. A large project is one that:
    • Will take over 1 year
    • Has over 300 team members
    • Involves people from a few different countries
    • Has a value of over US $1,000,000

31. If you do not manage projects of this size, you should spend considerable time before you take the exam imagining that you are working on such a project. Consider how project management and risk management are different when you have a large project.

32. Do not study risk management in isolation. You must understand how risk management fits into the project management process. What are the inputs to risk management, and how do the outputs of risk management affect the project management plan.

33. Review general project management concepts, including leadership styles, the communications management process, and organizational structures.

34. Do not spend all your time understanding the calculations that can occur in the Perform Quantitative Risk Analysis process. The more important topic is understanding the Monitor and Control Risks process. This topic is heavily tested on the exam.

35. Remember that the exam is trying to keep those who are not experts on risk management from passing the exam. Keep this focus in mind when you take the exam. Make sure your lack of knowledge or experience does not trick you into selecting the wrong choice.

36. A trick for taking the risk certification exam is to:
    • Read each question once
    • Figure out what part of the risk management process is being asked about (e.g. risk identification)
    • Figure out what part of the project you are in (e.g. monitoring and control and moving back to planning)
    • Based on this, pick the best choice.
    • If you are unsure of your answer or cannot pick an answer, mark the question for review and look at it again at the end of the exam. You should mark about 25 questions or more on the exam.

This method will help you better understand the question and to get confused less often about what the question is asking about.

....

TRICKS OF THE TRADE®

Common Risk Management Errors and Pitfalls

The exam may describe situations where the wrong thing is being done to see if you realize it is wrong. So I have a trick for you. Listed below are some of the common risk management errors people make. This list will be extremely valuable in helping you to select the best choices on the exam.

- Risk identification is completed without knowing enough about the project.
- Project risk is evaluated using only a questionnaire, interview, or Monte Carlo analysis and thus does not provide specific risks.
- Risk identification ends too soon, resulting in a brief list (20 risks) rather than an extensive list (hundreds of risks).
- The processes of Identify Risks through Perform Quantitative Risk Analysis are blended, resulting in risks that are evaluated or judged as they come to light. This decreases the number of total risks identified and causes people to stop participating in risk identification.
- The risks identified are general rather than specific (e.g., "communications" rather than "poor communication of customer's needs regarding installation of system Z could cause two weeks of rework").
- Risks are not identified using the cause-risk-effect format.
- Some things considered to be risks are not uncertain; they are facts, and are therefore not risks.
- Whole categories of risks (such as technology, cultural, marketplace, etc.) are missed.
- Only one method is used to identify risks (e.g., only using a checklist) rather than a combination of methods. A combination helps ensure that more risks are identified.
- The first risk response strategy identified is selected without looking at other options and finding the best option or combination of options.
- Risk management is not given enough attention during project executing.
- Project managers do not explain the risk management process to their team during project planning.
- Contracts are usually signed long BEFORE risks to the project are discussed.

The following are things about risk management that people miss on exams.

- Everyone, that means all stakeholders and maybe even people who are not stakeholders, should be involved in identifying risks on projects.
- Risks are things that can get in the team's way or can help the team. Therefore, the risk management process should receive serious attention.
- Threats to the project can add time and cost to the project schedule and budget. This is why risk management is such an important activity. It saves project time and money and improves quality and customer satisfaction.
- The key focus of the Perform Qualitative Risk Analysis process is subjectively evaluating individual risks—to form a short list of risks that will move further. The key focus of the Perform Quantitative Risk Analysis process is to determine the amount of risk in the project by calculating a numerical figure of the time and cost impact of risks.
- There should be risk response plans in place for almost all problems that occur.
- Having to hold last minute meetings to deal with a disaster is an indication that your risk management efforts were inadequate and that you should redo them.
- Risks should be reviewed throughout the life of the project.
- One of the topics on the exam that even experienced project managers have a hard time with is what should a project manager be doing when the work is being done to manage risks. Remember that risk owners and risk action owners are assigned to each risk? So what is left? Review the Monitor and Control Risks chapter of this book again. If you can say to yourself, "Of course I would be performing these functions," then you are ready for these most difficult questions.
- Companies should have risk governance in place. Review all the standards for risk management that a risk governance body might create and then assume that you have those standards when taking the exam.
- Many companies try to hide the fact that they have risks, and may even discourage discussion of risks. Assume that risk management is an accepted and supported function in the organization unless the questions say differently.
- When you take the exam, assume that risks are communicated to all parties on the project and even risks that relate to politics or other issues you might think would be hushed up, are discussed openly.

- Think of reserves as a checking account; you need to account for every dollar you put in and every dollar you spend. Getting more is extremely difficult.
- Remember that management reserves are usually outside the authority of the project manager and therefore cannot be used without management approval.

....

After You Are Certified

Come back to RMC Project Management after you've earned your RMP. We can help you continue your training and earn PDUs to maintain your certification through our advanced instructor-led and e-Learning courses and products. See you there!

The PMP® and CAPM® Exams

Are you surprised to find a chapter on the PMP and CAPM exams in this book? Risk management is one of the most difficult topics for people on the PMP and CAPM exams. In addition to helping you apply risk management on your real-world projects, this book will increase your risk management knowledge to better prepare you for the risk management portion of those exams.

The following provides an overview of both the PMP and CAPM exams.

The Exams

Keep in mind two things. First, the exams (especially the PMP exam) are not tests of the information in the *PMBOK® Guide*! Second, you cannot just rely on real-world experience to get you a passing score on either exam. For both the PMP and CAPM exams, it is critical to have training in project management! This does not mean that you need weeks of training or a master's certificate in project management to take the exam. But the training does need to include and promote the terminology and best practices of project management.

Warning: The exams change frequently! Visit www.pmi.org for complete and up-to-date details about the exams. Any differences between what is listed here and what is listed on PMI's Web site should be resolved in favor of PMI's Web site.

The PMP® and CAPM® Exams

A Summary of the Exams

CAPM			
General Education	PM Education/Experience	Number of Questions	Time to Take the Exam
High school diploma/ global equivalent	1500 hours experience or 23 hours PM education	150	3 hours

PMP					
Category	General Education	PM Education	PM Experience	Experience	Number of Questions
One	Bachelors degree	35 contact hours within last eight years	4,500 hours	Three years within last eight years	200
Two	High school graduate	35 contact hours	7500	Five years within last eight years	

Applying to Take the Exams

You can submit applications for either exam by mail or online. PMI's turnaround time to review electronic applications is much faster than those submitted by mail. If PMI accepts your application, you will receive a notice authorizing you to make an appointment to take the exam. You may be subject to an audit of your application, however. Be aware that an audit will delay your approval to take the exam. You will likely take the exam on a computer, as PMI is quickly moving to offer computerized testing around the world in many languages.

Watch out! Once you receive your authorization notice, you must pass the exam within one year! In some instances, testing centers do not have openings for several weeks.

PMI often makes changes to the way the exam is administered. Therefore, read the authorization notice carefully for any differences from the information described here.

What Are the Exams Like?

The PMP exam includes 200 multiple-choice questions with four answer choices per question. The exam must be completed in four hours. The CAPM exam includes 150 questions with four answer choices per question and must be completed in three hours.

The CAPM exam is knowledge-based, whereas the PMP exam is knowledge, application, and analysis-based, and includes more situational questions. The questions for both exams are randomly generated from a database containing hundreds of questions. The questions may jump from topic to topic and cover multiple topics in a question. You get one point for each correct answer. There is no penalty for wrong answers.

For many people, the toughest knowledge areas on the exams are project management processes, procurement management, and risk management. The toughest process groups are monitoring and controlling and initiating. Make sure you study these carefully.

The exams often present questions from a large-project perspective. Large projects can easily get out of control if the project manager does not practice proper project management and instead spends time on such activities like solving problems rather than preventing them. You should have a large project in mind when you take either exam. Think of a project that is new to the organization (it has not been done before), utilizes resources from many countries, has more than 200 people on the team, lasts longer than one year, and has a value of over US $1,000,000.

Warning: The PMP exam may not be like any exam you have taken before. The exam is written psychometrically, and there are questions on the exam that even experts find difficult! Do not get frustrated!

Taking the Exam

You must bring your authorization letter from PMI to the test site as well as two forms of ID with exactly the same name you entered on the exam application.

Once you arrive at the test site, you will be given scratch paper and pencils (and possibly even earplugs or a headset) and have the chance to do a 15-minute computer tutorial (if your exam is given on computer) to become familiar with the computer and its commands. **Note:** The testing center will require you to exchange your scratch paper if you need more during the exam.

When you take the exam, you will see one question on the screen at a time. You can answer a question and/or mark it to return to it later. You will be able to move back and forth throughout the exam.

When you finish the exam, you will have multiple chances to indicate if you are done. The exam will not be scored until you are ready or your time is up. If you pass the exam, the computer will print out a certificate and a report, and you will officially be certified. If you do not pass the exam, PMI will be notified and will send you information on retaking the exam. You will have to pay an additional fee to retake the exam.

Why Take the Exam?

Let me quote one of my students: *"The exam has changed my life. (Could I be more dramatic?) The process of studying for the exam, taking your class, and passing the exam has changed how others look at my abilities."* By passing the exam, you can say that you have passed an international exam designed to prove your knowledge of project management. That is impressive. There are other benefits. Should I put this in writing? PMI's salary survey regarding the PMP certification has found that PMP-certified project managers are paid at least 10 percent more than those without the certification in the United States (and even more in some other countries). I have had many students who have received a US $15,000 bonus AND a 15 percent raise when they passed the PMP exam. Others have said they got a job over 200 others because of their certification. In this economic climate, having the PMP or CAPM certification can be the reason you get a job, keep your job, or are promoted. These are good incentives to finally get around to taking the exam.

Materials to Use

RMC's PMP and CAPM exam prep products are used in more than 43 countries around the world. The following resources are available for the PMP and CAPM exams.

PMBOK® Guide

You should review PMI's *PMBOK® Guide* in preparing for either the PMP or CAPM exam.

Project Management Training

Many of those who fail the exam do not have adequate project management training. Don't make this mistake. Try our:

- *PM Crash Course™ book*
- Project Management Tricks of the Trade® course
- CAPM Exam Prep course (online or classroom-based)
- PMP Exam Prep course (online or classroom-based)

Exam Prep Systems

RMC has created systems for both the CAPM and PMP exams. Our materials are designed to work together! The exam prep books cover the knowledge you need to pass the exam. The *PM FASTrack®* exam simulation software helps you test and apply your knowledge. And our *Hot Topics* flashcards helps you improve your recall of important terms and information on the exam.

The PMP Exam Prep System includes the following resources:

- *PMP® Exam Prep book*, **by Rita Mulcahy:** This is the best-selling project management exam preparation book in the world. In addition to study materials, games, exercises, Tricks of the Trade®, and information about common mistakes, this book offers more than 400 test questions (enough for two full exams). It also includes a chapter dedicated to making sure you pass the exam on your first attempt.

- *PM FASTrack® Exam Simulation Software for the PMP Exam*, **by Rita Mulcahy:** This software was created with the assistance of a psychometrician (just like the actual exam). The program's database of 1,500+ questions allows you to take exams by knowledge area, process group, keyword/concept, PMP, and SuperPMP simulation. All questions are cross-referenced with RMC's *PMP® Exam Prep* textbook, so you can quickly and easily go back to work on your weak areas. Why be surprised when you take the actual exam? Find your gaps before the exam finds them for you.

- *Hot Topics* **Flashcards (in hard copy or audio CD format), by Rita Mulcahy:** These flashcards can help you prepare for the exam in a way that fits into your busy schedule. Now you can study 300 of the most difficult to recall exam-related concepts at the office, on a plane, or in your car with these portable and extremely valuable flashcards—in hard copy or audio CD format.

The CAPM Exam Prep System includes the following resources:

- *CAPM® Exam Prep* **book, by Rita Mulcahy:** This book is the worldwide standard for people studying for the CAPM certification. In addition to 12 comprehensive chapters, this book includes games, exercises, Tricks of the Trade®, and common pitfalls and mistakes—as well as enough sample test questions for nearly a full cAPM exam.

- *PM FASTrack® Exam Simulation Software for the CAPM Exam,* **by Rita Mulcahy:** How would you like to know you are going to pass the exam before you take it? *PM FASTrack®* for the CAPM Exam is an exam simulation software program containing more than 600 questions and three testing modes. This software utilizes the same testing and evaluation engine as the best-selling PMP exam software. It features automatic question bank updates (for people with Internet connections), as well as comprehensive grading and reporting capability.

- *Hot Topics* **Flashcards (in hard copy or audio CD format), by Rita Mulcahy:** These flashcards are part of both the PMP and CAPM Exam Prep Systems. With the choice between the audio or hard copy format, over 300 of the most important and difficult to recall exam-related concepts are now available for study as you drive, fly, or take your lunch break.

© 2010 RMC Publications, Inc. • (952) 846-4484 • info@rmcproject.com • www.rmcproject.com

1. A contingency plan is different than a fallback plan in that a fallback plan:
    A. Is implemented after a contingency plan.
    B. Is created before a contingency plan.
    C. Will be managed by the project manager while the contingency plan is managed by the risk owner.
    D. Will require management approval, while the contingency plan does not.

2. Which of the following is generally NOT an output of the Plan Risk Responses process?
    A. A revised project management plan
    B. Data precision ranking
    C. Residual risks
    D. Secondary risks

3. Which of the following is NOT a correct statement?
    A. Risks can be identified during project closure.
    B. Risks should be part of project go/no-go decisions.
    C. Numerical evaluation of risks is the most important part of risk management.
    D. The project manager should attempt to have a complete scope of work before beginning risk management.

4. You have just been asked to take over a project that is in execution from another project manager. Which of the following is the FIRST thing to do regarding risk management?
   A. Identify risks.
   B. Determine if risk responses have been completed for all identified risks.
   C. Review historical information for the project.
   D. Look for new risks based on your own experience.

5. The Plan Risk Management Process results in:
   A. A risk register and risk management plan.
   B. Risk response plans.
   C. The assignment of risk owners.
   D. A risk management plan.

6. Which of the following BEST describes avoidance of a risk during the Plan Risk Responses process?
   A. Do nothing and say, "If it happens, it happens."
   B. Eliminate the threat by eliminating the cause.
   C. Assign the risk to someone else.
   D. Reduce the probability of occurrence.

7. During execution of the project, a risk has been identified that you and the team missed during the Identify Risks process. Which of the following is the BEST thing to do?
   A. Look for more risks.
   B. Implement a workaround.
   C. Report the situation to management.
   D. Identify risk responses for the new risk.

8. Which of the following are risk response strategies for opportunities?
   A. Exploit, share, mitigate
   B. Enhance, transfer, avoid
   C. Accept, enhance, share
   D. Accept, mitigate, exploit

9. A subjective evaluation of the probability of a risk is determined during what part of risk management?
   A. Identify Risks
   B. Perform Qualitative Risk Analysis
   C. Perform Quantitative Risk Analysis
   D. Plan Risk Responses

10. Your project has 31 stakeholders, a completed project charter signed by three managers, a CPI of 1.2, a risk threshold of 55, 13 contingency plans, and a risk score of 72. The project is in the middle of project executing, and the last two project team meetings were completed on time with contribution from all the team members.

    Management has expressed approval of the project management plan, has provided input to project risk identification, and has gotten involved during the Plan Risk Responses process. The project manager, however, gets a call from the management team expressing deep concern about the project. Why might this be?
    A. There are too many stakeholders, and the charter should be signed by only one person.
    B. The cost for the project is too high as reflected in the CPI.
    C. The project is too risky and needs to be adjusted.
    D. There are not enough contingency plans to allow fallback planning.

11. A risk review includes all of the following EXCEPT:
    A. Changing the order of top risks.
    B. Adjusting to the severity of actual risks.
    C. Documenting the effectiveness of contingency and fallback plans.
    D. Monitoring residual risks.

12. A risk trigger is defined as:
    A. An early warning sign that an identified risk is about to occur.
    B. A risk that has not occurred.
    C. Documentation created by a risk owner to report risks.
    D. A plan for what to do when a risk occurs.

13. There is a 20 percent chance that the software being developed for the project will have more bugs than planned, causing a 20-day delay to the project and an additional cost of $20,000. There is a 10 percent chance that the additional programmers needed for the project will have more expertise than predicted, saving 20 days on the project. There is a 50 percent chance that the installation will require some building reconstruction that has not been able to be predicted, resulting in a 60-day delay in the project and a cost of $9,000. As a result of this information, generally what amount of reserve would be required for the project?
    A. 32 days
    B. $29,000
    C. 34 days
    D. 36 days

14. What should you do about a residual risk on a project?
    A. Plan an additional response for the risk, as it is the result of either a contingency or fallback plan.
    B. Nothing. This is a risk you've decided to simply accept.
    C. Put the risk on the watchlist.
    D. Implement any assigned contingency or fallback plans for the risk if the risk occurs.

15. An identified risk has occurred, and a contingency plan has been implemented. Which of the following is the BEST thing for the project manager to do while the risk owner implements the contingency plan?
    A. Qualify the risk
    B. Adjust the severity of the risk response plan
    C. Create a fallback plan
    D. Help the risk owner

16. What happens when a risk is closed?
    A. The team can relax a bit.
    B. More attention is given to the watchlist.
    C. Some risk reserve may be returned to the company.
    D. Risks are never closed until the project is closed.

17. A project manager in your company runs a Monte Carlo simulation as the only risk management effort for the project. You have been asked to mentor that project manager to improve his risk management skills. Which of the following BEST describes what you should tell him?
    A. Make sure the Monte Carlo simulation includes the forecast of potential project schedule.
    B. You will need to have identified specific risks in order to control the project and decrease the project time and cost.
    C. You should make sure that you also determine the probability of any activity actually on the critical path.
    D. You should make sure you qualify the risks after the Monte Carlo simulation is completed.

18. Reporting formats and tracking processes are determined as part of:
    A. Monitoring and controlling risks.
    B. Determining roles and responsibilities.
    C. Planning risk management for the project.
    D. Planning risk responses.

19. An identified risk occurs, but the project manager cannot be reached. Which of the following should be done?
    A. Try to create a workaround.
    B. Implement the contingency plan that was used for a similar project, and be prepared to report the results to the project manager upon her return.
    C. Ask management for direction.
    D. Implement the contingency plan.

20. You are planning to identify risks with a group of people who are technically stakeholders for the project, but who will be only slightly impacted. These people are not experts in the work to be undertaken, but they have a lot of experience working for the company in their various departments and in their own fields of expertise. Which of the following would be the BEST method for identifying risks with this group?
    A. Nominal group technique
    B. Expert interviews
    C. Forms
    D. Sticky notes

21. Risk governance is concerned with:
    A. The roles and responsibilities of each risk owner.
    B. Creating the risk response plans for each risk.
    C. The impacts of a risk response plan on the other constraints of the project.
    D. Ensuring consistency in risk management practices throughout the organization.

22. A project manager is in the planning stages of her project when management agrees
    to allocate 75 hours of time to the project as requested by the project manager
    to support the project. The project manager has also learned that one of her top
    choices for team members has been provided and she has been given all eight of the
    needed resources. Management has approved $200,000 for the project instead of the
    $324,000 requested, and the project must be completed within eight months. Which
    of the following should the project manager do as a result of this situation?
    A. Include not having enough budget as an identified risk.
    B. Cut scope of work.
    C. Include a plan for the cost risk in risk response planning.
    D. Look for other cost risks.

23. The project manager has completed the Perform Qualitative Risk Analysis process
    when a stakeholder asks which activities are creating the biggest risk. When the
    project manager determines the answer to the question, he also determines that
    he should do something. Which of the following would be the BEST thing to
    recommend if you were asked for advice?
    A. Ask the stakeholders for additional risks because it is apparent that they were not
       involved in risk identification.
    B. Determine which risk is the greatest risk.
    C. Document non-top risks.
    D. See if it is possible to eliminate the activity.

24. The purpose of risk metrics on a project is to:
    A. Give the project manager an additional means of measuring success on the
       project.
    B. Measure the responses of individual risk owners and determine who is most
       effective.
    C. Measure how risk tolerances and thresholds change throughout the organization
       during the project.
    D. Create reports in the format required by management.

25. If you are a team member for a project, which of the following are you most likely to be involved with?
    A. Identify Risks process, Monte Carlo simulation, statistical probability analysis
    B. Plan Risk Responses process, Identify Risks process, risk owner
    C. Identify Risks process, risk owner, go/no-go decision
    D. Plan Risk Management process, Plan Risk Responses process, Perform Quantitative Risk Analysis process

26. One of the stakeholders for a project is strongly arguing that a certain risk exists on a project. The other stakeholders disagree. The stakeholder is so sure that the item identified is a risk for the project that he comes to see you in person to discuss. Which of the following should you do?
    A. Add the risk to the list of risks.
    B. Talk to the stakeholder to calm him, but do not add the risk.
    C. Ask management to mediate.
    D. Try to gain substantiation for why the risk should be added.

27. Which of the following is NOT an input to risk management?
    A. Kickoff meeting
    B. Network diagram
    C. Schedule
    D. Project team

28. In order to identify the most risks from the attendees during brainstorming, it is important to:
    A. Keep a list of all risks identified.
    B. Make sure you are prepared with forms for the participants to fill out.
    C. Make sure that those who talk a lot are provided the time to respond.
    D. Refrain from evaluating responses while risks are being identified.

29. A risk rating is different than a risk score in that a risk rating is:
    A. Used to calculate the probability of a risk.
    B. Used to calculate the risk score.
    C. Divided by the risk score.
    D. Multiplied by the risk score.

30. Which of the following BEST describes why a network diagram is an input to risk management?
    A. It shows dependencies.
    B. It is created by the team and therefore has team input.
    C. It shows where paths converge.
    D. It shows what needs to be done to complete the project.

31. The project manager has implemented the plan for identifying risks but does not feel confident that all the possible risks have been identified. Which of the following would be the BEST risk identification technique to add?
    A. Nominal group technique
    B. Brainstorming with the stakeholders
    C. Expert interviews
    D. Affinity diagram

32. What is done during the Plan Risk Responses process?
    A. Figure out what to do about all the risks.
    B. Figure out what to do about each top risk.
    C. Figure out which risks are really facts.
    D. Perform a Monte Carlo simulation.

33. Which of the following BEST describes the focus of the Delphi technique?
    A. Reorganization of the identified risks into categories
    B. Gaining a group's opinion
    C. Looking at records from past projects to identify risks
    D. Gaining expert opinion

34. When completing your project, 20 risks have occurred and 18 contingency plans have been implemented. Two stakeholders have identified four new risks, and qualitative risk analysis and risk response planning have been completed for these risks. One employee was hired by the company and subsequently identified as a stakeholder for the project and has participated in an expert interview to identify his risks.

    If this is all the project manager has done to control risk, which of the following did the project manager forget?
    A. She should have qualified risks during the expert interview.
    B. Quantitative risk analysis should have been done for the four new risks identified.
    C. A risk review meeting should have been held.
    D. Two more contingency plans should have been implemented.

35. A risk action owner:
    A. Will implement response plans if a risk occurs.
    B. Will ensure risk responses are effective.
    C. Is responsible for investigating the best actions to take in responding to the risks he or she owns.
    D. Evaluates the level of risk activity on a project and determines if the actions taken affect other planned responses.

36. Early in the Perform Qualitative Risk Analysis process, a risk receives a low data quality assessment rating. What should the project manager do?
    A. Do not include the risk in the Perform Qualitative Risk Analysis process.
    B. Improve the understanding of the risk.
    C. Hold a brainstorming session.
    D. Test the assumptions.

37. An identified risk occurs. What should the project manager do FIRST?
    A. Understand the legal implications of his actions.
    B. Nothing. The trigger has also occurred, and the risk owner should be taking action.
    C. See if the severity of the planned response to the risk should be adjusted.
    D. Implement fallback plans.

38. You are planning a new project that is understood to have very little risk. The project will have a duration of five months, is being completed for your own company, and is low priority for the company. Based on this data, which of the following is the BEST thing to do?

A. Omit the Perform Quantitative Risk Analysis process.
B. Spend only one day on risk management.
C. Start the Plan Risk Responses process with only the most vocal stakeholders.
D. Spend the same amount of time as previous projects on the Perform Qualitative Risk Analysis process, as there could be risks that have not been identified.

39. In the Identify Risks process, all the risks had a high data quality assessment rating and assumptions were tested. The probability and impact of each risk has now been identified qualitatively. What did the project manager miss?

A. Probability and impact scales should have been determined.
B. Stakeholders should have been involved in the risk response planning.
C. A risk status report should have been created.
D. A Monte Carlo simulation should have been done.

40. A project is determined to have the highest risk rating of any project within the company. The project has 35 risks and 14 stakeholders and was determined to be one of the most important projects for the company. The Identify Risks process went smoothly, and in the Plan Risk Responses process, contingency plans were created for most of the risks. What should the project manager do?

A. Create contingency plans for the remaining risks.
B. Eliminate some of the root causes of risks.
C. Make sure risk identification is, in fact, complete.
D. Consider the project to be less important to the company because of its risk rating.

41. Risks can be identified during which part of the project management process?

A. Project planning
B. Project initiating
C. Project executing
D. All parts of the project management process

42. A very high-priority project is a main reason to make sure which of the following is done?
    A. Risks are quantified.
    B. Risks are identified.
    C. Risk responses are planned for top risks.
    D. Risks are identified by key stakeholders.

43. During an expert interview, two of the risk team members explain why they are there, compliment the interviewee, ask an open-ended question, and then proceed to ask their previously prepared questions. Which of the following have they done wrong?
    A. They should have complimented first, and then explained why they are there.
    B. They should not have used previously prepared questions, as they diminish the flow of ideas.
    C. It would have been better to ask one previously prepared question and then go on to ask the open-ended question.
    D. They should have asked more questions to clarify the response(s) to the open-ended question before asking their prepared questions.

44. Updates to the risk register after the Plan Risk Responses process include:
    A. Contingency and fallback plans for each risk, triggers, finalized risk owners
    B. Triggers, outcomes of risk audits, secondary risks
    C. Finalized risk owners, secondary risks, amount of contingency time and cost reserves needed
    D. Contracts, secondary risks, risk probability and impact ratings

45. Though there are many ways risk owners can be used in risk management, they are BEST used during which parts of the risk management process?
    A. Identify Risks and Plan Risk Responses
    B. Perform Qualitative Risk Analysis and Identify Risks
    C. Monitor and Control Risks and Perform Quantitative Risk Analysis
    D. Plan Risk Responses and Monitor and Control Risks

46. You have a 20 percent chance that there will be a £20,000 price increase in a piece of equipment before you can place an order. This would cause a two-week delay in the project, to gain approval for the increase in cost. You also have a 5 percent chance that you will need to pay £200,000 for an insurance policy on the delivery of materials because the seller may not be able to provide insurance for the shipment. If they cannot cover the insurance for the shipment, the seller has told you that they will give you a £10,000 price decrease. What is the expected monetary value of these risks?
    A. £13,500
    B. £220,000
    C. £14,000
    D. £210,000

47. When can risks be closed?
    A. When the risk team lowers the impact value
    B. When the time in which the identified risk can logically occur passes
    C. When the team needs to focus on new risks
    D. They can never be closed

48. A stakeholder tells the project manager that there is a risk that some funding might be removed from the project. Which of the following is the BEST thing for the project manager to do?
    A. Try to obtain additional funding.
    B. Obtain additional information so that the risk can be defined.
    C. Have the stakeholder provide proof that the risk exists.
    D. Hold a brainstorming session with the team to deal with the risk.

49. You have been identifying risks when a stakeholder informs you of a major risk that you had not previously identified. The stakeholder knows little about the risk other than that it exists. He cannot help you understand the risk or qualify it. Which of the following would be the BEST thing to do?
    A. Hold a brainstorming session with the team.
    B. Ask management if they know anything about the risk.
    C. Ask the next expert you interview.
    D. Include the risk and your need to understand more about it in a special message to all the stakeholders.

50. Stakeholder tolerances and thresholds should be identified during:
    A. Perform Quantitative Risk Analysis
    B. Plan Risk Management
    C. Identify Risks
    D. Plan Risk Responses

51. While the project manager was planning the project, he completed the Plan Risk Responses process and determined the reserve. However, when a senior manager looked at the reserve, she deleted it from the project management plan and called it a pad. What should the project manager do?
    A. Delete the reserve, and try to make up the time or cost while managing the project.
    B. Find a way to hide the reserve in the estimate for some activities, and make sure the team does not know that this has been done.
    C. Explain that the reserve is needed in the same way that activities are needed, and support this statement with detailed analysis and justification.
    D. Get the team together to determine a strategy for managing the project without the reserve.

52. A project manager has had a lot of experience with system design, but little experience managing system design projects. She is working on a new project that is a medium-priority project for the department and has to complete the project in a relatively short period of time, making sure the accounting and finance departments' daily work is interrupted as little as possible. The Monte Carlo simulation has shown only a 60 percent chance of completing the project within the time allowed. Because the project manager is new to project management, you have been asked to advise her. Which of the following is the BEST choice to recommend?
    A. Make sure the requirements are finalized before you begin design.
    B. See if you can get the project to be a higher priority.
    C. Fast track the project.
    D. Ask the accounting department when would be the most convenient time to interrupt their work.

53. Data quality assessment and determining probability are parts of which part of risk management?
    A. Identify Risks
    B. Perform Qualitative Risk Analysis
    C. Perform Quantitative Risk Analysis
    D. Plan Risk Responses

54. Which of the following is NOT true about a Monte Carlo simulation result of a 70 percent probability of completing the project on time?
    A. The number is not a problem for medium-priority projects.
    B. The project could be crashed.
    C. The probability of completing the project within the cost constraints should also be known.
    D. The project could be fast tracked and Monte Carlo simulation redone.

55. During the end of planning, the project manager has a meeting with management to go over the list of major risks identified. Management notices one of the risks and says that it would not be politically correct to include that risk in a list that will be seen by the department who may cause the risk. They ask the project manager to remove it from the list. What is the BEST thing for the project manager do?
    A. Remove it from the list, and make sure such a problem does not happen again.
    B. Determine why the risk was identified in the first place.
    C. Tell the manager that they cannot remove the risk since it is a project risk.
    D. Ask the manager for ideas about what can be done to eliminate the risk before the project gets started.

56. A project team is performing risk management and is discussing answers to the question, "How will we know in advance that the risk is about to occur?" The project team must be involved in which of the following?
    A. Determining risk triggers
    B. Looking at secondary risks
    C. Creating workarounds
    D. Determining the quantification of a risk

57. Which of the following is an example of a risk?
    A. Team members are located across the country in ten different cities.
    B. The customer is known for requesting additional scope in the middle of every project.
    C. The results of our planning efforts indicate that we will not meet the deadline imposed by management.
    D. We do not have adequate resources to complete this project.

58. The project has finally begun the executing phase when a risk occurs. The risk owner is well aware of the risk threshold for the project, and the contingency plan is understood. This particular risk posed a problem during planning because the risk team could not identify a fallback plan. However, the data quality assessment went well for the risk, the project charter is clear, and the project management plan was approved. In this case, what is the BEST thing for the project manager to do?
    A. Nothing.
    B. Let management know the impacts of the risk on the project if the contingency plan fails.
    C. Join the risk owner in completing the contingency plan.
    D. Crash or fast track the project.

59. Deciding how to approach risk management is a key focus of which part of the risk management process?
    A. Plan Risk Management
    B. Perform Qualitative Risk Analysis
    C. Plan Risk Responses
    D. Perform Quantitative Risk Analysis

60. When completing your project, 20 risks have occurred and 18 contingency plans have been implemented. Two stakeholders have identified four new risks, and qualitative risk analysis and risk response planning have been completed for these risks. One employee was hired by the company and subsequently identified as a stakeholder for the project. She has participated in an expert interview to identify her risks.

Which of the following would be the BEST thing to do next?
A. Identify probabilities for all the risks.
B. Hold a risk review.
C. Complete lessons learned.
D. Identify risk triggers.

61. A risk owner is BEST defined as:
A. Someone from management.
B. The person who determines the qualification for the risk.
C. A project stakeholder.
D. The person who is responsible for responding to the risk.

62. The risk rating for the project is determined during which process?
A. Plan Risk Management
B. Identify Risks
C. Perform Qualitative Risk Analysis
D. Plan Risk Responses

63. Management is BEST involved in which of the following parts of risk management?
A. Approving the risk management plan
B. Helping to determine risks
C. Planning responses to risks
D. Approving the list of risks and the qualification plan

64. Which of the following is NOT correct?
A. Opportunities are used to balance risks when calculating expected monetary value.
B. Risk owners could help determine risk resources.
C. Risk audits are performed to identify additional risks.
D. Contingency plans are planned responses.

65. Which of the following things done (or not done) by a project manager would increase risk to the project?
    A. Not performing conflict resolution
    B. Using a work authorization system
    C. Not being involved in the procurement process
    D. Being involved in contract negotiations

66. During project planning, the risk team identified several risks. Some of these risks would only be a problem during the detail design phase. Once that phase was complete, the risk would no longer be relevant. At this point in the project, the team has completed the detail design phase and those risks did not occur. What is the outcome of this?
    A. The risk team should reevaluate the risks.
    B. Some risk reserve may be returned to the company, and the risks can be closed.
    C. The risks can be closed, and the reserve can be used for a team celebration.
    D. Some risk reserve may be returned to the company, but the risks remain open.

67. If during planning the team finds ways to eliminate potential problems so they cannot occur, what are they doing?
    A. Changing the scope
    B. Padding the estimates
    C. Risk response planning
    D. Gold plating

68. What can you do about risks that cannot be eliminated?
    A. Create workarounds and fallback plans.
    B. Create contingency plans and fallback plans.
    C. Create a contingency plan.
    D. Perform a Monte Carlo simulation.

69. In the execution of the third phase of the new product design project, the vendor that the team had wanted to work with because of their experience in the field is not available. What should they do?
    A. They should let the project manager and the sponsor know that the project will be delayed until the vendor is available.
    B. They should call a meeting with the project manager and the functional mangers to decide how to handle the situation.
    C. They should start checking around to see if there are any other vendors who do the same work.
    D. They should contact their second- and third-choice vendors, as described in the plan.

70. While in the execution phase of the project, a new risk is identified that will seriously jeopardize the success of the project. What should be done?
    A. Determine a response strategy.
    B. Advise the sponsor and the customer immediately.
    C. Evaluate the risk for probability and impact and determine a response strategy.
    D. Contact the stakeholders to get their advice on how to respond to this risk.

71. Which of the following is an example of the avoidance risk response strategy?
    A. The team member does not know how to do the work, so training is scheduled.
    B. The team member keeps adding extra features to the product.
    C. The team member causes a lot of problems so is removed from the project.
    D. The team member is so over-allocated that he cannot do the work assigned.

72. What does the response strategy of transferring the risk accomplish?
    A. It makes another party responsible for the risk.
    B. Nothing, since it is still your project.
    C. It avoids any possibility of residual risk.
    D. It makes it impossible to calculate the cost impact of the risk.

73. During the execution phase, there are an inordinate number of change requests received. What should the project manager do about that?
    A. The project manager can do nothing except process the change through integrated change control.
    B. Prevent all changes by having solid requirements before starting execution.
    C. Put a limit on the number of changes any one person or group is allowed to submit.
    D. Find out where the changes are coming from and what could be done to eliminate the root cause.

74. Which of the following are risk response strategies for threats?
    A. Exploit, share, mitigate
    B. Accept, transfer, avoid
    C. Accept, mitigate, share
    D. Accept, mitigate, exploit

75. If an organization doesn't have consistency within its risk management practices and tends to have widely varying results as to the effectiveness of risk management, they need:
    A. Lessons learned
    B. A project management office
    C. Risk governance
    D. To practice proper risk management

1. **Answer:** A

   Explanation: You need a contingency plan to be created and take place before a fallback plan, so choice B cannot be the best choice. Since all plans are managed by the project manager (although they may be implemented by others), choice C cannot be the best choice. All plans may require management approval, so choice D is not the best choice. Thus, choice A is the best choice.

2. **Answer:** B

   Explanation: Choice B is done during the Perform Qualitative Risk Analysis process.

3. **Answer:** C

   Explanation: Risks can be identified during all parts of the project (choice A), including closure. Imagine that a seller is hired during project closure to store project documents. New risks that were not thought of previously could come to light when that company comes to collect the documents. Many people forget that risks are as important as cost and time in making a go/no-go decision (choice B). Though it is not always possible to achieve, the project manager should attempt to have a final scope of work (choice D). Quantitative risk analysis (choice C) may or may not be important on the project.

4. **Answer:** C

   Explanation: There are many correct answers to this question, but what is the first thing that should happen? Choice D is certainly something you could do. However, you wouldn't do it first. Historical records will tell you what risks have been previously identified and if any risks you identify are truly new. You need to look at what was done already when taking over any project. That is the role of historical records in this instance. Choices A and B should also be done, but what has already been done, as identified in the historical records, will determine how risk management should continue under your leadership. Choice C is therefore the best choice.

5. **Answer:** D

    Explanation: The Plan Risk Management process results in a risk management plan (choice D). The risk register, risk response plans, and assignment of the risk owners come later in the risk management process.

6. **Answer:** B

    Explanation: Avoidance does not mean ignore (choice A); rather, it means eliminate (choice B). Choice C relates to transferring the risk. Choice D relates to mitigation.

7. **Answer:** A

    Explanation: Sometimes shorter questions are not easier! Although choice D will need to be done eventually, the Perform Qualitative and Quantitative Risk Analysis processes should come before the Plan Risk Responses process. Although an attempt is made to identify all risks during planning, risks will always be identified while the work is being done, if for no other reason than new information about the project will be available. Thus, there is no reason to always report only one instance of a new risk to management (choice C). You should carefully reread the question if you picked choice B as the best choice. The question says that you identified a risk, not that a risk has occurred. Therefore, a workaround is not needed. Many project managers have difficulty realizing that a problem may be an indication that something worse has happened or will happen. Many project managers do not take problems as potential indications of more problems. One missed risk MAY mean that you missed others or that there was a flaw in your risk management plan or its implementation. This makes choice A the best answer.

8. **Answer:** C

    Explanation: The correct answer is choice C. Mitigate, transfer, and avoid are all response strategies for threats.

9. **Answer:** B

    Explanation: Subjective evaluations are done during the Perform Qualitative Risk Analysis process, and numerical evaluations are done during the Perform Quantitative Risk Analysis process. Thus, choice B is the best choice provided.

10. **Answer:** C

Explanation: More than one person might sign a charter and there could be hundreds of stakeholders on projects, so choice A could not be the best choice. The CPI is greater than 1, and therefore good, so choice B could not be the best choice. There is no information provided to say that there are not enough contingency plans (choice D). A risk score of 72 is higher than the allowable threshold, which indicates that the project risk has increased. When the risk score for the project is higher than the risk threshold, the project is too risky and needs to be adjusted. Therefore, choice C must be the best choice.

11. **Answer:** C

Explanation: Documenting the effectiveness of contingency and fallback plans is a part of a risk audit. Remember that a risk review looks forward in time, while a risk audit looks backward at what has already occurred.

12. **Answer:** A

Explanation: A risk that has not occurred (choice B) is called a risk, not a trigger. Risk triggers may be identified by a risk owner, but not created by them (choice C). A plan for what to do when a risk occurs (choice D) is called a contingency plan. The only correct choice in this case is option A.

13. **Answer:** A

Explanation: Since there is not a cost impact listed for all the risks, choice B could not be the best choice. This question would be calculated as (0.2 x 20 days) – (0.1 x 20 days) + (0.5 x 60 days) = 4 – 2 + 30 = 32 days. The second item listed is an opportunity and should be subtracted from the risks, making choice A the best choice.

14. **Answer:** D

Explanation: Residual risks are the risks that remain after the Plan Risk Responses process. Although residual risks include those you've accepted (choice B), they also include any other risks that remain on the project. Therefore, choices B and C aren't the best options. Choice A describes secondary risks, not residual risks. Choice D is the best answer.

15. **Answer:** B

    Explanation: Qualitative risk analysis (choice A) and planning contingency plans (choice C) should already be done. A project manager should only need to help the risk owner if the risk owner has asked for assistance (choice D). Otherwise, the risk owner should be prepared in advance to implement the contingency plan without assistance from the project manager. The project manager will be needed (on critical path activities) to make sure the plan is adequate (choice B), and if it is not adequate, to adjust it accordingly.

16. **Answer:** C

    Explanation: Option C is correct. Choice A may happen, but it's not the best answer. Choice B is partially true but the focus should be more on all open risks, not just the watchlist. Choice D is just wrong. When the time has passed in which a risk may occur, it is closed.

17. **Answer:** B

    Explanation: Many project managers make the mistake of thinking a Monte Carlo simulation represents the entire risk management effort. Choice D could not be the best choice as the Perform Qualitative Risk Analysis process occurs before the Monte Carlo simulation is done during the Perform Quantitative Risk Analysis process. Choices A and C could be outputs of Monte Carlo simulation, but they are not the most important things you would tell the project manager in this particular scenario.

18. **Answer:** C

    Explanation: In the Monitor and Control Risks process (choice A), you use the reports and tracking processes determined during the Plan Risk Management process (choice C). Therefore, choice C is the correct answer. Roles and responsibilities (choice B) are also determined during the Plan Risk Management process. The Plan Risk Responses process (choice D) happens later in the project.

19. **Answer:** D

    Explanation: This should not be a problem. The result of risk management efforts should be a plan for each risk identified. In this question, the problem is caused by a risk event. This means that the risk was previously identified. If identified, there should already have been a response plan in place. Therefore, the best choice is D.

20. **Answer:** A

    Explanation: Because these people are experienced, there is a high probability that a risk could be identified that the project manager or risk team have not uncovered. Choices C and D would not allow any interaction, and thus would not be the best choices. Choice B would take too much time for little return. Therefore, the BEST choice is A.

21. **Answer:** D

    Explanation: The best choice is D, because risk governance takes an organizational view of risk management to ensure it is practiced consistently. The details of each risk management activity of a single project are not the primary focus of governance.

22. **Answer:** B

    Explanation: The cost situation is not a risk; it is a fact. Therefore, it is handled as part of project planning rather than in risk management.

23. **Answer:** D

    Explanation: The process of risk management is to decrease threats on the project. This should not only include an analysis of the largest threat but also the activities with the largest threat. Choices B and C do not address the problem of the riskiest activity. Since no evidence is provided in the question indicating the stakeholders were not involved, choice A could not be the best choice. The best response to the riskiest activity is to try to eliminate it. If that does not work, attempts should be made to decrease the activity's probability or impact rating. Therefore, choice D is the BEST choice.

24. **Answer:** A

    Explanation: Risk governance involves creating metrics for an organization that project managers can then use on their projects as an additional means of measuring whether their efforts and the project are successful. Therefore, choice A is the correct answer. Metrics may be used to help assess the effectiveness of risk owners and risk responses, but that is only one area in which they may be used. Therefore, choice B is not the best answer. Risk tolerances and thresholds (choice C) should have been determined in the Plan Risk Management process and shouldn't regularly change throughout a project. Metrics are a measurement tool, not a reporting tool, so choice D is incorrect.

25. **Answer:** B

    Explanation: It is unusual for a project team member to be involved with risk management planning. A go/no-go decision is made by management with information from the project manager. Monte Carlo simulation is a computer simulation completed by the project manager. Therefore, neither A, C, nor D can be the best choice.

26. **Answer:** D

    Explanation: This question requires the project manager to attempt to determine the root cause of the concern. This will require some proof or substantiation of the risk (choice D). If substantiation is not available, the project manager may still choose to add the risk. Therefore, D is a better choice than A. A is the second choice.

27. **Answer:** A

    Explanation: A kickoff meeting occurs at the end of planning and therefore after the Plan Risk Management, Identify Risks, Perform Qualitative Risk Analysis, Perform Quantitative Risk Analysis, and Plan Risk Responses processes have been done.

28. **Answer:** D

Explanation: It is always important to keep a list of risks identified (choice A), but that will not increase the number of risks identified by the attendees. Forms (choice B) are not generally a part of brainstorming. If choice C had said, "Make sure those who do not talk…" it might be one of the best choices. Not evaluating responses is one of the key things to remember about brainstorming, making choice D the best choice.

29. **Answer:** B

Explanation: A risk rating is used to calculate the risk score by multiplying the probability rating and the impact rating of each risk to obtain a risk score, making choice B the best choice.

30. **Answer:** C

Explanation: Choices A and B are true, but not answers to the question—they do not explain why they are inputs to risk management. A work breakdown structure shows what needs to be done, while a network diagram shows when it needs to be done, so choice D could not be the best choice. Any place where multiple paths in a network diagram converge into an activity makes that activity riskier, making choice C the best choice.

31. **Answer:** D

Explanation: Nominal group technique (choice A) and expert interviews (choice C) are slow, and do not have a reasonable chance of uncovering something new when risk identification has been planned and then implemented. Brainstorming with the stakeholders (choice B) may seem like a great idea, but if you selected this one, you missed something, as the stakeholders have most likely already been involved. Affinity diagramming (choice D) sorts risks in a way that helps new risks become more visible, and therefore would be the best choice.

32. **Answer:** B

Explanation: Choice B is the best answer. Choice A is wrong, as we do not plan responses for risks on the watchlist. Choices C and D would have been done before this step.

33. **Answer:** D

    Explanation: Choice A relates to affinity diagramming. Choice B relates to Nominal group technique. Choice C relates to historical records.

34. **Answer:** C

    Explanation: Choice A is not necessarily the best choice, because qualitative risk analysis could have been done as part of an expert interview either while identifying risks or as a separate session. Quantitative risk analysis (choice B) is not required for every project and may be skipped. Since each contingency plan could address more than one risk, it would be allowable to have 18 plans for 20 risks (choice D). Risk reviews (choice C) are critical to the project, which makes this the best choice.

35. **Answer:** A

    Explanation: On projects in which the risks can have severe consequences, there may be both risk owners and risk action owners. The risk action owners are responsible for implementing the response plans if their risk occurs (choice A), while the risk owners would ensure the risk responses are effective (choice B). Choice C is incorrect because potential risk response actions are investigated during risk response planning and are not necessarily the responsibility of the risk action owner. The risk action owner is responsible for his or her assigned risk; this person is not responsible for evaluating the effects of that response on other risks, so choice D is incorrect.

36. **Answer:** B

    Explanation: Choice D is another step in the Perform Qualitative Risk Analysis process, and does not solve the problem. Choice C may not be the best way to improve the data quality assessment rating. Just because a risk has a low rating does not mean its probability or impact will be low; it means that there is not yet enough of an understanding or enough information about the risk to qualify it. Therefore, choice A could not be the best choice. Choice B is the BEST choice.

37. **Answer:** C

Explanation: Fallback plans (choice D) are only needed if the contingency plan does not work. Legal implications (choice A) are always important, but that understanding would have been gained in the Plan Risk Responses process, not when the risk occurs. If the project response is well planned, choice B could be an option. However, without further information about the identified risk, its severity, and the specific response planned, the BEST choice would be C.

38. **Answer:** A

Explanation: If this project was completed in a consulting environment, the best choice might be different, since detailed costing of the risks might be helpful. However, in this case, the project is for the project manager's own company and the overall risk is known. Remember that the project management process (particularly stakeholder involvement, the work breakdown structure, the network diagram, and finalizing the schedule) will provide the project manager and others with a good overall understanding of the risk of the project. Since the amount of time spent on any aspect of risk management should be adjusted to the needs of the project, choice D could not be the best choice. Based on the situation described, there is no reason to ignore some stakeholders (choice C) or to limit the efforts to only one day (choice B). Some projects may involve stakeholders in other locations or other countries, and therefore require more than one day simply for communication to take place, not just for effort. Since the project is low priority, the BEST choice would be to omit the work needed to quantify risks (choice A).

39. **Answer:** A

Explanation: Choices B, C, and D are done later in the risk management process. Choice B is done in the Plan Risk Responses process. Choice C is done in the Monitor and Control Risks process. Choice D is done in the Perform Quantitative Risk Analysis process. Only choice A would have been done before the probability and impact of each risk is identified.

40. **Answer:** B

    Explanation: The response to a risk may be acceptance, not the creation of contingency plans, so choice A could not be the best choice. There is no reason to suspect that risk identification is not complete (choice C). Choice D is not the best choice, as the risk rating should not affect the importance of a project. Because this project has the highest risk rating and contingency plans were found for most risks, the only thing left to do is change the project. Only choice B changes the project and is therefore the best choice.

41. **Answer:** D

    Explanation: Risks can be identified at any time in the project management process. Therefore, the best choice is D.

42. **Answer:** A

    Explanation: Choices B, C, and D should be done for low-priority as well as high-priority projects, so they could not be the best answers. One of the criteria for determining if the Perform Quantitative Risk Analysis process should be done is the priority of the project. Therefore, choice A is the best choice.

43. **Answer:** D

    Explanation: Since no meeting should begin without a stated purpose, choice A could not be the best choice. Previously prepared questions help make the interviewer look prepared (choice B), but the second part of the choice is wrong; they do not diminish the flow of ideas—they increase it. Since previously prepared questions come after open-ended questions in order to get the interviewee's individual thought, choice C could not be the best choice. Choice D represents a common error of those doing expert interviews. We tend to want to jump to our questions when what the interviewee has to say is the real purpose, and may be a more valuable outcome of the interview. Choice D is therefore the best choice.

44. **Answer:** A

    Explanation: Only choice A is completely correct. Outcomes of risk audits (included in choice B) are added to the risk register after the Monitor and Control Risks process. Amount of contingency time and cost reserves (included in choice C) are added to the risk register after the Perform Quantitative Risk Analysis process. Risk probability and impact ratings (part of choice D) are determined in the Perform Qualitative Risk Analysis process, and are added to the risk register at the end of that process.

45. **Answer:** D

    Explanation: At the very least, risk owners are used in the Plan Risk Responses and Monitor and Control Risks processes, making choice D the best choice. They are not always used (or named) in the Identify Risks process (choices A or B) and might only be used for some projects in the Perform Quantitative Risk Analysis process (choice C).

46. **Answer:** A

    Explanation: In this case, the real cost of the insurance is £$190,000. Therefore, that number should be used in the calculation. (0.05 x £190,000) plus (0.20 x £20,000) = £13,500. Probability x Impact = Expected monetary value. The expected monetary values of each risk are added together.

47. **Answer:** B

    Explanation: Option B is correct. Choice A is wrong because the risk would not be closed just because the impact value was lowered; it may move to the watchlist, however. Choice C is not correct since the team needs to watch all the open risks. When the time passes in which a risk might occur, the risk can be closed, so choice D is incorrect.

48. **Answer:** B

    Explanation: Many people make the mistake of forgetting to properly name risks. In this case, a risk of losing funds is not defined enough for the project manager to determine the appropriate action. That is why choice B is the best choice. Holding a brainstorming session (choice D) would not solve the problem. Choice C is not productive until the real risk is identified. Perhaps it really is, "Management is planning to cut the funding for this project, causing the need to crash or fast track the project." Or perhaps the real risk is, "The X activity cost estimate will not be enough to cover the cost of the equipment, resulting in a cost overrun that cannot be recouped by other activities." Choice A implies that the project manager asks for more funding without getting additional information or satisfying him- or herself that the stakeholder is correct. Therefore, it cannot be the best choice.

49. **Answer:** D

    Explanation: Though all the choices are correct, there is only one BEST choice. Look for the choice that best solves the problem, not just addresses it. Choice D does that, because it quickly reaches the most people who are most likely to know the answer to the question.

50. **Answer:** B

    Explanation: Stakeholder tolerances and thresholds should be identified during the Plan Risk Management process (choice B). These factors will help in determining the severity of risks to the company and the appropriate responses. They should be identified before any of the other risk management processes begin.

51. **Answer:** C

   Explanation: There are two common errors listed as choices in this question. Many project managers do everything with the team, and rely on meetings for everything (choice D). This is a key trait of an inexperienced and ineffective project manager. The second common error is to have the attitude of "yes boss," as illustrated in choice A. A project manager is not a pushover; he or she is required to push back instead. In this instance, the project manager can substantiate the need for the reserve. The reserve is not a pad; it is for specific events, just like project activities are for specific work.

   Removing reserve (choice A) or hiding it (choice B) are considered unethical, as that would provide a false sense of the real cost of the project. When you use risk management, it is up to you to inform management that you are making a change in how projects are planned, what that change is, and why it is important. Then, once project plans are developed, stick by your decisions. Since one of the top things management complains about regarding project managers is that they do NOT push back, you might receive a more favorable response than you expect. Go for it for the benefit of the team, the project, and the company!

52. **Answer:** C

    Explanation: Here again is an example of a question with more than one "correct" choice, but only one BEST choice under these circumstances. Think, "Where is there a problem?" Nothing says that interrupting the departments is a problem, or that it was not taken care of in planning the project. Therefore, choice D could not be the best choice. Many projects have medium priority (choice B), and there is no indication that a higher priority here will really solve the problem. There is no indication that the requirements were not finalized on this project (choice A), leaving only choice C as the BEST choice.

    The problem here is the 60 percent probability. It is wise for project with medium and high levels of importance to have the confidence that they can meet the required time and cost constraints. The only solution to this problem listed is choice C. Fast tracking puts more activities in the network diagram in parallel (concurrent) and therefore will shorten the length of the project (while adding risk). When that change is made, the Monte Carlo simulation would be rerun to determine if further project adjustments are needed to improve the probability of completion within the allowed timeframe.

53. **Answer:** B

    Explanation: Though probability can also be determined (numerically) in the Perform Quantitative Risk Analysis process, the only part of risk management where both activities are done is the Perform Qualitative Risk Analysis process.

54. **Answer:** A

    Explanation: For most medium- to high-importance projects, a Monte Carlo simulation result of 70 percent is not good enough. For less important projects, the extra effort, adjustments to the project, and analysis required to improve the result may not be worthwhile, making choice A the only statement that is not true. Either fast tracking or crashing could improve the Monte Carlo result for this project; therefore, choices B and D are true statements. There is a good chance that reducing the time of the project may impact the cost so it would be wise to know the cost probability, making choice C also a true statement.

55. **Answer:** D

    Explanation: This could be a common occurrence with risk management, but it is not a bad one. Such risks should be worked out with management. They should not be ignored (choice A); they should be dealt with. Only choice D deals with the problem and solves it. Choice C does not solve the problem. Choice B would not need to be done, as the project manager should already know the answer and such activities do not deal with or solve the problem.

56. **Answer:** A

    Explanation: A risk trigger can be determined by asking the question provided. Therefore, choice A must be the best answer.

57. **Answer:** B

    Explanation: Choices A, C, and D are facts, not risks, and should be dealt with in other parts of project planning.

58. **Answer:** A

    Explanation: A project manager always seems to think he or she has to do something, but in this case, the "something to do" has already been done during planning. It is not always possible to come up with a contingency or fallback plan. In such cases, the risk is simply accepted. The risk owner knows what to do. The potential impact should have been assessed during risk response planning and communicated to management as part of the contingency reserve discussion (choice B). If the contingency plan did not include the project manager's involvement in implementing the plan for this risk, then the project manager would be getting in the way if he or she tried to help (choice C). Crashing and fast tracking would already have been done (choice D). As compared to Question 37, more detail is provided, so choice A is the best choice.

59. **Answer:** A

    Explanation: This question is dealing with the whole risk management process. Therefore, choices B, C, and D could not be the best answers. It is during the Plan Risk Management process that a decision is made on how to approach risk management.

60. **Answer:** B

    Explanation: Choices A and D should have already been done, even for the additional risks identified. Though many people collect lessons learned (choice C) during the project instead of just at the end, this is not the most important thing to do in this situation. Lessons learned are only required to be complete during project closure. A risk review (choice B) revisits all risks and risk response plans. With so many changes to risk on this project, such a review may uncover changes to the risk response plans that are needed to better control the project. Therefore, it would be best to hold a risk review.

61. **Answer:** C

    Explanation: I keep trying to make these questions easy, but then I find tricks to really test your knowledge and they become hard! Should I be sorry? A risk owner may be involved with determining risk responses (choice D) or qualification (choice B), but not always. A risk owner could also be someone from management (choice A), but not always. This makes C the best choice.

62. **Answer:** C

    Explanation: In order to rate risks, one must have begun to collect information on them. Therefore, choices A and B could not be the best choices. The risks need to be rated before you know which ones to plan responses for (choice D). Therefore, choice C is the best option.

63. **Answer:** A

    Explanation: Management may not need to approve the list of risks or qualification plan (choice D). They would be involved in planning responses (choice C) and helping to determine risks (choice B), but the risk management plan is part of the project management plan. Since management approves the project management plan, the best choice is A.

64. **Answer:** C

    Explanation: The main purposes of a risk audit are to determine if risk owners are assigned to each risk and to determine if they are effective.

65. **Answer:** C

    Explanation: Choice C is correct. Option A is not necessarily the correct choice, as the project manager does not always need to be involved in resolving conflicts. Choices B and D are not correct, as they can help reduce risk.

66. **Answer:** B

    Explanation: Choice B is correct. Choice A is something that should be done in any case. Choice C would be an unethical use of the funds. Choice D is incorrect, as the time in which the risk might occur has passed, so the risk is closed.

67. **Answer:** C

    Explanation: Choice C is correct. The team is eliminating risks. This does not change the scope (choice A), and it is not adding things the customer did not ask for (choice D). Padding is not allowed (choice B).

68. **Answer:** B

    Explanation: Choice B is correct. Choice A includes workarounds, which are unplanned responses. Choice C is only half the answer. Choice D is done as part of quantitative risk analysis.

69. **Answer:** D

    Explanation: Choice D is correct. We assume the team did risk response planning and that there is already a plan in place. All the other choices imply risk response planning wasn't done.

70. **Answer:** C

    Explanation: Choice C is correct. You can't do options A or D until you evaluate the risk. And you don't have enough information to advise the customer or sponsor (choice B) until you evaluate the risk.

71. **Answer:** C

    Explanation: Choice C is correct. Choice A is a contingency response. Choice B is gold plating and should not be done. Choice D is a risk, not a response.

72. **Answer:** A

    Explanation: Choice A is the only correct answer. Transferring a risk makes another party responsible for the risk.

73. **Answer:** D

    Explanation: Choice D is correct. Choice A is not proactive. Choice B is a good idea, but you cannot stop ALL changes, and it's too late at this point in the project. Choice C is unethical.

74. **Answer:** B

    Explanation: The correct answer is choice B. Exploit and share are response strategies for opportunities.

75. **Answer:** C

    Although all of these answers could be correct to some degree, the best answer is risk governance, choice C.

Accomplishing Risk Management when Doing High-Level Estimating

There are two common instances when a project manager may have to perform risk identification quickly:
- When asked to come up with an initial project estimate of time or cost
- When responding to proposals as a seller

Though many project managers complain about this, there is nothing wrong with management asking for a quick, high-level project cost or time estimate. In fact, this is a great opportunity for you to get involved in creating realistic estimates. The problem is that most project managers do not know how to create such quick estimates. Even if they are experienced with estimating under these conditions, they often neglect to take risk into account.

How do you come up with a high-level estimate under these circumstances? In these situations, risks can be identified at a high level in the work breakdown structure instead of the detailed activity level. Follow these steps:

1. Perform an expert interview with the person who assigned you the project immediately upon their asking you for the estimate or assigning the project. This will enable you to obtain a better understanding of the work, as well as to begin identifying risks.
2. Collect background data and historical records. Look for existing information about risks experienced on similar projects within your company. If you often receive requests for high-level estimates, it is in your best interest to work to make such information exists. (See the discussion on the value of historical information in

Chapter 2 of this book, What You Need Before You Can Effectively Begin Risk Management.)

3. Have a charter (at least a verbal one). Make sure you know what is included in a charter and request all of that information the moment you are asked for an estimate. Be prepared. Try to get a signed charter, to confirm that this is a real project, rather than just hypothetical.

4. Ask the person assigning you the work who might have insights into the project and who they anticipate might be part of the project team.5. Perform expert interviews by phone with others not on the team, but who may have insight into risks.

5. Assemble a team to create a high-level work breakdown structure.

6. With the team, estimate work packages based on historical costs, schedule estimates, and best guesses. You could use one-time estimates at this stage, or use three-point estimates to better understand the ranges.

7. Identify risks for each high-level work package. Brainstorming risks of these high-level work packages, and take into account the risks identified by others in step 5. Document these risks in a risk register.

8. Perform qualitative risk analysis using a 1 to 10 scale. Continue to document risks in the risk register.

9. Quantify the probability, cost, and time impact of the top risks by educated guess. Document the results in the risk register.

10. Create a reserve based on the probability and impact guesses and add that number to the estimate.

11. Add the estimates, add the reserve needed, and then provide an estimate in a range. ("If the charter remains the same, the project should cost between $75,000 and $125,000 and take between six to nine months.")

Note that this process does not involve risk response planning; doing something about the risks. There is usually not enough time if you need to create an estimate quickly.

No matter how you create an estimate, the end result is that you have to provide your team's best guess. Certainly you want to make sure that you provide a realistic estimate, even if it is in a range. Although the process described here is not foolproof, it is a proven method to improve accuracy and to create documentation to support the estimate you provide. Remember that an estimate must consider risks.

If the project is approved, you can take review the risk register and other documentation created here, add any new information and then refine your estimates to an activity level.

You will then create an estimate detailed enough to be used in managing the project and against which to measure project performance.

Risk Categories and Lists of Risks

The following is a list of risks compiled by Rita Mulcahy, PMP, as a result of two international risk studies and with contribution from over 141 individuals and companies.

WARNING: This list, if improperly used, could hurt you because:
*   This is not a complete list of risks. It does not include all activity risks or all project risks! It cannot be used as a checklist! Besides, using checklists can give a false sense of security that all risks have been uncovered for a project.
*   Lists can limit thinking, if improperly used, because people tend to see only those risks ON the list and overlook what is NOT on the list.
*   More than a list is needed to properly perform all of risk management. Assessment of overall project-related and activity-related risks are required parts of risk management. Lists do not help you assess overall project risk.

How to Use This List
*   Identify risks for your project and for each activity using your own process and the help of the team and stakeholders
*   Then, and only then, have the team and stakeholders review these lists to see if they generate any further risks for YOUR project
*   Once you have a more complete list of risks, follow the rest of the risk management processes: Perform Qualitative Risk Analysis, Perform Quantitative Risk Analysis, Plan Risk Responses, and Monitor and Control Risks.

Risk Categories and Lists of Risks

Please Note

Make use of the cause-risk-effect columns in evaluating your own projects. The causes listed here might trigger an idea about a different risk on your project.

Many of the risks listed are not as project-specific as recommended. However, they may suggest possible related risks for your project.

Many of these risks could be placed in more than one category. This is a matter of opinion. Some of the risks could also be causes, and causes could be listed as risks. These things do not matter. The list provided here is to help you generate ideas for your specific projects, not to provide you with exact risks.

When you review the list, you may laugh at some of the easily preventable problems some of the contributors have contended with. Such problems show us just how much risk management is needed and how, if all the stakeholders work together, we can easily make improvements to our projects.

As this list has been compiled from many different sources, it includes some industry-specific wording or "terms of art." Please take this list "as is." No explanation can be given for these words.

Send your list of risks to Rita Mulcahy, PMP, at risk@rmcproject.com for inclusion in future updates of this book. You could help others even as these lists help you.

Do not forget to check out our Web site (www.rmcproject.com/risk) for other information about risk management. Please have a copy of this book with you, as you will need to provide information about the book in order to gain access to this part of our Web site.

Risk Categories and Lists of Risks

● ● ● ● **Table of Contents**

Risk Categories and Lists of Risks

List of Potential Risk Categories

The following are very high-level areas of risk, causes, or even effects on projects. Use this list as instructed on the first page of this appendix.

- Acceptance criteria
- Administrative procedures
- Age
- Aging workforce
- Approvals
- Assumptions
- Attrition
- Authority
- Availability
- Bankruptcy
- Bribes
- Bugs
- Business units
- Buy-in
- Cash flow
- Change control
- Changes
- Chemicals
- Choice of technologies
- Communication
- Communication channels
- Communication methods
- Company organization
- Compatibility
- Competence
- Competing goals
- Competition
- Competitors
- Components
- Computers
- Computer software
- Conflicting requirements

- Conflicts of interest
- Construction
- Contracts
- Cost
- Critical path
- Culture
- Currency
- Customer
- Customer acceptance
- Customer requirements
- Customer support
- Customer's end user
- Customer's competition
- Dependencies
- Documentation
- Drug testing
- Due dates
- Egos
- Electrical
- End users
- Environment
- Errors
- Ethics
- Exchange rates
- Experts
- External
- Fast tracking
- Financial
- Fit
- Follow-through
- Foreign Corrupt Practices Act
- Form of company organization

- Form of project organization
- Fraud
- Functional managers
- Funding
- Geographic constraints
- Goals
- Gold plating
- Government
- Government regulations
- Handoff
- Hardware
- Health
- Help desk
- Hidden objectives
- High volumes
- Incorrect assumptions
- Inexperience
- Information distribution
- Injury
- Integration
- Intellectual property expectations
- Interfaces
- International
- Knowledge base
- Labor
- Lack of progress
- Lack of project management knowledge
- Lack of project management training
- Lag
- Language
- Laws
- Learning curve
- Legal
- Lessons learned
- Letter of credit

- Licenses
- Logistics
- Make-or-buy decisions
- Management
- Manufacturing
- Marketplace
- Measure progress
- Medaling
- Meetings
- Mergers
- Metrics
- Milestones
- Modules
- Motivation
- Multi-location issues
- Multiple projects
- Negotiation
- Network
- New methodology
- New technology
- Objectives
- Obsolescence
- Operations
- Other organizations
- Other projects
- Packaged software
- Padding
- Permits
- Personal agendas
- Personalities
- Politics
- Poorly designed project
- Poorly designed solution
- Power/politics
- Presentations
- Priorities

- Procedures
- Procurement
- Product development life cycle
- Profit
- Progress
- Project closure
- Project management (including lack of project management, time, cost, scope, quality, communications, human resources, procurement, integration)
- Project management plan
- Quality
- Religious beliefs
- Reorganization
- Reporting
- Request for Proposals (RFP)
- Requirements
- Resistance to change
- Resource availability
- Resource owners
- Resources
- Revenue
- Risk management (or lack of risk management)
- Rollouts
- Schedule
- Scope
- Scope creep
- Scope of work
- Security
- Senior management meddling
- Shipping
- Slack
- Software
- Span of control

- Special provisions
- Sponsor availability
- Stakeholders' interests
- Standards
- Storage
- Storm
- Strategies
- Subsurface conditions
- Supplier
- Support
- Technical opinions
- Technology
- Terrorism
- Theft
- Thresholds
- Tolerance levels
- Trainability
- Training
- Transportation
- Turnover
- Unclear requirements
- Unions
- Unrealistic schedules or budgets
- Users
- Vandals
- Virtual teams
- War
- Warranties
- Weather
- Workload

Examples of Opportunties

Cause	Risk	Effect
The components might fit together so easily	that they could be manufactured as one part	saving the project time and money
A supplier determines that there is room for growth in its market and invests in R & D	which creates a new component for the project that is cheaper or easier to maintain	thus saving the project time and life cycle cost
A competitor may release new technology	that could also be available for a project another company is working on	resulting in saved time on the project
Changes in customer requirements	may include components already included in the project	thereby increasing the market and interest in the product
If much of the work from the prior Latin American eBusiness project (including payloads for order create/order response/order cancel response transactions) is leveraged	the work on this project would be easier	resulting in decreased cost and schedule duration
Due to having an opportunity to travel to a foreign country	the availability of contract assistance may be higher	which would result in a higher quality project team
Because the supplier department doing the work has more talented resources than those assigned to this project	a complaint by the customer or a peer review by the supplier could result in the assignment of more skilled resources before development begins	reducing the risks to the project and perhaps shortening the schedule
Due to program products including new features	design and development of additional code may not be necessary	which would result in a shorter schedule and less money needed to complete the project
Due to organizational decisions to utilize offshore suppliers	the cost of software development may decrease	which may lead to decreased project development costs for internal customers

Cause	Risk	Effect
Due to new tools becoming available on the market	a system's test time could be dramatically reduced	leading to a shorter schedule than originally planned
Decreased cost of a key component	could lead to a product that has a lower production cost than the initial target	thus saving money on the project
Due to properly trained employees and perfect market conditions	demand for the product or service might be greater than anticipated	resulting in higher profitability for the company overall
Due to detailed efforts before the contract was signed	the supplier could apply value engineering ideas	resulting in lower equipment and construction costs
Due to not having adequate information technology support	a creative approach to analyzing data may be discovered	which could decrease project time
A fire causes a review of possible missing records	leading to inconsistencies among existing plant records found	preventing a regulatory problem

Additional Opportunities

- We can leverage existing functionality for the next project
- The historical records and lessons learned will help the next project doing a similar implementation
- This project provides experience that can be leveraged by entering new markets
- Less manual effort than expected on the project saves time
- When the project is completed our company will be experienced with projects like this and thus can increase business
- The contract language may be less restrictive than we thought
- Beating the competition to market will make our company the exclusive provider of this new product
- A business unit within company works with an outside software developer on unit testing, yielding fewer errors in delivered software
- Integration of organizational units (sales, support, service) will lead to business growth
- Training or cross-training from other business units will result in additional availability of people qualified to work on this and similar projects
- Alliance between IT and business
- Good project documentation allows quick disaster recovery
- Circuit is delivered early, so data migration can begin sooner than originally scheduled
- Software is programmed on faster and with fewer problems than anticipated
- Bids come in lower than expected, saving cost on the project
- Land acquisition occurs sooner than planned, allowing us to begin the building phase of the project before winter sets in
- The team works together more effectively than expected, allowing the project to be completed faster
- Show value of project management (not just overhead)
- Improved confidence of stakeholders means they require fewer meetings and reports later in the project
- Newly discovered efficiencies on this project will reduce cost of implementation for the next customer
- Finding a problem before the government does keeps us in compliance, and avoids possible fines
- Finding an efficiency in a workgroup that could be applied to another project adds value throughout the organization

Risk Categories and Lists of Risks

List of Risks

Cause	Risk	Effect
Aerospace and Defense		
The unique hardware is a new development	that may not be delivered on time	forcing schedule delay and potential deviation from design-control approach
The flight software being created in the project has never been created before	resulting in late delivery of flight software	may offer less time to verify performance requirements at the system level prior to launch
Ability of payload requirements to continue to expand without requiring risk-adjusted benefit/cost analysis for each proposed enhancement	may prevent closing on design and mission planning in a timely manner	increasing cost and project schedule
Discrete electronic part problems	may lead to recalls that force rework or retesting of delivered hardware	thus impacting the schedule
A new system	may not perform to requirements	resulting in difficult mission design and partial loss of science
Lack of a completely networked, integrated and controlled schedule	increases the risk of late deliveries and incorrect assessment of schedule slack	resulting in a lack of project schedule control
A modal survey occurring late in the program	may not allow sufficient time to correct structural design problems	resulting in schedule delay
A determination must be made as to what the plane will carry	which may lead to internal payload mass growing beyond baseline aerodynamic design limits	resulting in significant cost and schedule growth

Cause	Risk	Effect
The late installation of a clean room	may result in the potential inability to prove contamination control processes	leading to the inability to verify procedures
New equipment fabrication	may continue to slip in the schedule	resulting in a delayed start of integration
Late development of computer cards	may delay delivery of other hardware	resulting in shortened flight software development time and reduced schedule margin prior to launch
Multiple organizations responsible for development	may result in variances in assumed objectives and nonalignment of effort	resulting in extra cost and schedule to complete the project
The communication equipment design must be ordered without government frequency allocation	offering the risk that they could be the wrong frequency or that the design would have to be changed or equipment re-ordered	adding cost and delay to project
Presently unforeseen atmospheric changes	may cause the need to redesign some components	leading to schedule delay or a failed project
A change in geopolitical environment	may require changed components beyond that expected in the project	causing the need to make changes to other components beyond their design limitations
The market for planes is ever-changing and there is a history of one competitor adjusting based on what others do	which may lead to a change in how the competitor markets its product	requiring changes in the design beyond what was planned for in the project
The market for planes is ever-changing and there is a history of one competitor adjusting based on what others do	which may lead to a major component of the competitors' new product not being well-received in the marketplace	causing the need to speed up completion of the product another company is working on

Risk Categories and Lists of Risks

Cause	Risk	Effect
A failure in security of confidential information on this project	may change how competitors plan their projects	causing a need to change an existing project
The success of underwater or low space personal aircraft building contests	may make a project obsolete	causing project failure
The market research function may stop focusing on a product while doing marketing research	thus missing a new trend in requirements	resulting in scope changes
The number of inches the seats should be spaced on the plane will depend on market research. Because of changing consumer needs, that research will not be done until late in the project. If the market research department has many products it will be researching	the seat spacing requirements could be ignored or come even later than planned	causing the need to eliminate one row of seats and redesign the locking mechanism if the research shows changes in needs
Design Procurement and Construction		
At Site During Erection/Construction		
Improper/inadequate soil assessment	may result in unplanned sub-soil conditions	causing a delay in the commencement of construction and replanning required for construction
Lack of proper planning and coordination between the home and site offices	may result in equipment already dispatched from the sub-supplier's works, with access to the site not properly established	causing a delay in the equipment reaching the site and consequently causing project schedule slippage

Risk Categories and Lists of Risks

Cause	Risk	Effect
Local politicos, unruly elements, etc.	may cause access to site to be denied or challenged	resulting in a delay in the start of construction, leading to slippage in the project schedule
Improper packing and handling	may cause damage during storage	resulting in breakage of equipment, necessitating repair or replacement
Improper provision of security at site/deteriorating law and order condition at site	may result in theft	causing a time and cost increase for the project
Improper engineering design discovered during the construction of the main deck	may cause design problems and errors, such as equipment out of dimension and not fitting right	resulting in the work needing to be torn down, generating additional risks as well as cost
Untrained or improperly trained workforce/unskilled workers	may lead to defective workmanship	resulting in rework
The XYZ equipment being supplied by a company new to this area of manufacturing	may result in a manufacturing defect in the equipment	causing time and cost increases for the project, even though the supplier can be levied for liquidated damages
The inefficiency of the supplier	may cause payment disputes between the supplier and his employee	leading to a delay in the project schedule
Misinterpretation of the EPC contract	may cause a delay due to the dispute between the client and the customer regarding payment	leading to a delay in project implementation
Communication problems between the home and site offices	may result in non-receipt of design drawings	leading to a slip in the project schedule

Risk Categories and Lists of Risks

Cause	Risk	Effect
Faulty planning	may result in the out-of-sequence receipt of materials at the site	leading to a delay in the project schedule
Faulty planning	may result in over/under deployment of personnel at the site	leading to a delay in the project schedule
Backfill		
Due to heavy rains and extremely wet, heavy soil	the weight of the soil could cave in a portion of the foundation	which would result in a delay in the completion of the backfill while rework is done
Due to the excavator hitting rock on the job previous to ours	he might be delayed in arriving on our project	which would lead to a delay in the start of the backfill
Due to the excavator having an equipment failure	he may be late in arriving	which may lead to a delay in the completion of the backfill
Business Risks		
Due to a change in governmental policies (regulations)	the project funding may be stopped	which may result in premature closeout of the contract
Due to a change in government	the percentage of domestically manufactured items may be increased to encourage the domestic market	resulting in loss of profit
As a result of technologic advancement	the equipment or software currently used may be outdated	resulting in new training requirements or a delay in approval
As a result of environmental impacts	the project site may be shifted to another location	resulting in new establishment or a major scope change etc.
Commercial Risks		
Due to a missing of "zeros" in pricing while bidding	the final value of the contract price may either be too low or too high	resulting in a loss of face as this is addressed with the buyer

Risk Categories and Lists of Risks

Cause	Risk	Effect
Due to too much dependence on spreadsheet formulas while bidding	addition or multiplication errors may result in loss of bid or a bid with an extremely low price	resulting in a loss of face as this is addressed with the buyer
Due to exchange rate fluctuations	the contract and/or the equipment price may become high or low with respect to the initial bid price	resulting in a change from anticipated profit
Due to a company's policy to select the lowest-cost bidder	the project manager may choose an inferior product or supplier	which may result in rework, a dissatisfied customer, or delay in project delivery
Due to poor battery limits definition in the bid documents	the bidder may be asked to include additional work during execution of contract	which may result in arbitration or disputes
Dispatch and Transit Risks		
Narrow bridges/pathways/ non-receipt of clearances/ landslides/monsoon damage to roads/rails/bridges etc.	may cause a delay in consignments reaching the site	causing slippage in the project schedule and/or liquidated damages for delay
A hike in petrol/diesel prices/ changes in service tax and other governmental policy changes	may cause a transporter's strike	resulting in no movement of goods, slippage in project schedule, liquidted damages for delay
Governmental policies	may cause a trade embargo on a supplier's country	resulting in a delay in supplies, slippage in project schedule, liquidated damages for delay
A short circuit/improper handling of flammable material	may cause a fire in transit	resulting in a delay of project supplies, slippage in schedule, liquidated damages for delay

Cause	Risk	Effect
Unscrupulous truck suppliers/ no security	may result in a loss of trucks/ consignments	causing a delay in supplies if a consignment is not found, necessitating reorder, an increase in project cost and a time delay
Faulty planning	**may result in using an improper route survey**	causing a delay in supplies reaching the project site, leading to slippage in project schedule
Excavation		
Due to rain, snow, or ice	a delay in the excavation may occur	which would delay the start of forming the foundation footings
Due to hitting rock in the excavation	dynamite and extra equipment may be needed	which would lead to a delay in the completion of the excavation
Due to not hitting bearing soil in the excavation	engineering (and possible rework) may be needed	which would lead ot a delay in the completion of the excavation. A delay in the completion of the excavation would lead to a delay in the start of the forming of the foundation footings
Due to hitting an active spring in the excavation	additional manpower and equipment could be needed	which may lead to a delay in the start of forming the footing for the foundation
Due to the ground freezing during the winter months	the excavation may be delayed until warmer weather arrives	which would lead to a delay in the start of excavation
Due to the legal survey	undisclosed easements or other encumbrances could be identified	leading to a delay in the completion of the staked survey for the project

Risk Categories and Lists of Risks

Cause	Risk	Effect
Flatwork (Inside)		
Due to frost in the soil	the flatwork would need to be delayed until the ground thaws	which would delay the start of flatwork
Due to rain the night before the inside flatwork was to be placed	the foundation may need to be pumped out	which may cause a delay in the start of the inside flatwork
Due to pilferage of job site materials	there may not be enough gravel to grade the basement for the placement of concrete	which may delay the start of inside flatwork
Foundation		
Due to hitting inadequate bearing soil in the excavation	engineering may determine that piers, instead of spread footings, are required to adequately support the structure	which could lead to a delay in the completion of the foundation
Due to heavy rain the night before the footings were to be poured	the excavation may fill up with water which would need to be pumped out	which would delay the start of the foundation
Framing		
Due to high winds during framing	the framing carpenters may not be able to tilt walls up	which would delay comletion of the framing
Due to snow during framing	the framing carpenters may take the day off	which would delay completion of the framing
Due to rain during framing	the framing carpenters may take the balance of the day off	which would delay completion of the framing
Due to lumber not showing up at the appointed time during framing	the carpenters may have to make work	which could delay completion of the framing
Due to half the carpenters not showing up for the work the first day of hunting	the work may slow down to 40 percent during that day	which would delay completion of the framing

Risk Categories and Lists of Risks

Cause	Risk	Effect
Due to one of the carpenters cutting himself badly with a saw	production oculd stop the subsequent emergency first aid and evacuation of the injured man to the hospital	which would delay completion of the framing
Due to the owner giving the rough-in carpenters $300 each as a Christmas gift	the carpenters may take the day off	which would delay completion of the rough-in framing for the job
Lumber and Windows		
Due to a mistake at the mill	the windows may not be completed in time to arive at our job on the designated day	which may result in extra labor man hours delaying completion of the framing and an additional charge by the framing carpenter
Due to a number of drivers not showing up for work at the lumber yard	the first load of lumber might be late in arriving on the project	which could delay the start of framing
Due to a new forklift operator at the lumber yard	the lumber may arrive loaded in reverse order	which could delay the start of framing
Due to a remote site	the lumber delivery driver may have trouble finding the location of the project	which may delay the delivery of a critical load of lumber
Due to lumber being stolen from the job site the night before the framing was to have started	the framing carpenter may only be able to work part of a day while a reorder is placed	which would result in a delay in the completion of the framing
Permits		
Due to the city plans examiner being ill	there may be a delay in acquiing the building permits	which would lead to a delay in the start of excavation for the project
Due to record building starts, the building rough-in inspection	may take 20 days to obtain versus the standard two days	which would delay the start of insulation installation

Risk Categories and Lists of Risks

Cause	Risk	Effect
Plumbing		
Due to rain the night before the ground rough plumbing is to be installed	the foundation may need to be pumped out	which may lead to the late mobilization of heavy equipment and late start of the project
Due to several plumbers not showing up at the plumbers shop for work on a Friday	there may not be a plumber available for our job	which would delay the completion of the ground rough plumbing
Due to heavy rain the night after the ground rough plumbing is installed	the plumbing could float	which may delay the start of inside flatwork
Subsurface and Miscellaneous		
Due to constructing in a congested industrial area	relocation of overhead and underground utilities may be required	which may lead to the late mobilization of heavy equipment and late start of the project
Due to having to relocate public utilities	it may be necessary to coordinate and schedule the public utilities involved	which may result in delays due to the untimely response of public utilities
Due to building in an area that has extensive previous constructions	it is probable that hidden obstructions could be discovered once construction begins	which would lead to extra cost involved to remove previously unidentified hidden material
Due to insufficient soil testing prior to construction	underground water may be discovered	which would delay the project and could result in extra cost to resolve the problem
Due to improper testing for hazardous materials	latent contaminations could be discovered	and may result in extra cost and time for remediation of hazardous materials
Due to upgrading an operating facility	the coordination of shutdown may be required to minimize impact to the ongoing operation	and could result in delay to the schedule

Cause	Risk	Effect
Due to sole sing equipment	the supplier may not be concerned about delivering on time	and could impact the project schedule and cost
Due to poor field coordination by the general supplier	out-of-sequencing activities	could result in extra work for trades
Due to missing details on drawings or in specifications	assumptions by the supplier	may lead to errors in the field
Due to not requiring deliverables such as schedules to be pay items on the schedule of values	schedules may not be submitted as specified	which could make it difficult to establish baselines and properly quantify progress
Due to not properly monitoring the submittal progress	submittals may be forgotten until they impact the project	and lead to late equipment or material deliveries
Due to not preparing a training manual in advance of equipment turnover	the owne may not be trained and prepared to operate the equipment	resulting in late turnover of responsibilities and extended guarantees
Due to allowing the early delivery of equipment and materials	the owner may assume the risk that the supplier properly protected the equipment and material from the elements. However, when the time for installation comes	it may be discovered the equipment and material have been damaged, requiring replacement, resulting in a delay to the schedule and extra cost
Due to renovating an operating wastewater treatment facility	excessive wet weather	may cause flooding into areas under renovation
Due to extensive excavation in a heavily congested area	geotechnical problems such as soil movement could occur	resulting in unsafe conditions that would require soil stabilization in order to proceed with construction
Due to stockpiling soil in an area of extensive excavation	geotechnical problems such as unforseen pressure against sheeting could occur	and cause out of plumb problems with sheeting

Cause	Risk	Effect
Due to paint being applied to bulding or equipment when temperature or humidity are not being closely monitored	poor performance by the product	would invalidate the guarantee
Due to allowing one general supplier to perform both new construction and renovation within the same project at the same location	labor forces and supervision may be insufficient and not properly balanced	causing one area or the other to fall behind schedule. The renovating would usually suffer because there is generally more cost associated with new construction
Due to a lump sum contract	there may be some conflict about work items or quantities that the supplier states were not included in lump sum quote	which could result in extra cost and schedule impacts
As the result of allowing the construction manager to self-perform the concrete work	the suppliermay optimize durations for the concrete work and minimize durations for the finish trades such as electrical and mechanical	which could lead to delays in finish and turnover of an area
Technical Risks		
Due to varying site conditions	scope change may occur	which may lead to cost an/or schedule overrun
Due to a recent revision in applicable standards	design parameters may change	which may lead to scrapping of designs done already or major revisions of those designs
Due to incorrect inputs while entering data for analysis	the results may give erroneous output	which may lead to a poor decision on when to start construction
Due to incorrect scaling of route maps or site maps	the quantity take-off (BOM) estimate may be less or more than the actual	resulting in cost overruns

Cause	Risk	Effect
Due to a reliance on the owner-supplied as-built drawings	the supplier may be carried away by wrong/outdated inputs	resulting in a claim by us to the owner for damages
Due to incorrect date entry format (US system to UK system)	the computer outputs may give wrong validity/expiration dates	causing system failure
Incompativle analysis and design software between the approving organization and the performing organization	could result in training the performing organization's personnel quickly to become familiar with the new software	which may lead to errors and delay in design approval
There is not enough time to complete the construction and management is desperate for time savings	leading to "Approved with Comments" drawings being used for construction	which may lead to demolition or major change when the "Approved for Construction" drawings are released to site
Transporation and Shipping		
Due to high waters at the landing point	the jetty could flood	which could lead to fishing/ pleasure craft or other coastal traffic striking an underwater object
Due to a delay in the start date of the project	the tidal charts used in the planning process could be incorrect	which may lead to a larger amount of required dredging
Due to the wave actions of previous tides	rocks may be swept into the barge landing area	which could lead to movement (rocking) of the barge during load transfer
Due to variations in tidal predictions	the actual tide may be lower than predicted	which may lead to structural damage to the barge bottom during berthing
Due to environmental effects	adverse weather conditions may occur	which may lead to delaying the discharge operation until operational limits are met

Cause	Risk	Effect
Due to substituting a barge of different dimensions than used in the design of the dock	variations in height may occur	which would lead to the use of a bridging ramp to accommodate variances in height
Due to improper lifting operations	a loss of the load may occur	which could lead to damage of the cargo
Due to transporting an abnormally heavy load	collapse of the road surface may occur	which could lead to damage of underground services
Due to need to transfer the abnormal load from marine vessel to the barge	fall of the load from a height may occur	which could lead to damage of the cargo
Due to transporting cargo through a foreign country	unforeseen permits may be required	which may lead to delay in transport schedule
Due to traveling timeframes being at night	personnel injury may occur	which may lead to not meeting our planned stopping points on schedule
Due to working over and near water	falling into the water may occur	which could lead to drowning
Due to mobilizing the transporters	damaged/worn tools may be used	which could lead to injury to the operator or damage to the equipment
Due to a change in political leadership during the life of the project	requirements to legally transport the cargo may change	which could lead to additional permitting requirements
Due to hiring a foreign supplier to perform the haul	contract issues may not be understood the same by both parties	which may lead to additional expense
Due to using a hydraulic transport system	hydraulic lines may burst during the haul	which could lead to delaying the haul
Due to planning the haul route over private land	easements must be obtained from the owners	which may lead to additional expense

Cause	Risk	Effect
Due to not meeting the discharge schedule	the barge may attempt to float on the rising tide	which would lead to suspending discharge operations
Due to weight of the transport vehicle and load	road surface dimpling may occur	which may lead to repair activities after the haul is complete
Due to insufficient water depth at design tide	the barge could bottom before reaching the dock	which would lead to a loss of time and require additional dredging
Paucity of manpower, unplanned load on manpower, improper estimation of quality /quantity of manpower	may lead to a delay in detailed engineering	causing a slippage in project schedule and liquidated damages for the delay
Bureaucracy in the owner's organization/ long approval processes/ incompetent personnel	may cause a delay in the owner's approval of suppliers	leading to a delay in placing orders, a delay in project supplies, a slip in project schedule, and liquidated damages for the delay
Bureaucracy in the supplier's organization/ long approval processes/ incompetent personnel	may cause a delay in the supplier's input for engineering	leading to a delay in detailed engineering, a slip in project schedule, and liquidated damages for the delay
eBusiness		
A trading partner is using a different software version. While the eBusiness hub can handle the translation,	differences in versions may not be discovered until installation	resulting in at least a two week delay in project completion

Cause	Risk	Effect
There has not been any fit/gap analysis done on the project while creating the scope of work	therefore, results of business rules fit/gap analysis between our trading partner and us could show unanticipated gaps (potential gaps could be itemized as part of the detailed risk analysis)	causing project delays or a "showstopper" situation
If adequate time and available data from the trading partner are not obtained early enough	the preliminary rough estimates could be outside of reasonable window of accuracy	and the revised estimates could come as a shock to the sponsor, causing credibility issues
If incoming orders for the Latin American AS/400 order entry system cannot be separated from those for another regional order entry mainframe system and/or sites that are on the new SAP system	there could be no way to ensure that incoming orders are going through the proper routing channels	causing poor quality in the end product
In leveraging code from an existing Latin American eBusiness application	the existing application does not contain all the data required to create the needed documents	and project delays could occur as time is taken to fill the gaps or find alternatives
There are still unknowns in the scope of work	and the "smart e-mail" approach may be used (to indicate what has changed with an order) and/or if a monitor program is developed (to allow CSRs to monitor inbound transactions)	causing an increase in the cost and duration of the project

Cause	Risk	Effect
Use of new corporate project management standards along with incorporating a new CIDX chemical industry standard eBusiness implementation framework	introduces two new frameworks that must be incorporated into one and then followed	which may increase the cost of this project
If the technical learning curve using new resources and regarding the B2B integration tool is not anticipated and built into the estimates	costs could be estimated incorrectly	resulting in cost and/or schedule overruns
The back end Latin American order entry system's compatibility with the required and/or agreed upon transaction flows is unknown	which may result in gaps between the systems	causing project delays
If we do not have frequent oral and written communication with virtual team members in Philadelphia and Brazil and if the intranet site is not adequately maintained	we risk communication breakdowns and "runaway" sub-teams	resulting in a cost overrun
If the Brazil tax and other legal requirements are unclear	missing crucial functionality—or worse—not satisfying legal requirements could result	causing a legal problem
Since the trading partner requires usage of the discontinued order cancel and order cancel response transactions	there could be some work needed after this is implemented when the trading partner goes to the next version of the software (which may not include these transactions)	resulting in a schedule delay for the project

Cause	Risk	Effect
If it is not clear what the eBusiness hub's simulation testing system could and could not include	there could be problems when testing with the trading partner	resulting in a loss of customer satisfaction
This project requires the use of data provided by the trading partner's computer system. That system is currently being implemented and is replete with problems	which may cause the trading partner to discontinue implementation	resulting in a need to decide to either reduce the scope to fit the go-live in before the moratorium or delay the go-live until after the moratorium
Since the eBusiness hub's simulation server is limited	it could be critical to obtain real sample data from the trading partner early on	or run the risk of increased error when testing begins with the trading partner
Information Systems		
Contract		
Supplier selected is doing work time/materials versus the usual fixed bid	therefore, lack of experience in accurate record keeping for this form of contract	could lead to costs being billed inaccurately
Because the contract time/materials is unlike previous releases, which were done under fixed price contracts, and the supplier is seldom critical of a customer-requested change	scope could creep	which could cause the project to be late and more costly
Customer		
Because there is resistance from users when replacing their current software application with a new software application/system	there could be sabotage	which would result in a delay of the project

Cause	Risk	Effect
Because a good relationship with the customer cannot be maintained	there is a lack of trust	which may require more meetings and extra hand-holding
Because the supplier is dependent on the customer for test data	it may not be available as soon as required	causing testing to begin later than it should to meet the requested due date with adequate quality
Due to little effort by the customer to gain support for the project	customer personnel could actively work against the project	which may result in project goals not being met on time as well as important information not being available
Because the customer is completely dependent on the supplier for technical knowledge about the application software and underlying software tools	opportunities for a more satisfactory solution could be missed	causing both the customer and their customers to accept unnecessarily reduced functionality
Because the customer plans to rewrite the application and bring it in-house within 12 to 18 months	cancellation of the project might occur	causing a schedule delay of more than two months
International		
People from eight countries are working on this project and most are not attuned to working with different cultures	which may cause misinterpretation of language or cultural issues	resulting in low morale and the need to increase training and team building
The current economic climate has many changes in the value of the currencies in use on the project	which could cause a large fluctuation in the value of the dollar	posing the risk of additional costs

Risk Categories and Lists of Risks

Cause	Risk	Effect
People from eight countries are working on this project and most are not attuned to working with different cultures	which could cause a change in foreign and domestic laws or missed laws	resulting in inadvertent illegal activity
Due to problems with immigration	one or more traveling project team members may be delayed or not allowed to proceed	which could cause a delay in the project
Due to customs requirements and restrictions	key software or equipment may be delayed in transit	which could cause a delay in the project
Due to differences in holiday schedules	the full project team may not be available at certain times	causing rework
Due to language requirements	the number of qualified suppliers may be lower	which could result in a project team of lower quality
Due to different business practices	the system selected for the US-based operations may not be adequate for the international business units	which could result in a poor quality system or an increase in project duration and cost due to higher programming requirements
Due to poor flight availability	traveling project team members may not be available for a full working week	which could result in a delay to the project
Due to purchasing hardware from multiple international sources	incompatibility could result	which could cause a delay to the project while obtaining the correct component(s)
Due to poor e-mail or voice communication (slow delivery or poor quality) internationally	key communications may be delayed	which could result in project slippage
Due to language differences	the definition of roles and responsibilities for the project team may not be fully understood	which could result in failure to select the best resources
Due to not understanding international labor laws and regulations	improper procedures may be followed	which could result in delay of resource availability

Risk Categories and Lists of Risks

Cause	Risk	Effect
Due to terrorism	facilities could be damaged or project team members may be killed or kidnapped	resulting in a delay to the project and/or increased cost
Due to language differences	the project manager may not adequately communicate requirements or schedules to project team members	which could result in a delay to the project or decreased system quality
Project Management		
Lack of funding has caused a mandatory 50-hour week for months with additional overtime to 50 hours being very common	which could cause rapid staff burnout for this high-demand industry skill	causing staff to burn out and leave the project
Due to no written information on past projects	additional time collecting data may be needed	resulting in less time being spent completing work
Due to a reorganization	people may spend time discussing the effect of the reorganization	resulting in project delay
Due to management announcing that a deliverable is be released on a certain date	employees might be pulled off their current work and another project might be started to meet that deliverable	causing delays in the project or dissatisfaction with management or loss of motivation and additional rework once the deliverable is met
Due to the existence of separate design and implementation teams	not all of the business areas are involved in determining the scope of work for the project	which could result in the system not being able to address all of the business requirements
Due to the existence of separate design and implementation teams, and because the implementation team has not been able to comment on the design	some of the design might not be able to be implemented in the real world	leading to changing scope very late in the project

Risk Categories and Lists of Risks

Cause	Risk	Effect
Due to the existence of two companion projects	there may be a lack of coordination between the projects	causing some misalignment of requirements and design
Because there is no comprehensive communications management plan	serious problems could linger at a lower level of project responsibility than they should	delaying the project and increasing stress on both customer and supplier teams
Neither management nor sales has told the customer that some of their requirements may not be met within their deadline	which may mean the customer might not adjust the requirements	resulting in lower profit on the project as the team adds the requirements using overtime or with additional resources not included in the original proposal
The team members are scattered throughout the country	which may cause communication to suffer	resulting in productivity being sacrificed
The evaluation time for tools/ methods is shorter than the company has ever had to deal with in the past	though this schedule has been approved by management, the reality of the timeline might not be adequate	resulting in delays
Quality		
Because there is no quality management plan	problems are likely to be discovered and solved after testing rather than being resolved early in the development life cycle	resulting in the potential for a release with significant known bugs
Because many of the rules to enforce referential integrity in the database are actually implemented in the application code	some table rows could be changed or deleted incorrectly	resulting (best case) in rework and (worst case) in the loss of customer data

Risk Categories and Lists of Risks

Cause	Risk	Effect
Because the supplier relies completely on the customer for many design decisions (e.g., web page navigation)	the interface might not be designed as well as it could be	reducing customer satisfaction
Because the design document refers to specific numbers (e.g., 0–120 days) without explaining the relationships among the numbers	at least one business rule could be misimplemented or an inappropriate dependency could be created	such that the application could not behave as it should
Because the supplier has no means for evaluating performance impact before the software is deployed	existing features that could share code with new features may not share code	resulting in slower user response times
Because this supplier/customer relationship and this application have a history of overrunning development schedules, resulting in significantly shortened systems and acceptance testing	this project could encounter the same pressure for reduced testing cycles	resulting in a deployed product of lower quality than desired
Because previous releases have had a high number of bugs and misimplemented features	the supplier may conclude that this is acceptable to the customer	and fail to improve the processes that can be shown to cause such poor results
Due to market changes or other priorities	the sponsor/fund source may run out of money or refuse to continue funding	which could lead to an abandoned project and/ or inability to deliver all functionality
Due to bad processes or other issues	historical data may be inaccurate and polluted	which would lead to bad system output and/or lowered quality of deliverables and low user acceptance

© 2010 RMC Publications, Inc. • (952) 846-4484 • info@rmcproject.com • www.rmcproject.com

Risk Categories and Lists of Risks

Cause	Risk	Effect
Due to bad communication or training or management	the system may work as needed but the process changes that need to occur may not take place	resulting in low user acceptance and negative impact on perception of the system and project team
Due to bad planning	the user/data volume may be greater than initial expectations	which may lead to slow service, dissatisfied customers, impact on network bandwidth, hardware (and therefore on other applications), system crash, etc.
Due to postponing quality assurance until the end of the project	a substantial amount of rework may be discovered at the end	which could lead to a slip in the delivery date
There have been three separate instances where the backup/disaster recovery mechanism failed. Though that system is being investigated, no changes will occur before the current project is completed	which may lead to failure in the system backup/disaster recovery mechanism	causing a loss of programming code or data structures and test data developed to date
Standards not yet agreed upon for the technologies are being used	despite the fact that new standards may emerge after project completion	leading to additional project work later to adhere to new technical or industry standards
Resources		
Infrequent meetings of the capital approval committee	may cause delays on capital spending approvals	resulting in purchase delays of computer hardware for testing and production installation, resulting in project delays
Due to the team not being co-located	some work might be duplicated	requiring additional work to determine which work should be completed

Risk Categories and Lists of Risks

Cause	Risk	Effect
Because the supplier intends to use the same resources on other projects	these resources may not be available when anticipated	and the projected delivery date could be missed
Because the supplier has significant staff turnover	new resources may have to be sourced and brought up to speed during development	which could add at least a month to the project and possibly much more
Because the supplier has been downsizing for many years and continues to do so	the supplier may choose to reassign resources among its projects	which could involve a substantial schedule delay as new resources are sourced and prepared. (Note: resources could include manager or physical space or work locations, etc., not just individual team members)
Due to having staff that is not properly trained in the development toolset	slow progress may occur	which could lead to missing the launch date
Due to overloading a critical resource	dissemination of vital information may be blocked	leading to poor decisions
Due to a critical senior-level resource becoming unavailable	the cross-training of the junior-level resources may not occur	which may lead to an ineffective team
Due to stakeholders not buying in	a gap between what is critical and what is not may occur	which could lead to a no-go decision for launch
Scope		
Because the supplier did not create a prototype of many of the user interface changes	some customer-expected functionality could be missing completely and not discovered to be missing until acceptance testing	resulting in last minute overtime

Risk Categories and Lists of Risks

Cause	Risk	Effect
Because the supplier plans to replace a core piece of the application (the e-mail engine) with an unidentified software package at the same time this release is being developed	reliability or scalability or other unforeseen technical issues	may impact the schedule for this release
Because the supplier has a good understanding of the application software but a poor understanding of the customer's business	the supplier could make undocumented assumptions about the business logic that could prove to be erroneous	and have to be re-implemented
Because the development team is in Maryland and the customer is in San Diego	problems discovered during coding and unit testing	could result in activity delays as business logic issues are discussed via telephone
Acceptance criteria for the project are unclear	which could lead to difficulty in obtaining sign-off on key milestones	resulting in additional work that is beyond the cost budget
Security		
Due to the high demand for a company's work, it has experienced more security breaches than most companies	which may lead to a security breach in one section of the company	delaying the project in order to assure management that there are no security breaches in their project
Supplier Risks		
A project requiring the involvement of small software suppliers in a fast-changing economy	may be at risk if the softwaresupplier is sold off by the parent company during or after software purchase negotiations	resulting in the project being stopped, or other, less optimally suited products being purchased instead, or the project being delayed due to changes in contract negotiations
Due to the number of suppliers	team turnover and personnel changes could slow the project	and cause deliverable completion to be late

Cause	Risk	Effect
Due to entrenched suppliers	the project might have to use older technology for development	which could delay the project and/or reduce the quality of the product and require additional unplanned maintenance
Since the software supplier's security does not conform to company policies	custom development could be required and the complexity of development will still need to be specified. If customization becomes overly complex	slippage may occur in delivery dates with increased customization costs or a security policy may need to be compromised
Because a supplier could merge with another supplier	products may not be available	causing a need to redesign the project
Because the supplier has no established design methodology	there is a high risk that multiple design cycles could be required before coding begins	which could cause development to start late, leading to overly optimistic activity durations in order to provide a customer-acceptable completion target
The software being used on this project has been around for a few years in a market where there are a lot of new products being released	which may cause a supplier to stop supporting the software	leading to change in architecture or approach
Because the supplier refers to the design as a "living document" and has no formal change control process	features could be added that the customer prefers not to have	resulting in decreased customer satisfaction
Because the supplier has been experiencing weakening financials for many years	the supplier, which is a division of a much larger company, could be sold to another company	causing substantial team disruption and problems including missed schedules and lost resources

Risk Categories and Lists of Risks

Cause	Risk	Effect
Because the supplier does not conduct internal design reviews	design elements may not be discovered until development is substantially complete	causing rework and/or retesting and schedule slippage
Because the supplier is inexperienced with code walkthroughs or other practices that reduce defects	bugs may not be detected until installation	increasing the time and cost required to fix any bugs found
Because the supplier's team has no previous experience with formal risk management	it is highly likely that workarounds could be employed for problems that could have been avoided or mitigated or transferred to another supplier	resulting in lowered morale and/or missed deadlines and higher cost and lower quality
Because the supplier has no formal process to relate application changes to the database schematic design	database design problems could be discovered late in the development process	requiring rework to fix the deficiencies
Because the supplier uses only a pure waterfall model for development	opportunities for fast tracking the project may be missed	thereby not taking advantage of time savings that could accrue to the project
Technology		
Because the software product is relatively new and the design technology may not have been proven	several releases may be required before the product is stable	which could lead to functional or technical defects
Because the software product has never been rolled out on a centralized platform with the volume of data required by the customer	it has not been proven that the product can scale to the required size	and additional resources may be required to performance tune the databases and from the software supplier to optimize code
Because software to be purchased is in beta	the date of final production release could slip	and increase the number of errors and bugs found in the released product

Risk Categories and Lists of Risks

Cause	Risk	Effect
Due to not having a solid scope management process	scope creep could occur	causing additional work or rework and dissatisfied users
Due to the length of the project	current applications may be functionally obsolete before rollout is complete	diminishing the business impact of the implementation
Due to the diverse stakeholders' difficulty in reaching consensus between standardization and local variation	the effectiveness of the implementation could be reduced	causing project delays
The project being implemented is in two business areas that share data for decision making	and piloting the system in one business area may cause a disruption to another business area	impacting their ability to carry out basic business functions
The software development project relies on data feeds from many legacy systems. Any area that cannot provide resources (people or test regions) to support this project	could introduce critical threads in the project path	and potential delays
Implementation of a new software product may cause increased demand on the help desk	which may cause long delays and inadequate answers to questions and possible use of a deployment team to answer questions	causing a possible delay to additional rollouts
The hardware team is replacing terminals with workstations	but if the deadline for workstation rollout is not met	temporary equipment may need to be rolled out or the project delayed
Because of inconsistent quality of data from the legacy system	unclean data may be converted to the new system	which may lead to substantial post-conversion clean up or distrust of the system by the user community

Risk Categories and Lists of Risks

Cause	Risk	Effect
Due to insufficient training or user acceptance	the system may not be properly used	and may result in insufficient accumulated data to support expected benefits
Due to an unstable development environment	loss of source code may occur	which would lead to duplication of work
Due to a poor understanding of the underlying data	an inconsistent design of the applications may occur	which would lead to a complete failure to meet the business requirements
Due to poor system architecture	a failure to meet the required performance metrics may occur	which could lead to a significant change in the system design
Due to a lengthy rollout of servers	technology advances may render the servers to be outdated by the project completion	which may lead to a need to purchase an alternative server before the project completion. Additionally, testing could be required to certify a second server
Because some of the key application modules are bumping against an absolute limit for source code size	some modules cannot be modified as anticipated	and could have to be restructured and/or rewritten
The client has been assured that new technology will meet their needs	but failure to realize the limits of technology	may cause extra costs to acquire new technology when the first fails
A newly created system has been in demand by excited end users for over a year	and due to overwhelming positive user response to the system	the application may crash when more users log on to the system than originally anticipated

Risk Categories and Lists of Risks

Cause	Risk	Effect
Information Technology and Telecommunications		
Environmental		
A project is being installed in a building with original electrical work from 1920	which could lead to a loss of power during business hours	resulting in customers not being able to have their service request processed within the 20 minute requirement
This project is being done in an area of the US that has frequent hurricanes	inclement weather and/or hurricanes could occur	which could result in lost time and damage to the infrastructure
Due to a facility power outage	air conditioning failure may occur	which would lead to shutdown of data center hardware due to hardware cooling requirements
Due to a facility power outage	a lighting failure may occur	which would lead to shutdown of data center due to an unsafe working environment
Due to an electrical grid failure	loss of power to the computer room's raised floor may occur	which could lead to lack of availability of customer facing systems
Equipment		
A server failure	could result in one hour's worth of transactions not being available on the fail-over server	causing the end user to revert to manual processes
If the supplier's release date is late	the retirement of the leased hardware could be delayed	resulting in added expense
If the customer does not support a request for additional equipment on the project	there may be an inadequate budget for equipment	resulting in restricting the development team's ability to perform work in parallel
Due to inadequate design	the network equipment may be greatly over-engineered	causing unneeded expenditures

Cause	Risk	Effect
Due to inadequate protocol design	the local and wide area networks may be congested with non-essential traffic	resulting in slow response to the user
A project involving complicated, tied-together networks	could be affected if modifications were made to any part of the network	resulting in one modification requiring changes on 10 systems
Due to inattention to "single point of failure"	the network could malfunction	resulting in large outages of communications
Process		
If the data conversion process fails prior to the 0900 Sunday production start time	the customer's service request could be delayed and a backlog could occur	resulting in extended work hours
Because service account managers may fail to use the agreed upon templates	internal communications could fail	causing a stakeholder to not be informed of a change that might affect their department
While recovery procedures for backed-up data are adequate (though more than Y of the stakeholders have identified this as an area of concern)	recovery procedures may fail anyway	resulting in extreme loss of data for the company that may not be able to be retrieved
If invitees fail to participate in the review of account management templates	it could be perceived as not having a high priority	thus sending a message of unimportance
If the fail-over server is moved during normal business hours versus a weekend move and a fault occurs in the production environment	production could be at risk of not having an equivalent environment	causing unforeseen production problems
If the IP address for production servers changes and it is not communicated to the other suppliers one week prior to the cutover	transactions could not process as expected the morning of the cutover	resulting in available resources not being used

Risk Categories and Lists of Risks

Cause	Risk	Effect
If the physical server move is not completed by Sunday at 0900	a production fail-over equivalent may not be available	and orders will not process within the defined 20 minute service level
If management does not support the testing activity	delaying all test activity until development is complete	the result could be components that do not meet quality standards
If project executing starts while plan project development is still in progress,	poor communications and/or poorly defined project scope or unverified scope could result	and delay in implementation
Project Management		
Because the client's motto is, "we know it all"	risks might be ignored to reduce the price	resulting in cost overruns that will have to be dealt with later
Extra documentation on a project is required in order to coordinate all activities of the team	causing a failure to properly record and report all project information	resulting in work being redone, sometimes several times
All levels of management do not buy into the project improvement effort	and this project could be perceived as "just another project that could eventually go away"	causing the effort to fail
The objectives of the software process improvement project are not communicated and understood by all stakeholders	causing communications to breakdown	leading to the failure of the quality improvement project
The software process improvement team's metrics are not regularly tracked and communicated to all stakeholders	which could result in a communications breakdown	resulting in lost momentum of the software improvement engine

Cause	Risk	Effect
Due to change controls (with new requirements) being defined late in the development phase	development of the changes may extend past the planned implementation date	which may delay the planned implementation date and also increase costs
Inability to measure project objectives (e.g., increased revenue)	may undervalue the contributions of the project	the overall program would not be seen as a success by the business
Changes to user requirements after analysis	if accepted via change management process	could impact subsequent project milestones
Due to not reviewing the lessons learned documentation from a previous similar project	certain previously identified constraints may not be considered	which may impact the project's quality, scope, schedule, and cost
Due to untimely responses from the stakeholders regarding the requirements issues	the analysis (requirements-gathering) phase may be delayed	which may lead to a delayed project schedule and software implementation date
Due to not properly identifying the appropriate stakeholders at the beginning of the project	certain information may not be available for project planning	which may result in a low quality implementation
Due to the increased number of projects being implemented throughout the year	projects may have to share implementation dates and combine their software packages	which may lead to multiple projects being backed out of production even if only one of them has a defect
Due to not obtaining approvals on various documentation or phase exits	the project team may not be able to move forward with planned milestones	which may delay the project schedule and planned software implementation
Due to a team's software release in a related application occurring on the same weekend as another team's project	the release could be delayed	leading to the insufficient time to test this project with the version of the related application that could be in production

Cause	Risk	Effect
Resources		
If insufficient resources are allocated during the customer test phase	a testing objective might not be met	resulting in a delay in production implementation
Due to poor planning in obtaining personnel resources to support various project phases	resources may not be available when needed	which could negatively impact the project schedule and planned software implementation date
If the proposed new hire for the software engineering process group is not given the proper authority	his/her effort could be undermined	and he/she could fail, as could the project objective
The company is currently reviewing the benefits programs it offers to employees	which may lead to major changes in benefits programs	causing decreased employee morale and productivity
Due to organizational decisions to utilize offshore suppliers	subject matter experts may be replaced	which may lead to longer development time for the project and decreased quality
Due to more and more projects requiring internet-capable test environments	internet-capable test environments are not always available when needed	causing a delay in the proposed project schedule
Due to new technology and software languages being utilized for a particular project	the project team software developers may not have the hands-on knowledge to develop the software efficiently	which may lead to poor quality and/or a delayed project schedule and a delay in the planned software implementation
Due to lack of participation by stakeholders in the design review	the design may not accurately depict the intent of the requirements from the stakeholders	which may lead to poor quality

Risk Categories and Lists of Risks

Cause	Risk	Effect
Due to lack of participation and focus by the stakeholders defining the requirements	gaps may exist in the requirement definitions	which may result in a low-quality implementation
Due to stakeholders' lack of education on the development methodology	phase containment may be impaired	which could most likely cause low quality and drive higher cost for the project. (Phase containment relates to completing the requirements prior to design and completing design prior to build or completing build prior to test, etc.)
Due to lack of required participation by one technology team	the analysis phase may not be completed as scheduled	which may cause a delay in the project schedule and additional costs
Scope		
Due to not completely understanding business requirements	the functional and technical evaluation groups might have their recommendations changed by upper management	resulting in distrust and confusion
Tool requirements never confirmed by the user base	could result in changing scope	causing an unknown amount of rework and delay
Lack of communication between X and Y	could result in change of scope and/or rework	and delayed implementation
Due to a recent reorganization and huge growth, a substantial number of new employees could be affected by a current project	all stakeholders may not be aware of the requirements definition	which may result in scope creep that impacts the end users' desired implementation date

Cause	Risk	Effect
Suppliers		
The references for the supplier were never checked	and misrepresentation (by supplier representatives) of the capability of the supplier products used as components in total solution may occur	leading to poor performance of the final solution
The project makes use of many underlying applications that the supplier has not been required to check for defects	which may lead to lack of supplier capacity to correct defects in underlying applications	resulting in delayed project completion
Due to exceedingly defective software delivered by supplier #1	additional software deliveries to correct defects may lead to supplier #2's inability to complete testing on time	which could jeopardize the ultimate project delivery date
Due to insufficient knowledge transfer of requirements to suppliers, consultants, suppliers, or staff working the engineering details of an IT project	detailed knowledge may be overlooked or lacking	resulting in incomplete design efforts
Technology		
Due to insufficient software application understanding	it may not be feasible for the applications developers to determine if the new hardware or operating system and software support systems could operate on new architectures/hardware and operating systems and the resultant costs to migrate from the old systems to the new systems could become prohibitive	thus causing drastic increases in time and costs required to move applications

Risk Categories and Lists of Risks

Cause	Risk	Effect
Customers do not have time to embrace the tool	and as time to accept the tool is short	it could result in rejection and/or delay in implementation
Due to new technology and software languages being utilized for the project	the project team software developers may not have the knowledge to accurately estimate the effort	which may cause a misrepresentation of funding requirements to the stakeholders
A web-based tracing tool requires a specific program to operate	and no clear plan exists on how to deploy this program	which means Activity L could be delayed beyond its float if the deployment takes more than five days
The customer has required desktop computers that have a unique configuration	but there have been technical problems installing multiple software packages	which may require the purchase of additional hardware
Due to insufficient design effort by the software technicians	the software may not be effectively developed	which may lead to poor quality
Due to requesting development support from multiple interfacing systems	certain systems may not be able to support the planned schedule due to resource or test environment constraints	which may lead to a delay in project schedule and the planned software implementation date
The software supplier has a history of coming out with new software releases without prior announcement	which may cause the need to evaluate the software for functionality on this project	which may impact resource availability and schedule for planned releases
Due to incorrect female connectors at either end of the physical cable	data transmission may become unreliable	which may cause major network outages
Due to non-data rated base cords (cord between PC and data wall jack)	data transmission may become unreliable	which may cause PC to function erratically or not at all
Due to poor routing of data cables beneath the desk	the data network may be adversely affected	which may cause total outage of the network segment

Cause	Risk	Effect
Due to poor quality in cabling in any of the disciplines	the network may become unstable	which may cause unexpected and erratic data transmission
Due to poor cabling marking	tracing cabling becomes labor intensive	which may cause excess expenditures
Due to poor cabling design	printers and other devices may not be installed	which may cause excess expense in installation costs
Due to non-standardization of network cards (NIC)	the maintenance of the network is greatly increased	which may cause an increase in installation and maintenance costs
Due to lack of standard replacement cards	non-standard cards could be installed in the network	which will greatly increase the maintenance efforts. Solution: Specify a 5% spare parts complement in NIC cards
Training and testing may need to occur during the same period of time	and because employees might be trained to use methods that change during testing	this may impact the training and support schedules
Many projects being undertaken at the same time will need to make use of IT infrastructure for training, testing and production	but equipment may not be available (hardware/ software/ DB instances)	which could result in missed deadlines and delayed delivery
Deliverables from a preceding project on which a company is dependant, as well as its future releases, may not be what was expected	which could result in an inability to deliver on planned future functionality	and could create an additional work effort on this project to bridge the gap between the two
Testing		
If the prior release testing is not complete by the user before the next release is made available	the planned install for the new release could be delayed	resulting in scheduling conflicts for the test team

Risk Categories and Lists of Risks

Cause	Risk	Effect
If the supplier's test objectives are not met by the end of the month	the customer test team could be delayed	resulting in idle time for testers
Due to testing/implementing "global software" for multiple international markets	one market (country) may incur a defect during test or implementation	which may delay the implementation in the other markets
If the supplier's response time to issues identified during nighttime testing is more than thirty minutes	the nightly test objective could be jeopardized	resulting in a schedule slippage for the dependent activity
Due to major reorganization changes occurring within the testing team, there are new testing resources and a new set of roles and responsibilities	which may lead to a delay in the schedule for testing	thus delaying the implementation of the project
Due to volume testing and functionality testing occurring simultaneously (to ensure the project is delivered on time)	functional defects may remain	resulting in the need to repeat volume tests if subsequent software changes to correct the defects are required
International		
Culture		
Due to a lack of understanding a country's customs	a project manager may unintentionally offend the customer	which may result in difficulty managing the relationship
Confusion about team member roles and responsibilities in a multi-national team	may lead to internal conflict and confusion	resulting in decreased productivity and a breakdown of a "team" environment
Not understanding the culture as it pertains to women	a female project manager assigned to a project may find she is not considered an equal	thereby compromising her ability to effectively manage projects or influence decision makers

Cause	Risk	Effect
If attention is not given to communicating	conversations and documentation may be misinterpreted	leading to incorrect actions or decisions being made that could change scope, increase costs, extend timeframes, and/or cause a project to fail or be cancelled
Making the assumption that people from other countries view business situations and opportunities the same as the project manager's home country	could cause the project manager to lose perspective of the customer's views	and cause the project manager to be alienated from the customer
The project manager is perceived to be biased	which may lead to a decrease in his team's continuity and productivity	which could jeopardize the project and eventually lead to dismantling the team
Not knowing the social, economic, and/or political makeup of a country or region	leads to accepting projects that require team personnel to go onsite in areas that place them in potential danger	which may cause strife and/or loss of members of the team
Failure to understand languages used in different regions of a country	may result in localizing software to the wrong dialect	causing a major rework resulting in additional costs and expanded timeframes

© 2010 RMC Publications, Inc. • (952) 846-4484 • info@rmcproject.com • www.rmcproject.com

Cause	Risk	Effect
Additional Risks: Culture		
• Missed opportunities to promote social interaction between team members away from work • The language of the host country cannot be typed on computers • The wrong language is used on documents • Not enough workers familiar with the project language or with the necessary technical skills are available • No software is available in the language of the host country • An incentive plan was created from the perspective of the home country, resulting in ineffective motivation of team members from other countries • The team is unprepared for the different languages spoken in the host country • The project expects continuity of quality from location to location in the host country when in fact there is none		
Currency		
Due to not understanding the role currency conversion plays in a project	the transaction based systems may use incorrect calculations	causing the system to fail user acceptance testing
Additional Risks: Currency		
• The conversion rate between the two currencies changes • To control possibility of loss, the supplier takes out arbitrage hedge or insurance • During the in-country effort, the customer's country experiences high inflation • Local government laws prevent transfer of monies to home country • Local government prevents profit being sent to home country		
Environmental		
The equipment to be used on the project has not been tested to work under the project's specific conditions	which may cause equipment to not work in the climate	which may lead to the need to do more work manually
Additional equipment is needed for the climate	but that equipment is not available	leading to extra cost and import duty to have it shipped overnight
The correct immunizations are not received	resulting in sickness	which leads to low morale

Risk Categories and Lists of Risks

Cause	Risk	Effect
The country's infrastructure is different than the home country	which may lead to damage from storms that would not be considered normal	causing loss of equipment
The country's infrastructure is different than the home country	which may lead to interruption of electrical power or brown-outs for part of the day or year	causing project delays
The transportation time was calculated based on good road conditions	but poor road conditions exist in the host country	leading to a need to find faster transport at higher cost
The schedule was calculated based on distance and not terrain	and staff encountered large rivers without bridges that needed to be crossed	causing delay or additional expense to go via the planned route
Ethics		
Secrets and property being stolen and sold to competitors	may lead to an accusation of fraud	causing time spent in lawsuits
There is a threat of fraudulent practices if greater amounts of money are not paid for the same amount of work	which may lead to the arrest of some of the project team for paying bribes	causing project delays
The economy of the host country is poor with many people living at the poverty level	causing a theft of property when legal recourse is limited	which could lead to additional cost to protect the remaining property
No research was done to determine if a license was required	leading country officials to ask to see the license	causing delay, loss of face, and additional costs
The team did not put a special clause in the contract conditioning delivery and contract on approval and receipt of export license	which may lead to the export license not being approved	causing a default of the contract

Cause	Risk	Effect
The team has never had to apply for an export license before	and may make a mistake by applying to the wrong agency	causing delay
After delivery is complete, it is discovered that warranty starts did not get a separate warranty license	which may lead to an inability to export items	causing the need to find another company who can provide those services in that country
If warranty export license is not renewed	it could lead to an inability to export items	causing the need to find another company who can provide those services in that country
The laws in the host countrycontradict the laws in the US	causing a constant need for legal review of actions	which could lead to delay
Additional Risks: Foreign Corrupt Practices Act		

- Payment is made to secure contract
- Payment is made to influence a company's position
- Payment is made to facilitate the performance of a contract, but can be interpreted to be for other purposes
- No specific audit trail is available on payments to foreign officials
- The company does not have explicit policies and procedures on FCPA
- Foreign competitors make payments to foreign officials to influence decisions
- This office makes payments to foreign officials to influence decisions
- Did not have agents and representatives sign company's FCPA and code of ethics policy and procedures

Legal Standards		
The laws of different countries are not understood by the team	which may cause it to develop products that do not meet the requirements of those laws	leading to project failure
Not taking a country's electrical standards into consideration when configuring hardware	may cause equipment to be configured for the wrong voltage	resulting in pushing out the project and significant additional costs for reconfiguring and reshipping

Cause	Risk	Effect
When importing team members from other countries to work on projects, the project manager must understand the host country's immigration laws pertaining to temporary work permits and sponsorship	otherwise, team members may find themselves in violation of government laws	and be required to leave before their work has been completed
Dimensions are given in metrics but are incorrectly converted to standard American equivalent	which may cause the equipment to not fit in the space allocated	thereby increasing costs for retrofitting and delaying the project
When shipping routes and procedures for clearing customs are not understood	shipments may take longer than expected to reach the customer	resulting in project delays and pushing out the project timeline
The import laws of the host country are being updated	which may lead to not being allowed to import into the host country because the product violates local environmental laws	which may lead to project failure
Due to the changing political nature of decision in the host country	it may be discovered that the company is responsible for recycling the product at no cost to the host country	resulting in a need to add scope of work to the project
Failing to take the international dateline into consideration when coordinating events between two countries	may lead to activity completion being early or late and/or deliverables arriving a day early or a day late	causing the need to perform acceptance testing before we are ready

Risk Categories and Lists of Risks

Cause	Risk	Effect
Additional Risks: Letter of Credit		

- During final stages of negotiation, a too low contract value may be accepted
- Did not negotiate the use of a corporate guarantee
- Customer destroys equipment
- Did not specify in the contract what is covered and what is not covered by warranty
- Did not specify who pays for shipping
- Did not specify turnaround time for repairs
- Did not get a warranty export license
- Did not specify payment with partial shipments
- Was not careful with all the details of the L/C
- Upon requesting payment from the bank, the bank found details of the invoice in error
- The invoicing is late for various reasons and the L/C expires
- L/C is not drawn on the company's local bank
- L/C is drawn on a bank in the customer's own country
- The bank is under governmental control
- Did not have the customer pay for bank charges
- The supplier wants to be paid in local currency

Manufacturing
Additional Risks: Customer

- The customer sells though their stock more quickly than anticipated and material cannot be obtained from suppliers fast enough to refill the customer's stock
- Lack of consensus (supplier and customer) on the implementation plan

Cause	Risk	Effect
Additional Risks: Facilities and Equipment		

- Space constraints/ physical plant limitations
- Mismatch of device's planned capacity versus reality
- Equipment may not fit into the available area
- Equipment is delivered on a truck without a power liftgate
- Facility may not have a level loading dock
- Doorways and hallways are too narrow for the equipment
- Equipment can't be brought to the appropriate room
- Equipment must be disassembled and reassembled using additional resources and time
- Equipment damaged in transit from manufacturer
- Replacement equipment must be manufactured and shipped

Additional Risks: Legal/Regulatory

- Because this line of products needs to be registered with the government for sale in this market, registration delays could delay the product launch

Additional Risks: Miscellaneous

- Supplier fire
- Raw material prices increase
- Tool comes in out of print or out of scope
- Raw material does not come in
- Drawings are not used or are not clear
- Detail on drawings not clear
- Internal scheduling problems with support departments
- Measurement lab equipment or process malfunction
- Research and development does not believe in project management
- There is no one project manager managing the research and development function
- Loss of project due to competition/market pressures
- Union problems
- Capacity problems
- Product is delivered to customer but does not perform
- Market passes the company by
- Management makes a decision not to accept the product when it is ready
- Customer cancels out or makes significant design changes that take the project off course
- Process problems

Cause	Risk	Effect
• Currency fluctuations • Government regulations • Economic conditions • Space limitations • Product weighs too much • Product is the wrong color/hue • Customer does not accept deliverables • Patent violation • Components interact negatively with each other • Components react negatively with other materials used by the customer • Materials too porous • Patent fear (customer) • Degradation of components • Competition offers a product that is the next generation after our company's product • Supplier does not produce to the right specifications • Supplier makes material substitutions • Need for rapid prototype • Equipment breaks		
Quality		
A high turnover rate in the production	may result in a lack of consistency in the output	causing more product returns
A strike or work stoppage affects the shipping company	which may result in suppliers receiving late delivery	resulting in a lack of time to perform inspection
If stability testing fails in a particular product/category	approximately $_____ in sunk costs may have to be spent	and the product may not be able to launch "as is"
If safety testing fails in a particular product/ category	approximately $_____ in sunk costs may have to be spent	and the product may not be able to launch "as is"
Since products are ordered prior to safety/stability testing being complete	suppliers might not meet customer's needs	and the customer could be liable for sunk costs of supplies valued at $_____ if product is determined to be unsaleable

Cause	Risk	Effect
Scope		
The original scope does not incorporate revised production levels	which may lead to planned equipment and throughput/capacity expectations not meeting the company's objectives	causing a redesign of the process
The equipment is scheduled to be retooled just before the project begins	but last minute mold/tooling changes	may result in unbudgeted costs
There are many senior stakeholders on this project who expect to be able to make changes to the project at any time	but design verification testing may show that proposed changes do not meet design expectations	resulting in the need for management to mitigate the scope of work with the senior stakeholders
Suppliers		
Due to aggressive project timing, finished goods could be ordered prior to safety testing being complete	but unsatisfactory safety testing results may occur, which could necessitate formula changes	and delay launch
Due to tight timing, QA inspections could be performed by the manufacturer utilizing the quality standards	leading to rejected product by the customer if standards are not well defined	resulting in wasted project efforts
Lead times and costs are pre-established because suppliers specified by the customer are being used. Although negations are in process	the customer may have provided inaccurate timing and/or costs	resulting in a launch that could be delayed
Supplies do not arrive in the expected packaging	requiring extra handling	and a delay of activity

Cause	Risk	Effect
Marketing and Sales		
Competition		
If brand positioning is not well defined and directed	cannibalization of the current brand could occur	thus reducing overall profitability of the program

Additional Risks: Competition

- Not recognizing our competitors
- Not recognizing competitors that solve the problem in different ways (candles versus incandescent lamps)
- Not making friends with competitors—giving them more reason than usual to work against us
- Bad-mouthing competitors makes us look bad/jealous/ insecure to our customers
- Not understanding our positioning in market (high/mid/low) and not understanding the penetration and competition strategies for those segments

Additional Risks: Distribution

- We may not think enough about how product will be distributed
- The cost of distribution is not researched
- The cost of supporting distributors may be underestimated
- The cost of finding distributors may be underestimated
- We may not know enough about specific distributors/partners
- We may not understand the mechanics of distribution
- The need to make it easy to buy our product may be underestimated
- Because we do not understand what motivates distributors, they could choose the easiest way to make their money

Additional Risks: Product Development

- Underestimating the costs of product development
- Underestimating the support costs of the product
- Not including enough G/A in the cost estimates of the product
- Overestimating profit margin
- Not understanding the problems that the customer wants solved with the product
- Not developing new products to sell to an existing customer base
- The customer may not make sure that the product team understands what they want to buy by letting them know what features of the product are going to "sell" the product and what things can "break the sale"

Risk Categories and Lists of Risks

Cause	Risk	Effect
Additional Risks: Sales		
• Overcommitment (technical and commercial) by sales • Ambiguity in specifications versus customer expectations • Mismatch in delivery committed by sales and delivery offered by product factory • Budget accuracy • Marketing changes may make the project unreasonable		
Additional Risks: Target Market/Customer		
• Not presenting our product to the market as we develop it to get their reaction • Not understanding our market's motivators • Overestimating the size of the target market • Not differentiating the market into segments (highest and lowest need/interest) • Not knowing the money available to purchase our product by our customer • Overestimating the need/desire for our product • Overestimating the penetration potential for our product		
New Product Development		
Competitors		
Due to schedules not being met	the competitor could beat the company to market with the product or service	which could result in decreased or increased sales of the product or service
Due to internal security leaks	information on the new product or service might be released to the competitor before the launch	which could lead to the competitor reaching the market first
Cost		
Due to inaccurate forecasting	the cost for the product or service might be higher than expected	which could lead to lower sales than projected
An increased cost of a key component	could lead to a product that does not achieve its production cost target	leading to project failure

Risk Categories and Lists of Risks

Cause	Risk	Effect
Environmental		
Due to concerned citizens	environmental/safety concerns could be raised about the product or service	which could lead to the product or service not being introduced
Equipment		
Due to equipment not being programmed properly	the product or service may not work properly	which could lead to customer dissatisfaction/ customer loss
Due to equipment not being physically available from the manufacturer	the product or service may not be available to the customer on the promised date	which could lead a to delay in the launch date and/or customer dissatisfaction/ customer loss
Due to inaccurate programming	the billing system might not be programmed properly	which could result in customer billing errors and customer dissatisfaction
Legal/Regulatory		
Due to ever-changing market-specific regulations, there is a probability that	certain formulations may not be acceptable for sale in specific markets	which may result in losing company revenue
Due to poor internal communication between departments	the product or service might conflict with contractual language	which could lead to legal action on the part of the customer
Marketing/Advertising/Sales		
Due to advertising materials not being available on schedule from an external supplier	the advertising materials may not be available for internal distribution	which could lead to a delay in the launch date of the product or service
Due to advertising materials—either internal or external—not being accurately created	the advertising materials could contain incorrect information	which could lead to customer or employee confusion, customer dissatisfaction, and/or customer legal action

Cause	Risk	Effect
Due to inaccurate forecasting	the anticipated demand might be higher or lower than forecasted	which could result in higher or lower sales than projected, leading to unavailability of product or service
Due to poor internal communication	advertising materials which appear in a foreign language might not be translated properly from English	which could lead to customer confusion/customer dissatisfaction
Due to poor employee morale toward the new product or service	employee sales efforts might not be maximized	which could lead to lower than projected sales
Due to inadequate/inaccurate training	the sales people might not be properly trained to sell the new product or service	which could result in lower than projected sales
Resources		
Due to inadequate/inaccurate training	the customer service staff might not be knowledgeable in the new product or service	which could lead to customer dissatisfaction
Due to a growing economy	key project staff might leave the company	which could lead to launch date delays
Due to inadequate/inaccurate training	the billing system staff may not be knowledgeable in the new product or service	which could lead to the billing system not being programmed properly
Due to internally-generated billing inserts not being available on schedule	the product or service may not be launched on schedule	which could lead to a delay in the launch date
Scope		
Due to poor internal communication	messages regarding a new product or service might not appear on the bill itself	which could lead to a delay in the launch date
Suppliers		
A single supplier for key components	may lead to non-availability or not meeting requirements	and cause project failure

Risk Categories and Lists of Risks

Cause	Risk	Effect
Pharmaceutical		
Additional Risks: Culture		
• Countries do not have the same immunization practices • Countries do not have the same clinical practices • Lack of awareness of country-specific regulatory constraints • Cultural influences affect the interpretation of standard operating procedures • Extended summer vacations in host country limit the availability of key decision makers, resulting in a delay in making decisions • Extended summer vacations in the host country limit the availability of key decision makers, resulting in possibly speaking to someone who may not be qualified to speak on behalf of the country • Lack of adequate procedures in the host country's language		
Additional Risks: Government/Regulatory		
• A delay in completing the appropriate government forms may result in government intervention in this project		
Quality		
Due to receiving inappropriate mammalian cell or bacterial cell lines from the primary investigators	research and development experiments have to be repeated on new material	which could result in increased costs and delays of other projects due to resource constraints
Due to inattention to validation/calibration/periodic maintenance schedules	laboratories and/or buildings could be shut down by quality assurance as being non-compliant with FDA regulations	which could result in increased overheads and project delays
Due to inattention to packaging and shipping policies for biopharmaceuticals	products may be stored under inappropriate conditions in transit	which could lead to degradation of the material to the point where it is unusable
Due to inattention to cell bank inventory control	master cell banks could be depleted of their past recovery due to repeated manufacturing runs	which could lead to increased costs and schedule delays while the bank is redeveloped and qualified

Risk Categories and Lists of Risks

Cause	Risk	Effect
Due to the shipment of an incorrect cell line or organism from a primary investigator's laboratory	research and development work may be done on a line that does not produce the proper material	which could result in significant waste of materials and man-hours before the error is discovered
Due to DNA mutation and sequencing changes	a protein may become unusable for its intended purpose	which could lead to the modification or closure of a project already underway
Due to contamination in cell culture flow paths	harvesting of material may have to be interrupted prematurely	which could lead to the need for additional runs and delays in providing agreed-to deliverable amounts
Due to inattention to fastidious growth requirements	cell culture harvests could vary in the amount of final material yield	which could lead to the need for additional fermentation runs and delays in deliverables
Due to unexpected cell qualification testing results	cell lines could be disqualified from use for production	which could lead to delays in projects while new cell lines are developed
Due to slippages in periodic maintenance shutdown schedules for production facilities	equipment and utilities could malfunction and become unusable	which could lead to delays for repair and requalification time
Due to failure to develop process documentation in a timely fashion	quality assurance may not grant permission for work to go forward on the project	which could lead to significant delays in scheduling
Due to stability study testing results that are out of specification	an investigation must be launched	which could lead to the rejection of an entire lot of material by quality assurance

Cause	Risk	Effect
Additional Risks: Quality		
• An increase in timeframes is necessary because a decrease in quality is not an option • Lack of or inconsistent training by not following standard operating procedures • Poor site selection, resulting in the need to recruit additional sites with the appropriate patient population • Patient data is not correctly captured • Inability to use clinical request forms from some sites because of the quality of the sites		
Scope		
Due to abrupt changes in deliverable amounts as defined by the primary investigators	additional production runs may have to be scheduled	which could lead to delays for both the project in question and for the rest of the projects in the queue
Due to difficulties in the scale-up of either production or purification processes	projects could be deemed as being too large and/or complex for the facility to handle	which could result in project cancellations at short notice
Due to unexpected utilities failures in the manufacturing areas	additional environmental monitoring must take place	which could result in project delays or (if testing reveals results that are out of specification) quality assurance may not be able to release the product to the investigator
Due to failure to plan for adequate production runs to cover not only the deliverable but also release testing/stability studies/retains	there may not be enough final purified material to fulfill all requirements	which could result in increased cost and extended schedules to allow for additional production
Suppliers and Supplies		
Due to reallocations of funding within the program	scheduled projects may be cancelled/reprioritized/have their scope reduced	which could lead to raw materials waste through product expiration and unnecessary man-hours spent in repeated turnarounds

Cause	Risk	Effect
Due to an increase in supplier costs for testing or materials	project initiating may be delayed while new suppliers are identified	which could lead to delays in other projects in the queue. Costs could increase if the increased prices are accepted
Due to delays with outsource testing suppliers	batch production records and CMC sections may not be completed in a timely fashion	which could lead to significant delays in product release time
Time		
Due to failing to take into account the longest lead times for materials to be received and cleared for use	projects may not be able to move forward as planned	which could result in missed delivery milestones and slippage of other projects in the queue
Due to unexpected issues discovered during the research and development phase of projects	the length of time that projects remain in this stage could increase significantly	which could result in higher development costs/ delays in product delivery/ and postponement of other projects due to resource constraints
Service and Outsourcing		
Contract/Supplier		
Due to the contract using an identified exchange rate for invoice calculation	the exchange rate fluctuation	could lead to a financial gain/ loss during life of project
Due to the multiple locations of equipment fabrication	the risk of locating competent local resources may be identified	which could lead to increased costs of having to locate resources outside of planned usage
Due to a supplier not having required management systems in place at the time of execution	the requirements of the contract could be executed incorrectly	resulting in rework when the quality is checked by the buyer

Risk Categories and Lists of Risks

Cause	Risk	Effect
Due to the lack of support from both the customer and the supplier	the schedule data may not be provided in any confident level	which could lead to every supplier missing the scheduled end dates for the project
Due to the customer's supplier inexperience	the contract administration may be poorly managed	causing an increase in non-reimbursable expenses
The contact language is foreign	which may cause a complete misinterpretation of the contract	resulting in the supplier inadvertently defaulting on the contract
Due to a reluctance from the supplier to engage an experienced bilingual contract administration resource	the contract may not be understood by all parties	resulting in cost overruns and extreme difficulty in continued goodwill
Due to a lack of contract review meetings with the customer at the start of the project	there could be contradictions in contract interpretations by all project team members	resulting in an adversarial relationship with the customer
Cost		
Due to nonexistent invoicing systems for this type of project by the supplier	the amount of effort for invoicing may be underestimated	resulting in the work being done by another party at additional expense
Nonexistent invoicing systems for this type of project by supplier	may increase the effort for invoicing	leading to an overrun on the estimate for project controls and a negative perception by the supplier
Because a contingency reserve was not allowed on the budget and because of the unit rate makeup of the contract	there may be a huge increase in changes	leading to a large number of variances and change requests which could take over six months to get either authorized or approved

Cause	Risk	Effect
Due to ignoring sunk costs	large amortizable costs may accumulate	which could result in the project being canceled (i.e., future expenses per account period)
Due to users not being available on a timely basis	the costs of the project may rise	which could eventually lead to reduced business value
Due to any related project(s) mismanagement and/or other reasons for failure	the business value originally projected might not be attainable	resulting in the canceling of all related projects
Project Management		
The inexperience of the supplier	may lead to an overall risk of overruns to the expended man-hours for the project	which could result in a lack of commitment by management to push forward project management concepts
The "trying to please a difficult customer at any cost" mentality	may lead to additional hidden project changes	resulting in a risk of increased costs to the projects
The lack of empowerment from project management to execute project activities as required	may lead to a lack of attention to project management during execution	resulting in total confusion on the project
Due to the lack of communication and documentation flow	timely and pertinent project data may not be communicated within the project team	resulting in inconsistent reporting of data to both the customers' and suppliers' management
Due to no formal change management system agreed to by both the customer and supplier	the risk of not being able to invoice for perceived legitimate changes to the scope of work	may result in major cost overruns to the supplier
Due to no formal system to capture rework for the project	project costs may become overrun	resulting in unjustified increases in the man-hours expended versus budgeted

Risk Categories and Lists of Risks

Cause	Risk	Effect
Due to not having a destaffing plan	costs may overrun	resulting in a large number of personnel charging to the project after the project contract expiration date
Due to the supplier not utilizing any project management software	the high risk of cost and man-hour overruns may be evident but not be quantified	resulting in unreimbursed costs
A lack of a project charter	may lead to a lack of a common vision internally or with the customer	resulting in an argument over what is and is not in the scope of work
The team members' opinions are not listened to	leading to an incomplete scope of work	resulting in the need to re-scope the project
Due to previously selecting one project from another informally	the wrong projects may have been selected	resulting in wasted project efforts as projects are terminated
The difference in content between a meeting, the minutes, and the approval of the minutes	may lead to deviations in the team members' actions	resulting in small issues having a great effect on the project
Due to the analysis and design deliverables not having a predefined format	work may not integrate	resulting in rework on a huge scale
Due to lack of coordinating projects with one another	poor utilization of resources could occur	which may result in lowering the business value originally projected
Due to simultaneous learning curves	human resources may be less productive	resulting in higher costs and/or a lengthier project schedule
Due to simultaneous project implementations	resources might become more difficult to schedule	resulting in increasing costs and/or risks for all related projects
Due to avoiding what is thought to be "gold plating"	fitness of use shortcomings may appear	which could result in extra work to satisfy the customer's requirements

Cause	Risk	Effect
Due to ineffective scope decomposition	less than optimal implementation may occur	resulting in a lower business value
Utility		
Contract/Supplier		
The supplier was selected without competition	which may lead to poor supplier selection to perform the needed activity	resulting in additional management by the buyer of the seller's activities
Due to adverse company and supplier relationship	posturing may set in	resulting in claims/ litigationlose-lose situation
Due to minimal company experience on the contract type (EPC)	contract language may be inadequate	resulting in poor quality/ claims/ litigation/schedule delays
Due to poor company practices	suppliers may go bankrupt	resulting in lost schedule/ litigation/execution of the performance bond provisions
Due to public bidding statutes and too much legal department involvement	liquidated damages/incentives may not be allowed	resulting in unaligned supplier/project goals (costing money/ schedule/quality/etc.)
Due to the project manager going to project management class	the project team may end up walking out of the project area with sticky notes on their shoes	resulting in part of the WBS not being input into the budget or schedule. (Humor me!)
One of the suppliers could merge with another supplier	causing products to become unavailable	resulting in the need to cut scope of work and not meet requirements
Due to X supplier merging with Y supplier	support/maintenance for product Z may not be available	resulting in the need to replace the components
Demand		
Due to regional power demand dropping	oversupply of electricity to the market may occur, resulting in lower market prices	making it uneconomical to run the plant or cover debt payments adequately

Cause	Risk	Effect
Due to shortages in natural gas supplies and gas transportation infrastructure	natural gas prices may increase	making it uneconomical to operate the plant and cover debt payments
Due to the changing supplier market from seller to buyer	the contract price may vary significantly from estimates	resulting in the need to save money in other areas of the project to compensate
Environmental		
Due to poor appearance or noise from a new power plant	neighbors may complain	resulting in poor relationships/ negative publicity/depressed property values
Due to bad or cold weather	construction personnel may lose productivity	resulting in additional costs to make up schedule/additional personnel/lost schedule float
Due to intruding in a neighbor's backyard	adjacent landowners may require perks such as paved roads/air conditioners/ fences/ trees/etc.	resulting in additional project costs and "me too" requests
Due to completing a more detailed geotechnical survey of the site	pockets of poor soil may be found	resulting in additional foundations and special designs at more cost
Due to the river overflowing	the construction site and access roads may be inaccessible	resulting in schedule delays and equipment damage

Risk Categories and Lists of Risks

Cause	Risk	Effect
Additional Risks: License/Permits/Legal		
<ul><li>Improper interpretation of engineering or environmental work used to prepare application</li><li>Regulatory agency rule or guidance changes to increase volume of required information</li><li>Regulatory agency rule or guidance changes to reduce volume of required information</li><li>Environmental permits not approved for construction and operation</li><li>Re-zoning fees changing</li><li>State agency guidance changes since the plant was originally licensed 20 years ago</li><li>New industry guidance published that reduces level of site-specific engineering work needed</li><li>Anti-nuclear activists raise unexpected legal issues</li><li>New operating experience identifies new technical issue for license renewal</li></ul>		
Project Management		
Due to inexperienced people managing the project to build and operate the plant	the project and plant may be over budget/incorrectly configured/suffer from poor quality	and be late going commercial
Due to company management changes (like this never happens!)	management may change the company/project focus	schedule delays/ frustration on the team's part
Additional Risks: Regulatory		
<ul><li>Creative application format may make regulatory agency review more difficult</li><li>Regulatory agency may not adequately manage government suppliers involved in review of application</li><li>Regulatory agency may reject previously approved industry guidance on engineering work</li></ul>		
Resources		
Due to human performance issues	a major explosion could occur	leading to personal injury/ death/ equipment damage
Due to a limited labor force	an adequate supply of qualified construction personnel may not be available	resulting in more incentive pay/guarantees of longer work hours/more stay bonuses, all of which impact the project budget
Due to inexperience	operational staff may misoperate the plant	resulting in death/equipment damage/power outages

Cause	Risk	Effect
Due to key players leaving the team	areas of the project may go uncovered for a period	resulting in delays and eating float
Technology		
Inattention to recordkeeping	may lead to a poor plant record management system	resulting in the inability to defend choices if regulatory problems occur
Poor information technology support	may lead to an inappropriate database system used to manage the large volume of information collected	causing rework to transfer the data into a new system that is more appropriate for needs

Risk Categories and Lists of Risks

Contributors

Rita Mulcahy and RMC Project Management have asked people around the world to tell us how they identify risks and what risks they have identified. Clients of RMC, RMC employees, those who attended Rita Mulcahy's presentations, people from PMI chapters and from PMI's Risk Special Interest group, individuals, and companies participated for a total of over 141 responses. This information is included in the risk list and also included throughout this book.

Many people contributed who asked that their names not be listed. Others contributed anonymously. We would especially like to thank the following contributors:

Anthony D. Adams, PMP
Kamran Akhavan
O. Arivazhagan, PMP
Rajiv Arora, PMP
Patricia Auger
Rodney G. Baker
Marie Beeson, MBA, PMP
Koenraad Béroudiaux, PMP, Ph.D
Todd M. Boley
Carolyn Boyles, MBA, PMP
Brenda Breslin, PMP
Ken Bunzel
Edgar Hernández Cañas PMP
Peter R. Ciment, Ph.D., DLM
Dave Davis, PMP
Robert J. Etten
Louise Fortuna
Norman L. Gideon, PMP
Charles G. Hamilton, PMP
Richard Hawkins
Louise Holzlohner
George Hopman
Colin F. Howey, PMP, P.Eng, MBA, ISP
Kathleen L. Huyge, PMP
Asim Khan PMP
Khalid Ahmad Khan, PMP

Erik Kosasih, PMP, MBA
Janeen M. Levin, PMP
Moises Guedes Lima
Virginia Lowe
Michael A. Mala
Jerry Manas, PMP
Lisa A. McFarland
Kenneth C. Meyer, PMP
Christine C. Miller, PMP
Daniel E. Miller, PMP
Ronald Saborio Montero, PMP
Joseph F. Moore IV, P.E., PMP
Guillermo Morales
Robert Moyich, PMP
Rita Mulcahy, PMP
Marlin Ness, PMP
Donald L. Nord, PMP
Nancy Palmateer, PMP
Eduardo Campello Peixoto, PMP
Ralph Pinney, PMP
Jeffery J. Pitman, PMP
Suman Rao
Peter Reekie
Timothy Roberts, PMP, CPIM
Paul Royer, PMP
Rolando Guevara Ruiz, PMP
Chet Ruminski

Anne Schilling
Shabnam Shaikh, PMP
Jacquie Sutliff
Trish Sutter, PMP
Chris Thain
Karen Threlkeld
Felix Valdez
Barry Vanek, PMP
Paul Webb, PMP
Michael Weins, PMP
Tony Williams
George Winn, PMP
Peter Wittenstrom, PMP
Wes Wong
Garry G. Young, PE, PMP
Shakir Zuberi, PMP

APPENDIX
3

Risk Chart Exercise

The following pages contain a blank Risk Chart, as well as a completed Risk Chart. List as many risk management activities and outputs as you can under each of the risk management processes. Compare your answers to the completed form.

Risk Chart Exercise

Risk Chart		
Plan Risk Management	Identify Risks	Perform Qualitative Risk Analysis
Activities	Activities	Activities
Outputs	Outputs	Outputs

Perform Quantitative Analysis	Plan Risk Responses	Monitor and Control Risks
Activities	Activities	Activities
Outputs	Outputs	Outputs

Risk Chart		
Plan Risk Management	**Identify Risks**	**Perform Qualitative Risk Analysis**
Activities	Activities	Activities
• Determine what you are going to do complete risk management on the project • Determine what risk management policies or procedures exist for use on the project	• Make a long list of risks using the cause-risk-effect format • Involve the stakeholders	• Test assumptions and evaluate the data quality of each risk • Subjectively determine the probability and impact of all risks • Determine which risks to analyze more fully in the Perform Quantitative Risk Analysis process and which to move directly to the Plan Risk Responses process • Document the non-top risks for review during the Monitor and Control Risks process • Determine the initial overall risk ranking for the project
Outputs	Outputs	Outputs

• Risk management plan	• Risk register
	• List of risks
	• Potential risk owners
		• Risk register updates:
		  ◆ Risk ranking for the project compared to other projects
		  ◆ List of prioritized risks and the probability and impact ratings
		  ◆ Risks grouped by categories
		  ◆ List of risks requiring additional analysis in the near term
		  ◆ List of risks for additional analysis/response
		  ◆ Watchlist (non-top risks)
		  ◆ Trends
		• Go/no-go decision

Perform Quantitative Analysis	Plan Risk Responses	Monitor and Control Risks
Activities	Activities	Activities
Numerically evaluate the top risks Perform Monte Carlo simulation	• Determine what you are going to do about each risk • Determine what will be done to eliminate risks while still in planning • Determine risk owners (if not already done) • Determine what will be done to change the probability and impact of each of the top risks—contingency planning • Create fallback plans to be used if the contingency plans do not succeed	• Ensure risk response plans are implemented • Look for risk triggers • Look for additional risks, then qualify and quantify the risks and plan responses for them • Evaluate the effectiveness of risk responses risk audits • Review the risk resopnse plans and look for more risks—risk reviews
Outputs	Outputs	Outputs

Risk register updates:
◆ Prioritized list of quantified risks
◆ Amount of contingency time and cost reserves needed
◆ Possible realistic and achievable completion dates and project costs, with confidence levels
◆ Quantified probability of meeting project objectives
◆ Trends
	• Risk register updates:
	  ◆ Risk response plans
	    ■ Contingency plans
	    ■ Fallback plans
	  ◆ Risk owners
	  ◆ Residual and secondary risks
	  ◆ Risk triggers
	  ◆ Reserves
	  ◆ Insurance
	  ◆ Contracts
	• Go/no-go decision
	• Project management plan updates
		• Risk register updates:
		  ◆ Outcomes of the risk reassessments and risk audits
		  ◆ Updates to previous parts of risk management, including the identification of new risks
		  ◆ Closing of risks that are no longer applicable
		  ◆ Details of what happened when risks occurred
		  ◆ Lessons learned
		• Change requests, including recommended corrective and preventive actions
		• Project management plan updates
		• Organizational process assets updates

GLOSSARY

Accept   Do nothing—"If it happens, it happens", or create a contingency plan

Affinity diagram   A method to identify additional risks and risk categories on a project

Assumptions   Things that are accepted as true, but may not be true

Assumptions testing   Looking at the stability (validity) of each assumption and the consequences if each assumption is false

Avoid   Eliminate the threat of a risk by eliminating the cause

Bar chart   A chart showing activity information; in risk management it is modified to include the risk score and risk owner

Brainstorming   A meeting to come up with ideas or solve problems

Budget   Amount of resources allocated to be spent on the project

Business risk   A risk of a gain or loss

Cause and effect diagram   A tool to evaluate the causes of risks

Cause-risk-effect format   As a result of (X), (Y) may occur, which would/could/may lead to (Z)

Cognitive bias   Bias due to a difference in perception

Common causes of risk   Instances where one activity, person, event, etc. is causing more than one risk

Communications management plan   A formal plan documenting how and in what form communications will be handled on the project

Contingency plan   Planned actions to be taken if the risk happens

Contingency reserve   An amount of time and/or cost added to the project to deal with known unknowns, i.e., identified risks

Contract   A legal agreement for the purchase or sale of goods and services

Corrective action   Changes implemented in order to bring performance back in line with the project management plan

Data quality assessment   Determining "How well understood is the risk?"

Decision tree   A model of a situation used to see the potential impacts of decisions by taking into account associated risks, probabilities, and impacts

Definitions of probability and impact   A standardized interpretation of the numbering system used to evaluate risks

Delphi technique   A process of seeking consensus of expert opinion

Earned value analysis   A method to quantitatively measure and monitor overall project performance against the project baseline

Enhance   Increase the expected time, quality, or monetary value of a risk by increasing its probability or impact of occurrence

Ensure compliance   Make sure policies, procedures, and plans are being followed

Estimates for time and cost   Anticipated time or cost of project activities

Evaluate the effectiveness   Measure to determine the results of actions taken

Expectations   Stakeholders' needs or intents that may be unstated, but are motivators or non-motivators for working on the project

Expected monetary value   The probability weighted average of all possible outcomes, calculated by summing all the quantitative probabilities times impact for risks on the project

Expert interview   A process for obtaining opinions or other input on the project from experts

Exploit   Increase the opportunity by making the cause more probable

Failure Modes and Effects Analysis (FMEA)   A tool to identify potential failure modes, determine their effects and identify actions to mitigate the failures

Fallback plan   Planned actions to be taken if the risk happens and contingency plans are not effective

Go/no-go decision   "Is the project too risky to continue, compared to the potential benefits?"

Historical records   Information from past, similar projects

Human resource plan A formal plan for when and how resources will be involved in the project, and what roles they will perform

Identify Risks process Determining specific risks by project and by activity

Impact The effect on the activity or the project if the risk (threat or opportunity) occurs

Input Something that must be done or information that must already have been collected before you can adequately complete the next process

Inputs to risk management Things that must be done or information that must be collected before you can adequately complete risk management

Insurance Assigns the liability for a risk to someone else

Iterative Repeated throughout the life of the project

Lessons learned What went right, wrong, or would have been done differently by past project teams if they could execute their projects again

Lessons learned management Ensuring that lessons learned are captured on all projects and made available for use on other projects

List of risks to move forward Risks that will be addressed in the Perform Quantitative Risk Analysis or Plan Risk Responses processes

Manage reserves Control the appropriate use of reserves

Management reserve An amount of time and/or cost added to the project to deal with unknown unknowns, i.e., risks that have not been identified

Methodology How risk will be handled on the project and what data and tools will be used

Metrics Standards of performance that, once evaluated, tell how work is performing against the plan

Mitigate Reduce the expected monetary value of a risk by reducing its impact or probability of occurrence

Mitigate the impact Decrease the impact of a threat or increase the impact of an opportunity

Mitigate the probability Decrease the probability of a threat or increase it for an opportunity

Monitor Oversee project performance and activities

Monitor and Control Risks

process Implementing the risk response plans as risks occur, looking for risk triggers, identifying new risks, and evaluating the effectiveness of risk responses

Monte Carlo simulation Computerized method of estimating that simulates the project to determine time or cost estimates based on probability distributions

Motivational bias Intentionally biasing results in one direction or another

Network diagram A dependency-sequenced organization of the project's activities

Nominal group technique A process of collecting and ranking risks contributed by a select group

Opportunities Possible events that may positively impact a project

Organizational process assets Company policies, procedures, templates, and historical information

Path convergence As illustrated on a network diagram, many activities leading into a central activity

Perform Qualitative Risk Analysis

process Subjectively analyzing the risks obtained in the Identify Risks process and deciding which risks warrant a response; creating a "short list" of risks

Perform Quantitative Risk Analysis

process Numerically analyzing the risks obtained in the Identify Risks process and deciding which risks warrant a response and analyzing the extent of overall project risk

Plan Risk Management

process Determining how risk management will be done on the project, who will be involved, and procedures to be followed

Plan Risk Responses

process Determining what can be done to reduce the overall risk of the project by decreasing the probability and impact of threats and increasing the probability and impact of opportunities

Pre-mortem Theoretical "evaluation" of a project before it has actually been done

Probability The likelihood that a risk (threat or opportunity) will occur

Probability and impact scales A standardized method of determining probability and impact of identified risks

Procurement management plan A formal or informal plan that describes what part(s) of the project will be purchased under contract or purchase order; it includes a plan for managing the sellers

Project background information Information from before the project was approved, articles written about similar projects, and other such information

Project charter High-level directive from the sponsor outlining the overall objectives of the project; it authorizes the existence of a project

Project constraints Anything that limits the team's options, e.g., scope, time, cost, quality, risk, resources, and customer satisfaction

Project management office (PMO) A department that supports project management within an organization

Project management process Initiating, planning, executing, monitoring and controlling, closing

Project scope statement A document which describes the approved product and project requirements

Project sponsor The individual or group who authorizes the project and provides the financial resources

Project team Those who will be executing the project management plan

Prompt list A generic list of risk categories

Pure (insurable) risk A risk of loss

Refine Change or modify

Reporting formats How the results of risk management will be documented and communicated

Reserve An amount of time and/or cost added to the project to account for risks

Residual risks Risks that remain after risk response planning

Risks Possible events that may positively or negatively impact a project

Risk action owner The person assigned by the risk owner to implement preapproved risk responses

Risk audit Analysis of what the project team has done for risk management to determine whether it has worked

Risk averse Unwilling to accept risk

Risk breakdown structure A graphic illustration of risk categories

Risk categories Common areas or sources of risk on similar projects

Risk exposure The level of risk on a project

Risk factors Probability, impact, expected timing, frequency of the event

Risk governance Oversight of the entire risk management process

Risk management department A department that supplies policies and assistance with project risk management efforts

Risk management plan A plan for how risk management will be done on a project, who should be involved, when risk management activities should be done, and how frequently they should be done

Risk management process A systematic and proactive approach to taking control of projects by understanding or decreasing the uncertainties

Risk owner The person assigned by the project manager to watch for triggers and manage the risk response if the risk occurs

Risk ranking A comparison of the risk scores for all risks on the project

Risk rating A number between 1 to 10 chosen to evaluate the probability or impact of a risk

Risk reassessment Looking for new risks when changes are made on the project

Risk register List of identified risks (threats and opportunities) for the project, and other information added throughout the risk management process

Risk reserve report A running balance of the remainder of the reserve

Risk response plans Documentation of what will be done to reduce the overall risk of the project by decreasing the probability and impact of threats and increasing the probability and impact of opportunities

Risk review Analysis of what the project team has planned for risk management to determine whether it is still appropriate

Risk score Calculated by multiplying probability times impact to obtain a numerical value for each risk

Risk team Those helping with the management of the risk management process

Risk thresholds Amounts of risk the company and key stakeholders are willing to accept

Risk tolerance areas Areas in which the company and key stakeholders are willing to accept risk

Risks Possible events that may positively or negatively impact a project

Roles and responsibilities Who will do what on the project

Root cause Underlying risk

Secondary risks Risks that are generated by a response to another risk

Share Retain appropriate opportunities or parts of opportunities instead of attempting to transfer them to others

Stakeholder register   Information about individuals and organizations who are actively involved in the project or who may affect or be affected by the project

Stakeholders   Individuals and organizations who are actively involved in the project or may affect or be affected by the project

Technical performance measurement   Measurement of factors such as strength of the concrete, measurable wind resistance of a building, meeting functionality requirements, strength of the plastic used in a product, etc. to identify deviations from the plan

Threats   Possible events that may negatively impact a project

Timing   When/how often risk management activities will be performed throughout the project

Tracking   How records of risks will be documented for the benefit the current project and future projects

Transfer   Assign the risk to someone else by subcontracting or buying insurance

Trigger   Early warning sign that a risk has occurred or is about to occur

Uncertainties   Unknowns

Work breakdown structure   A diagram that shows the decomposition of the project into smaller, more manageable pieces

Workarounds   Unplanned responses to unidentified risks that occur

INDEX

A

Accept   195, 196, 198, 200
Affinity diagram   95-97, 107
Assumptions   31, 80, 128-129
Assumptions testing   128-129
Avoid   195, 196

B

Bar chart   145-146, 263-264
Bias   131
Brainstorming   93-94, 107
Budget   51
Business risk   13

C

Cause and effect diagram   103-104
Cause–risk–effect format   74
Checklist   84-85
Cognitive bias   131
Common causes of risk   143-144
Communications management plan
34-35, 260-264, 290
Contingency plan   205-206, 209, 225

Contingency reserve   210, 225
Contract   218, 225

D

Data quality assessment   129-130
Decision tree   106, 179-180
Definitions of probability and impact   51
Delphi technique   102-103

E

Earned value analysis   254-255
Enhance   196, 199
Estimates   33, 259-260
Expectations   30
Expected monetary value   167-170
Expert interview   97-101
Exploit   196, 199

F

Failure modes and effects analysis (FMEA)
104-105, 106, 181
Fallback plan   206, 209, 225
Forms   82-83